The Global Rise of China and Asia

Abdul Razak Baginda

The Global Rise of China and Asia

Impact and Regional Response

2nd ed. 2022

Abdul Razak Baginda
Enfield, UK

ISBN 978-3-030-91805-7   ISBN 978-3-030-91806-4 (eBook)
https://doi.org/10.1007/978-3-030-91806-4

© The Editor(s) (if applicable) and The Author(s), under exclusive licence to Springer Nature Switzerland AG 2021
1st edition: © Abdul Razak Baginda 2020
This work is subject to copyright. All rights are solely and exclusively licensed by the Publisher, whether the whole or part of the material is concerned, specifically the rights of translation, reprinting, reuse of illustrations, recitation, broadcasting, reproduction on microfilms or in any other physical way, and transmission or information storage and retrieval, electronic adaptation, computer software, or by similar or dissimilar methodology now known or hereafter developed.
The use of general descriptive names, registered names, trademarks, service marks, etc. in this publication does not imply, even in the absence of a specific statement, that such names are exempt from the relevant protective laws and regulations and therefore free for general use.
The publisher, the authors and the editors are safe to assume that the advice and information in this book are believed to be true and accurate at the date of publication. Neither the publisher nor the authors or the editors give a warranty, expressed or implied, with respect to the material contained herein or for any errors or omissions that may have been made. The publisher remains neutral with regard to jurisdictional claims in published maps and institutional affiliations.

Cover illustration: Maram_shutterstock.com

This Palgrave Macmillan imprint is published by the registered company Springer Nature Switzerland AG.
The registered company address is: Gewerbestrasse 11, 6330 Cham, Switzerland

Preface

While the world was astonished for decades by the Japanese bullet train, the *Shinkansen*, which was launched in 1964, as an epitome of Japanese technological advancement, in July 2021, China unveiled its latest 373 mph slick-looking bullet train, making it the fastest land vehicle in the world. The train can complete the 754-mile trip between Beijing and Shanghai in a mere two and a half hours.[1] Such astonishing feats by China have become commonplace, mainly in the area of technology, including artificial intelligence, where sophisticated robotics have become a reality. China has indeed arrived on the global stage.

This book is, in essence, a revised edition of an earlier work entitled 'Dragon Diplomacy: Analysing China's Rise', published by Grosvenor Publishing House in 2020. While most of the text has remained relevant, this edition has been updated to cover recent events and incorporates more detailed academic discussion around a number of theoretical frameworks put forth by various scholars on issues related to China's rise.

It is not surprising that China has become a topic of enormous interest amongst individuals, groups, communities, societies and states alike. One manifestation of this is the countless books, articles and such written about the so-called Middle Kingdom, catering to a whole range of issues and interests. Armed with this challenge, I embarked on this book from what I hope is a different angle and with two personal perspectives. Firstly, I wrote with an Asian outlook—my ancestors lived in the Middle Kingdom (my maternal grandparents were from Su Zhou) and I live in multi-racial Malaysia, where ethnic Chinese still form a sizeable minority. My mother is ethnic Chinese and my father is ethnic Malay (his father came from Sumatra).[2] I could make the claim that China is my ancestral home, but such a claim would be much more romantic in nature than in the sense of real family ties.[3]

I have also spent considerable time living in the United Kingdom, where I completed most of my early and tertiary education. I was schooled in the Western liberal tradition and continue to spend time in the United Kingdom.[4] Arguably, my background, though not necessarily unique, gives me an interesting outlook on China.

The second perspective is of someone who lives in Malaysia. This is significant, particularly in relation to China, for a variety of reasons. The development of ties between these two countries could be summed up as moving from hostility to rapprochement to a close relationship, especially in the economic and commercial fields. During the early days, despite a number of irritants in relations between Kuala Lumpur and China, such as China's continued support for the ethnic Chinese-dominated Communist Party of Malaya, in 1974 Malaysia became the first non-communist Southeast Asian country to establish formal diplomatic ties with Beijing.[5]

Malaysia is one of the Southeast Asian countries that enjoys a high level of investment from China. While there have been criticisms and concerns on the various grand projects, it is doubtful that ties will be affected, as the reality of dealing with China will probably be dictated by *realpolitik* rather than prudence or good governance. In addition, Malaysia is one of several regional claimants to the much-disputed South China Sea, potentially putting it in conflict with China. Despite this, it has been far less involved in South China Sea disputes than Vietnam or the Philippines, which have been far more vocal and confrontational.

It is also relevant that living next to a giant requires considerable diplomatic dexterity because one is left with few real options. Countries such as Malaysia, which are in this position, often find themselves in a strategic bind. As the English writer and poet J.R.R. Tolkien said, 'It does not do to leave a live dragon out of your calculations, if you live near one.'[6] Historically, existing next to a powerful giant has led many to find themselves as part of its extended power base—as conquered people or occupied territories—as proxies or, if big enough, as enemies. Very few such countries have managed to protect their independence and simultaneously enjoyed adequate and accepted levels of respect and recognition. Finland did achieve this, however, when it had to rub along with the Soviet Union during the Cold War. Its specific status coined the term 'Finlandisation'.

With the exception of Tito's Yugoslavia, all of the Soviet Union's immediate European neighbours were subjugated under an arc of protection in the form of the Warsaw Pact. These countries were buffers against any impending threat from NATO. The Soviets had learnt a bitter lesson at the outbreak of the Great Patriotic War, which was sparked by the invasion of the USSR by Nazi Germany in June 1941. Germany had breached the Soviet–German Molotov–Ribbentrop Non-aggression Pact and the Wehrmacht were unleashed in Operation Barbarossa.[7]

Admittedly, most books on China with a global reach originate in the West and have the distinct perspective of viewing this emerging giant through the 'threat prism' of a Western world that for decades focused on the Soviets as the bogeyman. Following a short respite after the collapse of the USSR and the uncertainty of its break-up, the West had to review its perception of the threat from Russia when the charismatic Putin came to the helm.

The West has now clearly identified China as another nemesis alongside Russia. *Inter alia*, the Russia and China threats are pressing enough to fuel and sustain the West's military industrial complex, which historically requires periodic military escapades and adventurism for a variety of reasons, including to prove its continued relevance and to 'test' its 'inventions'. Even in the post-Cold War world, the US military has been unleashed on unsuspecting enemies, under the guise of fighting terrorism or of having, or more appropriately not having, weapons of mass destruction. The invasion of Iraq in 2003 by the US-led coalition was a shameful and blatant act of aggression and one that continues to cause untold misery and destruction. The invasion was predicated not on a mistaken premise but on a claim that decision-makers knew was fabricated to provide the *casus belli*. In other words, the United States was mendacious to the world. It is a wonder why those who took the decision to use force have not been brought to trial for war crimes at the International Court of Justice in The Hague. Perhaps this is an example of victor's justice.

The West regards China as a menace that will challenge its supremacy, in particular that of the United States. This has resulted in the demonisation of China. However, there is a certain degree of irony here. China's success is partly of the world's making: it was the huge foreign direct investment, mainly from the West, that turned China into the economic powerhouse it is today. It was the quest for reduced production costs that saw investment flood into China and so to some extent the West helped make today's China. It is no accident that China was, and probably still is, dubbed the 'world's factory'. For example, almost all Apple products are 'assembled' in China. To China's credit, it has used this capital investment to turn its economy into the second largest in the world.

There now exists a very strong negative narrative regarding China, which mainly, though not exclusively, emanates from the West.[8] China is often seen through the prism of a once weak country that has become very powerful and therefore must be stopped from becoming any more powerful. It is viewed as non-Western and non-democratic—not 'one of us'. This view has swept across the globe in the media and via academics and observers. All reinforce the view that China is the demon that will not only haunt the world but, inevitably, possess us all. Many critics of China have painted a very bleak and negative picture reminiscent of the way the West used to view the Soviet Union, which was described succinctly by President Reagan as the 'Evil Empire'.[9] The West's perception of China is often simplified in Manichean terms—the inevitable clash between good and evil. No guessing who is who!

While there is academic freedom and independence of thought, perhaps not surprisingly, many of the books that originate from the West pursue the China-threat argument to varying degrees. This was also the case in the Cold War years. Only then, it was the Soviet menace that commanded the headlines.

It is likely that any deviation from this line will automatically be dubbed 'pro-China' and not taken seriously or will be chastised. This 'China can do no right' script is overwhelming and takes precedence over any contrary view.

This state of affairs is tragic, for it boxes China into a corner. What follows is an almost crusade-like move to contain, check and even confront China. Any move towards recognition of China's rightful place in the world is viewed as fatalistic and even as a capitulation.

This is a dangerous path and a route that is not at all unique. Rather, it is a familiar road with potential catastrophic consequences. Most wars have been the result of states being placed on a collision course, and history is littered with examples of the rise of states and the inevitable cataclysmic showdown between the status quo and the ascending power. Perhaps the most tragic example of this came in those critical weeks preceding the outbreak of the Great War, which resulted in the death of millions; it was brought about by the egos of the leaders of competing European powers who one author has aptly referred to as 'The Sleepwalkers'.[10]

This book tries to view China with a much broader perspective, not in isolation but in comparison with other great powers, past and present. Critics of China are happy to lambast this new kid on the block but at the same time do not look at what other powers were and are doing.

It is hoped, therefore, that this book considers China in a much more balanced and even-handed manner, does not condemn it outright as a bogeyman or demon. It tries to navigate between the China alarmists and apologists. It attempts to challenge the dominant narrative and provide an alternative assessment of China's rise—to swim against the tide. This is an enormous challenge which may well end in failure. But try we must.

Enfield, UK Abdul Razak Baginda

Notes

1. *Robb Report*, 22 July 2021, robbreport.com
2. I often fail to comprehend what is meant when some in Malaysia refer to the ethnic Chinese as immigrants, when most Malaysians, including the majority Malays, are descendants of migrants. The exceptions are the truly indigenous people of the land, the *Orang Asli*, which, to borrow from the American nomenclature, could be appropriately called native Malaysians.
3. Because my mother was an orphan as a result of the Japanese occupation of Malaya, I failed to trace any living relatives in China. For my family background, see my father's autobiography: Abdullah Malim Baginda, *From Passion to Mission* (Kuala Lumpur: ICON Publishers, 2019).
4. I first went to the United Kingdom when I was 13 years old and attended a comprehensive school in Croydon. At the time, my father was studying at the London School of Economics.
5. For background on Malaysia's establishment of diplomatic relations with China, see Abdul Razak Baginda, *China–Malaysia Relations and Foreign Policy* (Oxford: Routledge, 2016). Technically, Malaysia was not the first as Indonesia had established official ties earlier in 1950, but suspended relations as a result of Jakarta's allegation of Beijing's involvement in the abortive coup of 1965.
6. J.R.R. Tolkien was famous for his fantasy tales, some of which have become Hollywood blockbuster movies, such as *The Lord of the Rings*.
7. For a brilliant account of this massive invasion of Russia, see Alan Clark, *Barbarossa: The Russian–German Conflict, 1941–45* (New York: William Morrow and Company, 1965).

8. Admittedly, the term 'the West' is a broad one and not homogeneous. Needless to say, this book recognises the over-simplified use of this term. Nonetheless, it is hoped that most will understand the meaning and context when such a term is used throughout this book.
9. This address was originally given to the National Association of Evangelicals in Orlando, Florida, in March 1983. See Ronald Reagan, *The Evil Empire Speech, 1983* (New York: Vintage Books, 1983).
10. See Christopher Clark, *The Sleepwalkers: How Europe Went to War in 1914* (London: Penguin, 2013).

Acknowledgements

This book is the result of years of interacting with a whole range of people, including academics. It would be next to impossible to list all those who have helped in my quest for knowledge, which is a life-long journey.

In writing this book I have travelled to many countries and talked with experts and observers. These discourses have been most enriching. I have spent time in various libraries such as that at the School of Oriental and African Studies in London and visited academics based in Peking University, the China Foreign Affairs University in Beijing and elsewhere. Special mention goes to Reitaku University, Japan, where I was a visiting fellow. My thanks go to Professor Lau Sim Yee there.

My special thanks go to Caroline Barber, who has been kind and patient in editing my manuscript. I would also like to express my sincere gratitude to my former supervisor at Oxford, Dr Rosemary Foot, who has always been helpful and an inspiration to me. In addition, my appreciation goes to the former president of my college, Trinity College Oxford, the Honourable Michael Beloff, QC, who has remained a constant in my life.

Towards the production of this book, I would like to record my appreciation to Ann-Kathrin Birchley-Brun from Palgrave Macmillan and Darin Jewell of the Inspira Group.

This work would not have been possible without the incredible support and help I have received from my parents, my wife Mazlinda and my daughter Rowena. Needless to say, all the faults and shortcomings of this book are entirely mine.

Contents

1	Introduction: Contextualising China	1
2	Examining China's History: Bringing the Past into the Future	33
3	The Multidimensional Elements of Chinese Power: An Assessment	51
4	Evaluating the China Threat: Between Perceived and Real	111
5	Regional Perceptions Towards China: Safeguarding Interests	137
6	Conclusion: Balancing Between Domestic and International Imperatives	175
	Select Bibliography	185
	Index	191

CHAPTER 1

Introduction: Contextualising China

What do a prophet and a general have in common? Centuries ago, both made profound statements about China. Prophet Mohammad, who lived in the seventh century, urged his people to go as far as China to seek knowledge. Some 11 centuries later, Napoleon Bonaparte counselled, 'not to wake up China, for when it does wake up, the world will tremble'.

Today, not only has China woken from its century-old hibernation, but it has moved so far ahead economically that it is now regarded as a superpower, with the strength not only to challenge the might of the United States but even, possibly, to surpass it. Therefore, China's rise has come at a time when the global order has remained much the same, in varying degrees, with the United States still maintaining its number one position, not only in economic terms, but as the pre-eminent military power in the world. This may well change in the future, leading to a new global order, with, perhaps, Beijing replacing Washington at the helm.

China has developed a strategic reach far beyond anything accomplished by its predecessors centuries before. Interestingly, during the Ming dynasty, Emperor Yongle dispatched Admiral Zheng He on seven voyages across the vast oceans, on huge vessels that dwarfed those of Christopher Columbus' fleet. Instead of colonising these territories, stretching as far as the Persian Gulf and African coast, and through Southeast Asian waters, the Chinese merely established commercial links while still projecting imperial power.

© The Author(s), under exclusive license to Springer Nature Switzerland AG 2021
A. R. Baginda, *The Global Rise of China and Asia*,
https://doi.org/10.1007/978-3-030-91806-4_1

Twenty-first-century China has also achieved this amazing feat, without firing a single shot. In a global environment in which access to finance has become much more challenging for developing countries and double standards[1] are ubiquitous, China is seen by many as a viable alternative source of funding to fuel their engines of growth. To some countries, China is a saviour, helping to develop and sustain their moribund economies or to jump-start them.[2] This seems especially the case with dictatorial or authoritarian regimes, many of which have been pushed away by Western states and financial institutions.[3]

When we were approaching the end of the twentieth century, prognostications abounded that the twenty-first century was going to be the Pacific century—it would see the shifting of the world's balance from the West to this economically dynamic region. Although China was collectively viewed through this geographic prism, as we now approach the beginning of the third decade of the new century, it appears that this economic titan is pressing far ahead of the rest of us; notwithstanding any economic slowdowns, China will continue to be at the forefront for decades to come.

What is significant about China is not just its exponential economic growth that has marvelled and dazzled the world, but that it is now a serious challenger to the United States' dominance and global supremacy. The decades-old unipolar world, which followed the end of the Cold War, has now been buried as China ascended to the global stage. Its rise has provided a direct challenge to the global order, which since the end of World War II has witnessed the preponderance of US power.[4]

To some extent, the arrival of Huawei's 5G technology across the world is the United States' second 'sputnik' shock. When the USSR became the first country to launch a satellite into space in October 1957, Washington had a reality check—the Russians had caught up in space technology which had much wider strategic implications and the Americans were caught napping! The significance of the recent revelation of Huawei's 5G technology is that China has, on the quiet, invested heavily in such areas and is catching up and overtaking the West. The West appears to be like the hare that thought it could afford to take a nap while waiting for the slow turtle to catch up. Catch up it did!

Today, the United States is no longer alone at the top of the hill. One after the other, China seems not only to match the former's achievements, but even to surpass them. For instance, with the American NASA Mars Exploration programme, which was established in 1993, the United States was back again at the forefront of space conquest. Suddenly, on 15 May 2021, it was revealed to the world that China's Zhurong rover had landed on the so-called red planet, from its mothership, the Tianwen-1 spacecraft. What was more shocking was that it took the Chinese a much shorter period to achieve what took the Americans decades. Riding on this success, the Chinese announced that, based on their long-term plans, they aim to send their first crewed mission to Mars in 2033, with the eventual realisation of its vision of setting up a permanently inhabited base there, in order to extract its resources.[5] Such an announcement was reminiscent of the famed John F. Kennedy's joint session of Congress speech in May 1961, when he caught the imagination of many about putting a man on the moon.

Such Chinese feats have been psychological shocks to the United States and the Western world. The reaction and response from the West is perhaps not surprising. It appears that everything must be done to check and subsequently undermine China's ability to challenge American global dominance. President Trump's mantra, 'make America great again', epitomises the idea that the United States' top position is slipping away and that it is imperative that it remains at the apex or, to some, regains this prized slot.

During the Cold War with the Soviet Union, the rivalry followed along ideological lines, but with China, this does not appear to be the case. Here lies the crux of the West's dilemma: although China is still ruled by the Communist Party, it is a far cry from what Marx and Engels envisaged. If these philosophers knew that capitalism was alive and kicking in a Communist Party-ruled country, they would be turning in their graves.

THE CHINESE MODEL: WORTHY OF EXPORT?

China's challenge appears to go beyond mere economic or even military might. There now seems to be a competition in the ideological dimension—not about Communist versus Western liberal systems, but rather a political–economic model that the vast majority of countries could well pursue. Given the heightened confidence level in China today, its leaders believe that the Chinese model could well provide an alternative to other more Western-biased models. In October 2017, President Xi announced that its official model of 'socialism with Chinese characteristics' is worthy of emulation by other countries. He said, 'It offers a new option for other countries and nations who want to speed up their development while preserving their independence, and it offers Chinese wisdom and a Chinese approach to solving the problems facing humanity.'[6] Interestingly, Xi not only mentioned the efficacy of its developmental model but ventured to project the Chinese-ness of their approach to cure the ills of mankind. While China is far from being able to overcome some of humanity's perennial issues, such as inequality and environmental degradation, the Chinese president has already projected its ability to do so. Such lofty statements do illustrate the extent of Chinese confidence in its model to provide for others to follow—signalling its ability to influence the majority of countries, which are still struggling to achieve modernisation.

The China model has many facets. While economic development is one obvious area, it is the political dimension that seems to strike a chord in many countries, including those in the West, which not only has pursued its own liberal-based democratic system but has also been advocating and even forcing its system to be replicated in the rest of the world. Today, the competition that China is putting forth on the table is not along the traditional ideological battle lines between capitalism and communism, but rather one that is much more complex, and which at the same appeals to many developing and authoritarian-ran countries. The divide is also predicated on democratic and non-democratic lines when looking at the so-called Chinese option, although it would be too simplistic to classify all states within such rigid classifications. The United States does recognise that the Chinese offer an alternative to its own liberal democratic values to the many countries that are considered non-democratic. According to one policy briefing group, the Chinese Communist Party (CCP) 'employs a suite of tactics to advance its strategic influence in countries around the world, in the process exploiting and exacerbating democratic weaknesses in target states', which has 'a pernicious effect on developing democracies'.[7] As such, 'if Washington's China strategy is to effect its desired change—a world where America is secure and remains the preeminent power—it must include investments focused on winning the competition of political systems'.[8] To advocates of the need for the United States to prevail over the Chinese on this issue, 'the goal of this strategy should be a world in which democracy is the predominant form of national governance because it is the model with the best chance of delivering peace and prosperity for citizens'.[9] As we shall see later, the Chinese model could well provide a serious challenge to the notion that democracy is the best form of political system to ensure long-term prosperity.

In addition to this political competition, one area that seems to be an increasing source of debate, going beyond the Western world, is whether the 'Chinese model' could be an alternative to the democratic–capitalist development paradigm that the West has long championed. The China model has been the subject of much discussion in the public domain, including among the intellectual community. In a much-debated work by Daniel A. Bell[10] on this subject, he presented his case by comparing what he described as 'electoral democracy', which hinges on the basic concept of one man, one vote, with 'political meritocracy', which he identifies China with. In favouring the latter, Bell identified four flaws of the former, based on the minimal element of free and fair elections—the tyrannies of the majority, the minority, the voting community and competitive individualists. In each flaw, he provided an alternative based on political meritocracy, which is based on the notion that the political system 'should aim to select and promote leaders with superior qualities, but what counts as merit varies from context to context'.[11] However, it must be pointed out that the selection of leaders in China has evolved, when compared to the early days of the People's Republic of China (PRC) under Mao Zedong, up to the present President Xi. Obviously, Mao led the communist revolution, not through a vigorous process of selection, nor due to his qualifications, but rather through a series of events that, one could argue, was due to circumstances, rather than some random 'throw of the dice'. However, Xi's rise to the helm of Chinese politics was certainly based on a much more 'competitive' situation together with having the right kind of experience that catapulted him to the pinnacle of the political hierarchy.[12] More likely, the present system emphasises a combination of factors, including the electoral process as well as experience and party positions. Interestingly, according to an academic, Baogang He, in essence, 'Chinese practices honor the one person one vote principle, but deal with some issues raised by Bell through an institutional design in which voting is only one component at one stage, and has about 20–30 percent weight in the whole decision process.'[13]

The contrast and merits of Bell's dichotomous democratic paradigms are stark when comparing Xi with Trump. Although some would argue that the latter was an aberration of the system, it could equally be argued that the system landed him there in the first place.

Nonetheless, perhaps one of the main issues of Bell's China model of political meritocracy is whether the imposition of meritocracy can be guaranteed as a way to select the best and most suitable leader to rule the country. At the end of the day, an individual or groups of individuals will decide, assuming that they all share a common consensus of what constitutes meritocracy. In addition, political meritocracy is invariably confined to a limited number of candidates. Finally, one wonders whether brilliance is the answer to all, for at the end of the day one could end up with 'the best and the brightest' but which for many different and complex reasons, may yet result in disastrous consequences.[14] Both Kennedy and Johnson were surrounded by the so-called best and the brightest, mainly from Ivy League institutions, but both were unable to extricate the country from the Vietnamese quagmire.

Another aspect of the so-called Chinese model, which could well be attractive to non-democratic states, is the notion that you can have economic growth and even prosperity without having necessarily to go down the democratic path. This contradicts the notion that democracy is a prerequisite to achieve growth and prosperity. Many in the West believed that when China opened up its economy and became integrated into the global economy, it would eventually become democratic, in the liberal Western sense. Put it simply, the Chinese model shows that economic liberalisation does not necessarily lead to political liberalisation. Harry Rowen of the Hoover Institution in 1996 predicted that China would become a democracy around the year 2015, based on China's steady and impressive economic growth, for when it becomes richer, it will become more democratic.[15] The fact that China is, at present, so far away from such a prediction speaks volume of the often-flawed argument that one size fits all. This has obviously punched a hole in the philosophical bedrock of the Western tradition, and it appeals to the many non-democratic states around the world. This has come at a time when the whole notion of democracy is being broadly criticised in many prominent circles in the West; the emergence of this new development model poses another threat to the dominance of the West.

However, a point that is often missed in the analysis of the so-called China model is that it is not necessarily a black-and-white model, such as a Western-style capitalist system of economic liberalisation and that of a liberal Western-style democratic system. It is perhaps more accurate to see the model adopted by China to be more of a hybrid that incorporates both the liberalisation of the economy with not just mere state intervention, but intervention that is even state-led, state-directed and state-guided. At the centre of the economy is the state, which is often authoritarian in nature, something which academic, Andrew J. Nathan, has termed

'Authoritarian Resilience', where, despite predictions that the system will lead to collapse, it has proven to be most resilient. He stated that the central theme for its success, though complex, can be summed up in the concept of institutionalisation, which is based on four aspects: 'the increasingly norm-bound nature of its succession politics; the increase in meritocratic as opposed to factional consideration in the promotion of political elites; the differentiation and functional specialisation of institutions within the regime; and the establishment of institutions for political participation and appeal that strengthen the CCP's legitimacy among the public at large'.[16]

While this model seems to attract many from the developing world, its universal applicability is somewhat limited, mainly due to the presence of the Communist Party, which has ruled the country since 1949. Even though the Party has evolved, the basic elements of one-party rule have remained unchanged. More importantly, the CCP has been able to adopt and change with the times, despite an uneasy start, when economic policies under Mao Zedong proved to be disastrous. As we shall see in the later chapters, it was the economic awakening of China in the late 1970s that catapulted the country to what it is today. Therefore, this one-party rule has survived due to its ability to bring prosperity to its peoples. The Party brought stability and at the same time was bold enough to seize the moment and embarked on economic modernisation. Without the stability in the country, it would have been a daunting task to open up the economy as it did from the end of the 1970s onwards. Very few countries, if any, share the same political evolution as China and at the same time to be economically successful, thereby rendering its model applicability somewhat limited. Many countries in the developing world, for example, have been grappling to find some degree of political stability, long enough for the economic development to take place.

There is another factor that helps explain why the challenge of China for the United States is taking a different twist. Looking at the heavy dose of criticism levied at China today—which comes mainly, though not exclusively, from the Western world—the conclusion one draws is that it is often predicated on a Western and non-Western divide, which may well include a racial dimension. This racial line is not uniquely used against China; it goes back centuries. When the Ottoman military forces were at the gates of Vienna in 1683, a new phrase was coined which has become part of the English lexicon: 'Barbarians[17] at the gate'. The whole concept of 'Orientalism' then became a philosophical foundation which underpinned

Western policies towards the rest of the non-Western world. Specifically, regarding an Asian power, the notions of the 'yellow peril' and the 'yellow hordes' do, to some extent, underline today's discussions about China. They remind us of the historical significance of Russia's defeat at the Battle of Tsushima during the Russo–Japanese war in 1905, not because of the war per se, but because it was the first conflict in modern times in which a European power was defeated by an Asian one. Following this, even the Pacific War had some racial undertones. Prior to the outbreak of the Pacific War, the British had a lowly impression of Japanese soldiers. In one assessment they were described as 'buck-toothed, slant-eyed, near-sighted, scrawny little people. Their slanted eyes make them poor night fighters, and prone to sea-sickness.'[18] One can imagine the humiliation of the British when they had to surrender to the Japanese when Singapore fell, with General Percival having to walk some distance while being filmed just before signing the instruments of surrender on the Island in February 1942. The defeat at the hands of the Japanese was described by Churchill as the 'worst disaster' and 'largest capitulation' in British military history. Less than a decade later, when Chinese troops crossed the Yalu River into Korean territory in 1950 in what was described as 'human waves', the 'yellow hordes' syndrome resonated in some Western circles.[19]

Concomitant to this is the tendency to view China from a Western perspective and by using a Western value system. Given the dominance of Western influence and thinking among the elites of the world, including in the scholarly world, it is perhaps not surprising that there exists a strongly negative assessment and outlook towards China. It is difficult to see China positively when one is wearing Western-tinted spectacles. China's political system is fundamentally different and in almost every other sphere the differences are also obvious. Culturally, socially, religiously and, since 1949, ideologically, China is significantly different from the West and even from the rest of the world. However, being different should not be a basis for negativity.

In a recent article appearing in *Harvard Business Review*, the authors argue that the assumption made in the West that economic liberalisation in China will lead to more political freedom, and the path of China will resemble that of Western nations, is wrong, due to the belief that economics and democracy are two sides of the same coin. However, in reality, in the case of China, 'growth has come in the context of stable Communist rule, suggesting that democracy and growth are not inevitably mutually dependent. In fact, many Chinese believe that the country's recent economic achievements—large-scale poverty reduction, huge infrastructure investment, and development as a world-class tech innovator—have come about because of, not despite, China's authoritarian form of government.'[20] It seems clear that much of what has been written or discussed in the West is within the prism of 'the Westernisation of China'. The same authors argue that, despite the views of many, 'the truth is that political reform in China has not stalled. It continues apace. It's just not liberal reform.' As we shall discuss later, the subject of democracy has been intensely debated within China itself, amongst both political elites and the intellectual community. It seems unreasonable to expect China, which has different historical experiences as well as cultural influences, to pursue a trajectory path similar to that of Western nations.

Putting China in Perspective

This book puts forth several basic premises against which China can be discussed and examined. It is important to place China in a proper context and perspective. The contextualisation of China rests on a number of pillars. Far too often what was once the Middle Kingdom is seen in isolation and viewed as a power that has risen from nowhere.

The first context, therefore, must be the historical dimension, which cannot be ignored when discussing China today. China's two millennia history of dynastic rule, during which time it saw itself as the centre of the world, must count for something. The very name, Middle Kingdom, conjures a particular image of China's sense of supremacy. China saw itself as self-sufficient; the outside world needed more from it than it sought in return. This will be discussed in Chap. 2, which advances the argument that, historically, despite its imperial nature, China was not a colonising power. Instead, it was very much an insular power—often with a false notion of its omnipotence. Internal divisions and rebellions have always been the main challenge for China's rulers.

In contrast to other former imperial powers, China seems to have been unique in being able to return as a great power. While the Greeks, Romans and British can indulge in nostalgia, the Chinese can reflect well on both their past and their present. Not surprisingly, Chinese leaders, when convenient, often draw on this historical continuity to demonstrate the enormity of the changes taking place in present-day China. For instance, in a speech made in November 2012, President Xi Jinping said, 'Our struggles over 170 years since the Opium War have created bright prospects for achieving the rejuvenation of the Chinese nation.'[21] The best illustration of this keen sense of historical context is the Belt and Road Initiative (BRI)—the modern-day equivalent of the Silk Road, which became a symbol of Chinese commercial and trade links during the imperial era when successive rulers wanted to create trade links between Asia and Europe.

Secondly, China is a great power and must be viewed within this context. Its behaviour has not been dissimilar to other great powers, which have common goals and aspirations, notwithstanding ideological differences. If there are any differences between them, it is matter of degree and scale and historical context. Today, countries, whatever their capability, are less likely to resort to the use of force than previously. And the rise of regional bodies and international organisations plays a restraining role on states' behaviour, although, as we have seen far too often, national and personal interests often override rational thinking and external restraints.

We sometimes view China through a moral prism, but the luxury of the moral high ground is often quickly sacrificed when it comes to national interest. When China takes action, there are critics who use a moral standard to hold China to account, perhaps unfairly, and who fail to apply the same standards to Western countries. Just look at Canada's Trans-Mountain pipeline project: Canada is a country that claims to put environmental issues at the core of its policies, but it is now constructing an oil pipeline that will cut across the country and devastate the environment in its path. The damage that will be caused by this project is rarely highlighted and has somehow avoided global headlines.

In addition, when discussing China, it is important to examine that country's behaviour and policies within the context of an ascending power. It has not yet reached its peak. Given China's enormous potential, it will surely continue on an upward trajectory, even if the speed of its progress varies. Chapter 3 will examine the re-emergence of China on the world stage.

Another perspective that should be considered, specifically in addressing the negativity that is often voiced about China, is that any study of this nascent globally influential power must be done in comparison with the United States. This is because it is America that leads the Western world and which, unfortunately, is also the biggest critic of China, no doubt because it has the most to lose from a rising China. As already pointed out, one of the main reasons why many Western observers are critical of China is that it is the only power that can match the might of the United States globally and has the potential to dislodge the United States as number one in the world. Concomitant to this, to lose top status to a non-Western power is probably the greatest insult to the Western world. To some extent, the 'yellow peril' has returned with a vengeance.

SALIENT POINT—CHINA'S INTERNAL DYNAMICS

The Democracy Debate in China

This book puts forward the argument that internal dynamics remain China's biggest challenge. To the world, a stable China is arguably the most important aspect of this growing powerful nation. It could be argued, though it would mean adopting a rather fatalistic stance, that for the rest of the world China under Communist Party rule is a better option than a democratic China. Democratic rule in China will lead to chaos because China has a massive population of 1.4 billion people to take into account. Anyone arriving in China, whether by air or land may be overwhelmed by the sheer number of people encountered. It is difficult to get one's head around the idea of more than a billion people living in this vast territory, all demanding the basic necessities of life—a roof over their heads, food on the table and clothes on their backs.

The thesis that 'democratic rule in China will lead to chaos' is intensely argued in the intellectual sphere. While China is often straightjacketed as a non-democratic state due to its one-party rule, a closer examination of the system would reveal such a classification as being far too simplistic. Yue Hu, of the prestigious Tsinghua University in Beijing, put forth a fascinating argument, which highlighted the use of the term 'democracy' in the Chinese political language.[22] Using computer-assisted text analysis of articles published over half a century in the *People's Daily* (the official newspaper of the Central Committee of the CCP), Hu concluded that the Chinese authority has applied a consistent refocusing strategy to frame democracy at both within- and cross-discourse levels over time and that with this, the framed discourse appears to be consistent with the fundamental values of Western democracies but works for the preservation of the authoritarian regime. This perhaps explains the constant usage of the term democracy in the Chinese political lexicon.

The Chinese have come out with their own interpretation of democracy within their own political setting. It focuses on the importance of checks and balances within the system. In this respect, they have constantly used the term, 'intra-party democracy', to denote adherence to democratic principles to ensure good governance. This recognition to emphasise on democracy within the party structure was spelt out in a communique published at the closing of the Fourth Plenary Session of the 17th CCP Central Committee, in September 2009, with the statement that the 'mission to manage the Party strictly has never been so arduous and urgent', and that 'many problems exist inside the Party that run counter to new circumstances and the Party's character, which are severely weakening the Party's creativity, unity and effectiveness in dealing with these problems', and that these drawbacks were regarded as 'severely harming the ties of flesh and blood between the Party and the people and the strengthening of the Party's rule'.[23] The communique also stated that 'deep changes in the world, the country and the Party have raised new requirements for Party building and all Party members should be aware and vigilant about the problems and solve them as quickly as possible', urging the members 'to be innovative, creative and never form ossified way of thinking and never stand still'.[24] Clearly, the Chinese political leadership felt that if China was going to compete in the global arena and perhaps even to move to its next level of growth, it needed some kind of 'creative' methodology, going beyond mere leadership. Some kind of internal reform within the institution of the Party was required. Hence, the concept of intra-party democracy surfaced. Not surprisingly, such a notion was severely criticised as merely cosmetic since the fundamental principle of one-party rule remained intact. To begin with, to expect a total democratisation of the political structure, in the same vein as within the Western liberal tradition is unrealistic as there is a firm belief within the Chinese political hierarchy, and perhaps even the country as a whole, that it would be suicidal for it to do so. As mentioned earlier, this book also subscribes to such a viewpoint.

Nonetheless, the fact that the political elites have understood the need to have pluralism in terms of ideas and solutions, albeit within the existing party structure, does bode well for its own internal dynamics. In other words, it is prudent to recognise the extent of its challenges and what is required to overcome them.

It must, however, be pointed out that even this notion of 'intra-party' democracy spurred an intense debate within the country. Cheng Li, in his article on this subject, highlighted some of the positions taken by Chinese leaders and the intellectual community on the basic concept of democracy and what kind of institutional changes should China pursue in achieving this.[25] The main argument put forth by the so-called anti-democracy group essentially identifies China as already democratic while at the same time states that CCP will not abandon its one-party rule. Such a position was voiced by Wu Bangguo, the Chairman of the National People's Congress and the second highest ranking member of the Politburo Standing Committee, who showed little enthusiasm for the concept of intra-party democracy.[26] Such a viewpoint was further reinforced by intellectuals, such as Li Lin, director of the Institute of Law at the Chinese Academy of Social Sciences, who accuses the West, in using the democratic argument, to 'contain, Westernize and split China'.[27] However, supportive of such a notion of democracy has perhaps, not surprisingly, come from the establishment. The then Chinese Premier Wen Jiabao defined democracy somewhat closer to the Western tradition, where he identified the three most important components, that of 'elections, judicial independence, and supervision based on checks and balances'.[28] He, however, fell short of mentioning the need to open up one-party rule to allow a multi-party system to emerge. Nor did he advocate the American notion of the three branches of government as a mechanism for checks and balances.

Going beyond officials, like Premier Wen, there are so-called liberal-minded intellectuals who have been 'actively engaged in political and scholarly discourse on the desirability and feasibility of democracy in China, often with the objective of refining the conceptual framework of Chinese democracy'.[29] One such scholar is Yu Keping, a professor at Peking University, who argued, among other things, that democracy is good universally. Supportive of intra-party democracy as being the best path for political development in China, he argued that 'incremental democracy is the optimal strategy for Chinese political reforms because gradual changes are compatible with China's historical experiences'.[30] He further explains that 'democracy requires sufficient political, economic, social and legal capital, and that improvement by the CCP in all of these areas will not only quantitatively increase democratic feasibility, but will also result in an eventual qualitative "breakthrough"'.[31]

What is significant about the above viewpoints expressed within political and intellectual circles in China is that it would be far too simplistic to argue that China is non-democratic and there is no pluralism of views. On the contrary, as has been seen, basic ideas of democracy and its practice are intensely debated. However, as most would agree, there will always be certain latent boundaries that public officials as well as intellectuals will not cross. Nonetheless, the idea that 'a democratic China will lead to chaos', perhaps, requires some qualification. However, it could be argued that the Chinese political leadership is fully aware of the demands for democracy from various quarters and that it needed to demonstrate that China will embark on further democratisation, but on its own terms and interpretation and not to be defined and determined by 'outside' and foreign concepts and practices. In other words, the Chinese are prudent enough to make policy adjustments and to ensure that its political system will be able to survive the rigours of globalisation, where not only the economy but also its peoples will have to be integrated into the wider world. It could even lead the world in the future.

Pursuant to the notion of imposing democracy on China is the mechanism of change. One of the key issues that are often missed in the argument is how will China transform itself into a Western-style democratic country, which would satisfy those that advocate that China should democratise. Would it be through a process of evolution—meaning over time, the Chinese system will undergo a reform period, which would allow a much more pluralistic political process, ending up with a much more diverse group of elites running the country? Or would it be through a revolution, whereby communist rule will be overturned and replaced with a much more democratic process of elections, predicated on a multi-party system? Surely, this revolution would be a violent one, with prolonged periods of chaos, with untold global ramifications. In addition to this scenario, surely the Communist Party would not be willing to merely give up its power base.

All considered, while many have envisioned China becoming a democracy, the discussion of transforming the system into one, is often ignored. Therefore, while we can discuss the subject of China becoming a democracy and the pressure upon it to be one, we are confronted with the realism of the process of transformation.

Notwithstanding this debate, it would be no easy task to bring democracy to such a large population, including people of diverse backgrounds and differing levels of political culture and maturity. There will be those who argue that India, with the second largest population in the world, has a vibrant democracy. However, what is the point of having democracy when poverty is ubiquitous? Underdevelopment and a severe income gap appear to be perennial issues in India, the largest democratic country on the planet.

Those who advocate democracy really are clueless about how this ideological fantasy would work in a country like China. One of the most absurd notions of the twentieth century was the belief that democracy was a cure for all political, economic and social ills. The idea of imposing democracy from outside is even more nonsensical. There are some who believe that democracy is like a magic wand—you just need to swan in and, hey presto, a society will be transformed into a full-fledged democracy.

As already pointed out earlier, China is seen as a non-democratic state, based on one-party rule, and that there is no alternative to this system, for no other political party is allowed to exist. However, elections and the process of selection of its leaders at the various levels undergo quite a vigorous process, which Bell[32] would describe as based on merit. In other words, while the CCP may have ruled China since 1949, of late, better and much more capable leaders have reached the top while climbing the greasy pole.

In addition, Western countries often view non-Western states through a democratic prism while ignoring that the basis of society differs from one another. The cultural element, with all its influences, is an important consideration when assessing a society that adopts a different political system. This has often led to the imposition of democracy to societies that may well be founded on a different tradition. It is like fitting a square peg in a round hole. Daniel A. Bell, in his discussion of the Chinese model, argues that 'Chinese political culture and history should serve as the main standards for judging political progress (and regress) in China'.[33] He further illustrates his point by suggesting the oddity of reforming American political institutions according to Confucian values would mirror reform of the Chinese political system according to the values of the American founding fathers or Kantian liberals.[34]

All the experiments in imposing democracy on a society and nation state have been a dismal failure. Even those that appeared to be successful at the beginning have turned out to be ephemeral successes. This was the case in Thailand where, after countless military coups, democracy seemed to have taken root and a succession of elected governments were formed. Then, all of a sudden, the military reared its ugly head again, seized power and remained in power for several years until elections were called. The general presiding over the coup then merely changed his clothes, set up a political party, stood for elections and won.

It should be pointed out that the advocates for democracy suffer from what can be called a 'democratic deficit', for the system they champion is itself flawed. There is no doubt that there has been an erosion of the practice of democracy, even in Western countries. Indeed, there has been much discussion about whether democracy is coming to an end. Cambridge

Professor David Runciman explores this critical question, arguing, 'Nothing lasts forever. At some point democracy was always going to pass into the pages of history.... But until very recently, most citizens of Western democracies would have imagined that the end was a long way off. They would not have expected it to happen in their lifetimes. Very few would have thought it might be taking place before their eyes. Yet here we are, barely two decades into the twenty-first century, and almost from nowhere the question is upon us: is this how democracy ends?'[35]

Calls for democracy seem hollow these days. Just look how the most powerful leader in the world, the American president, was elected. Historically, the turnout for presidential elections has been low, hovering just above the 50 per cent mark, and there has never been a US president who has won a landslide victory by receiving more than 70 per cent of votes cast. In the presidential election of 2018, which catapulted the unconventional Republican Donald Trump into the White House, Democratic candidate Hillary Clinton managed to garner more of the popular vote by almost 2.9 million votes. However, due to the Electoral College system, winning the popular vote did not secure a victory for Clinton. In that sense, the leader who has his finger on the nuclear button that could bring Armageddon to the planet only received the votes of about 25 per cent of those aged 18 and above who were eligible to vote. This most powerful leader, who does not represent the voice of the majority of his own citizens, could unleash his country's military force and invade countries and overthrow governments whenever he sees fit. One is reminded of the mass protests in the United Kingdom, in which then Prime Minister Tony Blair was urged not to involve British forces in the invasion of Iraq. When they first came on the political scene, Blair and New Labour embodied fresh ideas and style. However, when he stood shoulder to shoulder with President Bush over the invasion, against a backdrop of overwhelming public dissatisfaction, his image and standing suffered. The subsequent Chilcot Inquiry clearly placed Blair at the heart of this 'disaster', which, though successful in overthrowing Saddam Hussein, subsequently unleashed forces from across the sectarian divide and caused untold chaos across the Middle East and beyond.

In another example, under the 'first past the post' British electoral system, there are cases in which a party has received the most votes overall but still has insufficient seats to form a government. Britain's two-party system has helped to perpetuate the rule of either the Conservative or Labour party in British politics since the end of World War I. Such dominance has helped to marginalise smaller parties and relegate them to the backwaters of the political system. In addition, one need only look at the 2016 referendum on European Union membership. The Brexiteers' marginal victory (52 per cent) has led to one of the most chaotic periods in British political history. Scotland, where the majority wanted to remain, has become the victim of mob rule!

Often those who advocate democracy and critics of autocratic regimes themselves are not democratically elected. In a criticism to President Putin's claim that the liberal world view is obsolete, Donald Tusk, the President of the European Council which is not an elected position, has argued that it is authoritarianism, personality cults and the rule of oligarchs which are obsolete. Paradoxically, as one columnist with the British newspaper, *The Guardian*, put it, 'we increasingly see the rise of the unelected'.[36] Among others, the writer was referring to European Union bureaucrats who wield enormous power and influence.

With such an ideological deficit, advocates for democracy in China and other parts of the world do not have the moral standing with which to push such a flawed system. The West and the champions of democracy are themselves grappling with the rise of undemocratic tendencies in their own backyards.

One can imagine the chaos democracy would bring to China, bearing in mind that internal politics have historically been the critical factor that brought upheaval to that country. This book will argue that for China's neighbours, and even for the rest of the world, a stable China, irrespective of its political system, is probably best for everyone.

Defining Chinese Aspirations: Xi Jinping's 'The China Dream'

In focusing on the internal dynamics, in addition to the democracy debate, it is worthwhile to examine Chinese President Xi Jinping's concept of the 'China Dream', which provides us with a window on their aspirations as a future global power. Without referring to the term China Dream in his speech as the new General Secretary of the CCP at the Politburo Standing Committee Members' Meeting with the press at the Great Hall of the People in Beijing, in November 2012, he outlined the present expectations and hopes of the Chinese people. He said, 'Our people love life and expect better education, more stable jobs, better income, more reliable social security, medical care of a higher standard, more comfortable living conditions, and a more beautiful environment.'[37] About two weeks later, at the 'The Road Towards Renewal' Exhibition, held in Beijing, he first introduced the Chinese Dream, which henceforth became a buzzword and has stirred extensive debate amongst different groups, each trying to provide additional meaning and direction to what could best be described as something nebulous. Not surprisingly, the propaganda machinery, though much more sophisticated when compared to previous eras, went into overdrive to promote the idea of the China Dream.

Over the years, the term 'China Dream' has been built upon to create some kind of national agenda which the country could pursue and has been identified as a rallying point to galvanise the Chinese people. Today, it has officially become the 'Chinese Dream of National Rejuvenation'. To some extent, it is meant to stir up nationalism, for the speeches connected to this ideal are often imbued with a high dose of nationalistic fervour, with references of how glorious have been the achievements of China, and of its greatness, in the past and the future.

Most appropriately, during the 100th anniversary of the CCP, President Xi talked of the Chinese nation being a great nation, and he placed national rejuvenation at the core of the goals of the Party, historically as well as in contemporary times. He said, 'To realise national rejuvenation, the party has united and led the Chinese people in pursuing a great struggle, a great project, a great cause, and a great dream through a spirit of self-confidence, self-reliance, and innovation, achieving great success for socialism with Chinese characteristics in the new era.' The speech reached a crescendo when he concluded that 'it is certain that with the firm leadership of the party and the great unity of the Chinese people of all ethnic groups, we will achieve the goal of building a great modern socialist country in all respects and fulfill the Chinese Dream of national rejuvenation'.[38] Not surprisingly, the key elements mentioned by Xi here are the Party, unity and socialism (with Chinese characteristics) which, in effect, translated would mean that the CCP will ensure unity and bring prosperity to the nation.

There is no doubt that President Xi Jinping aspires to be remembered as a great leader who has given the Chinese people and nation the good life that all aspire to and dream of. As the famed American Civil Rights leader, Martin Luther King, had a dream, so too has Xi, for his dream is the dream shared by all Chinese for peace and prosperity. It is perhaps not surprising that Xi's agenda has been hailed as being monumental and he is regarded amongst the great Chinese leaders. Academic Elizabeth Economy, of the New York-based Council on Foreign Relations, even dubbed this as the third revolution,[39] with Mao and Deng, being the first and second respectively. This may be justified as the thoughts of Xi Jinping on 'Socialism with Chinese Characteristics for a New Era' were added to the Constitution of the CPC during the 19th Party Congress, held in October 2017, which has secured him a place on the same level as both Mao and Deng, where their ideas were also incorporated in the Party's constitution—the former's thoughts were established as the Party's guiding ideology at the 7th Congress in 1945, while the latter's theory on building socialism with Chinese characteristics was added at the 14th Party Congress in 1992.[40] Elizabeth Economy argues that 'What makes Xi's revolution distinctive is the strategy he has pursued: the dramatic centralization of authority under his personal leadership; the intensified penetration of society by the state; the creation of a virtual wall of regulations and restrictions that more tightly controls the flow of ideas, culture, and capital into and out of the country; and the significant projection of Chinese power.'[41]

In examining this national rejuvenation goal, there are several issues that clearly need discussion. The first is the role of the party and, in this respect, the idea of democracy within the confines of one-party rule has been discussed earlier. Secondly, it would appear that much of what lies in the dreams of the Chinese people—namely to secure their own personal prosperity in line with the nation's, which, in effect, would mean to be richer and have greater purchasing power, in order to buy more luxury goods and to enjoy a high standard of living—seems contradictory to what socialism represents, with or without Chinese characteristics, and that is the creation of a bourgeois society. According to Kerry Brown of King's College London, the China Dream seems to be 'the affirmation of a bourgeois China with all the paradoxes that that entails'.[42] To another scholar, these contradictions will grow in the future and that 'we should be alert to the potential of discontent coalescing into a significant political challenge', although she argues that 'there is no compelling evidence that Xi's revolution is in danger of being reversed'.[43]

Notwithstanding the paradoxes of the China Dream, the concept seems to be an evolving one, as speeches connected to the China Dream show, and it also entails the need to eradicate poverty as well as to achieve a greener environment. The focus on tackling the latter is a recognition by the state of the severity of this issue, not only as a frequent source of criticism from outside China, especially from the West, but also domestically.

No one visiting Beijing could fail to notice the lack of clear skies in and around the capital city.

The eradication of poverty does address the socialist ideals of creating a more egalitarian society, albeit with special Chinese circumstances or, the preferred official term, characteristics. To Beijing, to address poverty is to ensure that no one is caught in the poverty trap which appears a perennial problem facing many societies and countries. In this respect, China has indeed made impressive advances. To President Xi, the country was able 'to make the historic transformation of raising the living standards of its people from bare subsistence to an overall level of moderate prosperity'.[44] However, as we shall discuss later, given the massive number of people involved, the issue of poverty alleviation remains a critical area for the leadership and the Party. The growing income disparity is obviously one of those issues that garner constant attention, for it could well be a barometer to measure the success of the CCP. Not surprisingly, the state's commitment to ensure that poverty is reduced, if not eliminated, is periodically repeated by Chinese government officials. In one instance, in April 2021, at the press conference on the issuance of a white paper by China's State Council Information Office, entitled 'Poverty Alleviation: China's Experience and Contribution', officials reiterated not only a solemn commitment by the government but also as a priority of President Xi's work agenda.[45]

This remains so despite the official declaration that China has eliminated extreme poverty. President Xi himself announced this with much fanfare on 25 February 2021, declaring that China has won a 'complete victory' in its fight against poverty. Specifically, the Chinese president said that absolute poverty had been eradicated in the world's most populous country, in which 'over the past eight years, the final 98.99 million impoverished rural residents living under the current poverty line have all been lifted out of poverty. All the 832 impoverished counties and 128,000 impoverished villages have been removed from the poverty list.'[46] Although this is indeed an impressive achievement, some have pointed out that the definition and measurement of extreme poverty by the Chinese are flawed and set at a much lower threshold. For instance, in an article in the *Washington Post*, China's statistics bureau, in 2019, defined rural poverty as below per capita annual income of 2300 yuan (US$356). Previously, officials defined the poverty line as less than 4000 yuan (US$620) a year, or $1.69 a day—less than the World Bank's threshold of $1.90 a day and well below the $5.50 a day that economists recommend for upper-middle-income countries.[47] Therefore, notwithstanding China's sanguine official declaration, it remains clear that the Chinese leadership and government still acknowledge that combating poverty is a critical policy area that requires specific attention, as we have so often seen declared by officials.

It is important to acknowledge the existence of the China Dream, for although we could brush it aside as being rhetorical, it does provide us with an indication of the direction China is heading. This is central to any discussion of China's rise, for it does give us some inkling of Chinese aspirations and how it sees itself in the global order. According to a *Time Magazine* article, President Xi 'makes no secret of wanting to see China assume a position of international centrality'.[48] Clearly, it desires to be a power second to none, to 'rejuvenate the country', to reclaim what it had lost over the centuries and conjure again the Middle Kingdom, albeit, as a twenty-first-century version. To Professor Graham Allison, China wants to return to 'the predominance it enjoyed in Asia before the West intruded'.[49] However, there will also be constraints, as pointed out by China watcher, David Shambaugh, who, writing almost a decade prior to Xi's China Dream, cautioned against the tendency to view the Asian region as being 'China-dominant' as premature. He wrote, 'China shares the regional stage with the United States, Japan, ASEAN, and increasingly, India as well.'[50] It is true that when we look at China's rise in the region or in the world, we often tend to assume that China is alone and unrivalled and confronts no resistance or opposition from either prevailing powers or from regional countries. This will be discussed in later chapters.

Integral to making China a great nation is the military component, for in the words of President Xi, 'A strong country must have a strong military, as only then can it guarantee the security of the nation… It is a strong pillar for safeguarding our socialist country and preserving national dignity, and a powerful force for protecting peace in our region and beyond.'[51] As we shall see in Chap. 3, the modernisation of the People's Liberation Army (PLA) is driven by this goal of making China powerful, which to President Xi is to make China great again, a phrase used by the Chinese president a few years before the slogan 'Make America Great Again' became popularly associated with Trump.

This book will seek to answer perhaps one of the most pertinent questions—whether China will be a hegemonic power, dominating the world, along the same lines as the United States, or even worse, with untold devastating impact.

Salient Point—Regional and Global Dimensions

As the Western world, led by the United States, views China mainly through a threat prism, this book will address the contentious subject of how China is viewed in Chap. 4. There is even a Tom Clancy novel that portrays the fictitious and flamboyant Jack Ryan trying to deal with the Chinese threat. Earlier in the series, the bad guy is a Russian or a terrorist, which reflects the times in which those earlier books were written.[52]

Specifically, this book will propose that China is no more a threat to the world than the United States. In fact, in terms of their respective track records in the use of force beyond their borders, Washington has been far more active than Beijing. Notwithstanding interventions prior to the outbreak of World War II, and ever since the beginning of the Cold War, the United States has employed its military might, directly and indirectly, to intimidate, threaten, support insurgencies or overthrow regimes it deemed against its interests. We have witnessed US global interventions—in the Dominican Republic, Chile and Grenada in the Western hemisphere, the US disastrous intervention in Vietnam, and the more recent massive use of force in the overthrow of Iraq's Saddam Hussein. This book will examine and assess China's use of force since 1949 in Chap. 4.

In line with this argument, this book advocates the need for a greater understanding of regional countries' behaviour towards China. Chapter 5 will discuss how regional states view China and how the United States has tried to persuade them to join its own loose coalition against Beijing. Many of these states wish to remain neutral and do not want to be dragged into the American corner. Contrary to the United States' preoccupation with the threat posed by the new China, regional states might prefer to dance with the dragon rather than antagonise it. This work will explore Finlandisation, by which a country is urged to favour, or at least not oppose, the interests of a more powerful country, despite not being politically allied to it, from the perspective of regional states—in other words, the behaviour of states which are in close proximity to a global power.

In addition to this argument, it is relevant to discuss the approach of developmental peace, which could help us to understand and explain further how regional countries tend to view China, despite some great powers, such as the United States, perceiving it as a threat. According to Ling Wei of the China Foreign Affairs University, 'Since the early 1990s, the region has enjoyed dynamic economic growth and enhanced stability while accommodating the rise of China.'[53] She explored the analytical framework of developmental peace as 'a constellation of international practices to account for the long peace in east Asia'.[54] In essence, the prioritisation of economic development by regional states helps to sustain peace in the region. It could be further argued that when the stakes are high, the likelihood of breaching the peace is considerably reduced. Such an argument is predicated on the belief that economic development and the maintenance of security are linked. To Ling Wei, 'regional practices anchored by economic development promote growth and stability at the same time'.[55] Following this, the more countries place economic growth at the forefront of their national goals, the more likely will there be a reduction in conflict as well as incentives for them to resolve potential conflicts amicably. This approach in stressing economic development as a guarantee of peace and security could be seen in the policies of many regional countries, in their attitude towards China. As we shall see, despite outstanding issues with China, such as territorial disputes, regional states preferred to 'put aside' such problem areas and continue to pursue economic and trade ties with Beijing. This perhaps explains why such security matters rarely impact on commercial ties in regional states' relations with China.

It is interesting to note that while economic and security factors impact on one another, namely, any conflict could well disrupt economic growth in any country, it is the prioritisation of the former over the latter that seems to be the core of this developmental approach. When a state places economic growth at the forefront, it will be more inclined not to pursue security as its core interest. This does not mean that such states do not place importance on security. It is that these countries merely place greater emphasis on the economic factor as the overriding concern. To some extent, it is the de-prioritisation of security that will ensure the success of such an approach. Nonetheless, as stated before, the developmental peace approach does not put aside the importance of security, on the contrary it does, but only that it believes this could be achieved through economic development.

China has come to adopt such an approach, which explains, in general, why it has been less aggressive when it comes to disputed issues. It is more inclined to de-emphasise conflicts and instead focus on areas of cooperation, stressing economic, trade and commercial ties. In his study of China's policy in Africa, which is applicable to Beijing's approach in the other parts of the world, Wang Xuejun, from Zhejiang Normal University, argues that 'China's basic experience of maintaining internal stability is aimed at putting development the first priority, so China's idea for attaining peace can be summarized as "development peace", which is different from the liberal peace idea based on Western countries' experience'.[56] In order to illustrate the preference for development over military-based security, Wang used the UN peace missions, arguing that the reliance on the traditional approach of focusing on security instead of giving emphasis to development has proven to be inadequate. This led to a change in focus which was recommended by the Report of the Panel on UN Peace Operations in 2000 (also known as the Brahimi Report), which 'gives some recognition to the underplayed role and untapped potential that initial development work can bring to address the causes of conflict and to prevent the recurrence of conflict'.[57] While this report was specific to UN peace missions, such an approach indeed has a universal appeal.

However, it seems obvious that the developmental peace approach works when more regional countries adopt such an emphasis. As it is said, 'it takes two to tango'. In this respect, when it comes to bilateral security issues, it helps if both countries place economic development over security issues which could well jeopardise the former. This seems to be the case when one examines China's relations with the Association of Southeast Asian Nations (ASEAN), where the level of relations has seen significant improvement, from almost one of hostility in the 1970s and 1980s to one that is predicated on trade and investment, which have benefitted all round. In this respect, not only have ASEAN states placed economic development as central to its prosperity, China too has adopted such an approach.

However, as we shall see in later chapters, despite adopting such an approach, states still have to have some form of security insurance, by either building up their own military forces, engaging in military diplomacy or even relying on external powers, as a further guarantee of peace and security. For instance, the Five Powers Defence Arrangements (FDPA),[58] a legacy of the colonial era, brings the United Kingdom, Australia and New Zealand to the aid of both Malaysia and Singapore. Most recently, the United Kingdom deployed HMS *Defender*, a Type 45 Destroyer, which is part of the HMS *Queen Elizabeth*'s Carrier Strike Group, to the South China Sea, despite warnings coming from China. This Carrier Strike Group is on a global deployment, visiting 40 countries, including India, Japan, Korea and Singapore. According to the Royal Navy, while in the Pacific, ships from the Carrier Strike Group will mark the 50th anniversary of the FPDA by taking part in Exercise *Bersama Lima*.[59]

In the main, despite adopting developmental peace approaches, states will remain realistic about security issues for history is littered with conflicts that occur with or without economic considerations as its casus belli. Often, states are confronted with sovereignty issues which may not be such an easy factor to disregard over economic development. After all, safeguarding one's sovereignty is the raison d'être of a nation. As such, while countries would like to push for economic development, sometimes this has to be bypassed, in favour of traditional forms of security. This perhaps explains why states, including China, would resort to the real or threat of the use of force, as a way to deal with security-oriented issues. As we shall see in later chapters, despite adopting a developmental peace approach, generally reaping results, Beijing would abandon such an approach when it comes to reasserting its sovereignty over disputed territorial areas. China does not hesitate to deploy its armed forces, as a show of force, in order to show to claimants that it will never compromise when it comes to securing its territorial integrity and national sovereignty.

In addition, often without first establishing a stable security environment, it would be extremely difficult to get any meaningful economic development started. Therefore, it is often not a straightforward decision or choice to make regarding which should be given emphasis. The developmental peace approach seems to be more applicable when peace and security have already been achieved, making the shift in focus to development relatively easy. In other words, while states pursue a development peace approach, it is striking the right balance between development and security that is the key to success.

Nonetheless, the prioritisation of economic development as a way to maintain the state's security interest will remain the emphasis and focus, without unnecessarily jeopardising the more traditional approach to peace and security, that of arms and alliances. As the adage goes, 'if you want peace, prepare for war'.

The other issue this book will address is the whole question of China's global status. It is axiomatic that China's power influence today is global in nature and that its power structure continues to grow. Chinese industry is ubiquitous—not only in the products we use daily but, increasingly, in the higher levels of technology. In other words, China has come of age and has become a superpower—in a multidimensional sense that goes beyond mere military power. Further, China has achieved this global presence without firing a bullet and despite huge investment in its vast apparatus of military power. It has essentially used its economic strength as its main vehicle to achieve this status. Thus, as we shall see, it seems superfluous to talk about an emerging China when that country has been a global power in the past. Perhaps it would be more apt to refer to China as a re-emerging power. It was eclipsed as an imperial power following its decline in the nineteenth century, an overshadowing epitomised by the forced leasing of the lucrative island of Hong Kong to London after China's humiliating defeat at the hands of the British in the Anglo–China wars. As will be shown, China is probably one of the very few empires that, having once collapsed, has been able to rise again to take its place once more on the world stage.

This book will examine China's great power status and how it has re-emerged and subsequently spread its tentacles globally. China has already 'conquered' many parts of Africa, Asia and other regions with its domineering economic might. Its visionary BRI has come to symbolise Beijing's non-military approach to global presence, made possible with the assistance and cooperation of regional countries.

As we have seen, President Xi sees himself as the leader who will rejuvenate the country and lead it to the top of the world, as the most powerful and the most prosperous. To a large extent, Xi is blazing the trail for what might be described as post-socialism, which is the opposite of what Marx had in mind when he talked of a utopian society, although they both share the notion of an egalitarian society, with Chinese adoption of Lenin's pragmatic endorsement of the dominance of the Party in leading the proletariat. While China is undeniably a powerful nation, in all dimensions, it is trying to pursue a much more benevolent approach in its international position and behaviour. President Xi has focused, among other things, in improving the image of China, as it is increasingly sensitive to how the world views its rise. Although sometimes negative views on China are the result of its own policies and actions, Beijing feels that it has become a victim of a deliberate attempt by Western powers, in particular the United States, to project China's rise onto the global stage as negative.

A case in point is the debate over Huawei's 5G technology. Critics essentially make two basic points: the first is about the ability of Huawei, seen as subservient and a tool of the Chinese government, to eavesdrop on all of us and have our data at its disposal. While this will always be a possibility, has it not also been revealed that US-based companies Google and Facebook have leaked our personal data and, in some instances, have in a callous fashion made us all vulnerable to exploitation?[60] In addition, are we so naïve as to think that the Americans and other countries are not already listening in on us? The British GCHQ—the government's communication headquarters—which used to listen to the airwaves behind the Iron Curtain, is today focused on activities within the United Kingdom and other regions to address, among others concerns, the threat of terrorism.[61] So when people talk of Huawei having the ability to listen to our conversations and having access to personal data, have they missed the point that it is already taking place in our own backyard? It was already revealed that the United States had once intercepted German Chancellor Merkel's phone, which had caused a strain in bilateral ties. Even when it comes to having the ability to shut down Huawei-dominated technology, again, are we saying that Western-based companies have no such capability and that they will not be forced by the US government to use it? Critics of Huawei point out that the Chinese have legislation that compels Chinese companies to be part of the wider reach of the government. Conveniently, such critics have forgotten that the United States has its own Patriot Act which does the same and that other Western countries have different legislative provisions which they can use to force corporations to cooperate with them.

While embarking on an exercise to improve China's image, it is fast discovering that power often breeds power and with that discontentment. Throughout the ages, power has denoted a sense of invulnerability, often demonstrated through some wanton display or actual use of force. This was described by nineteenth-century British politician Lord Acton who said that 'absolute power corrupts absolutely'.[62] It could be argued that in order to mitigate such negativity, China wants to show the world a more positive image.

Having said the above, China has its fair share of challenges to overcome if it is going to be successful in the long run. Seen against China's long history, the period since the beginning of its present phenomenal rise seems a rather short time. Reminiscent of earlier emperors, Chinese communist leaders are painfully aware that it is the domestic agenda that will be the final determinant of its ultimate success. However, as China's rise has impacted on the world's stage, Beijing is aware that it needs to project a much more positive and benign stance, while at the same time, having to confront a number of contentious issues, mainly involving territorial disputes as well as having to fend off criticisms over its global behaviour, mainly spearheaded by the United States. To a large extent, China has to balance between its global aspirations and the often-negative impact on countries. As this book focuses mainly on Asia, this will be the prevalent theme that will emerge throughout the discussion of China's global rise and its regional impact as well as Asia's response to Beijing. As we shall see, regional countries have tended to be pragmatic in their approach when dealing with China while at the same time being cautiously sanguine.

Notes

1. Double standards have been common place in international affairs for centuries and it is interests that dictate policies, rather than those policies being predicated on ideal, altruistic notions. Many examples could be given here but the one that is so obvious is the close ties between the so-called champion of democracy, the United States, and the oil-rich absolute monarchical Kingdom of Saudi Arabia. Washington will use the democracy hammer when it wants to hit at dictatorial regimes that are against them, while ignoring this ideological factor when it suits them.
2. It cannot be denied that some of these regimes look to the Chinese for easy access to funds that are also used for personal and regime interests.
3. During the Cold War, some newly independent or liberated countries found themselves isolated by the West due to their left-leaning ideologies. For example, after Fidel Castro triumphantly marched into Havana in December 1958, having overthrown the US stooge Batista, Cuba tried to seek American assistance but was pushed away, leaving them with little choice but to move towards the open and willing arms of Moscow.
4. It is acknowledged that there have been periods of US power and its prestige being affected such as that following the end of American intervention in Vietnam, as well as the continuous debate of its decline. See Alfred W. McCoy, *In the Shadows of the American Century: The Rise and Decline of US Global Power* (London: Oneworld Publications, 2019); and Immanuel Wallerstein, *The Decline of American Power: The U.S. in a Chaotic World* (New York: The New Press, 2003).
5. 'China plans its first crewed mission to Mars in 2033', 24 June 2021, www.reuters.com.
6. Xi Jinping, *The Governance of China*, Vol. 3 (Beijing: Foreign Language Press, 2020), p. 12.
7. Patrick W. Quirk, David O. Shullman and Johanna Kao, 'Democracy First: How the US can prevail in the political systems competition with the CCP', *Global Governance and Norms*, September 2020.
8. Ibid., p. 1.
9. Ibid., p. 1.
10. Daniel A. Bell, *The China Model: Political Meritocracy and the Limits of Democracy* (Princeton, New Jersey: Princeton University Press, 2015).
11. Ibid., p. xvi.

12. For the rise of Xi Jinping, see Kerry Brown, *CEO, China: The Rise of Xi Jinping* (London: I.B. Tauris, 2017).
13. 'What Exactly Is "The Chinese Ideal?"', Review Symposia, *Perspectives on Politics*, Vol. 14, No. 1, March 2016, p. 148.
14. For an assessment of this group, see David Halberstam, *The Best and the Brightest* (New York: Ballantine Books, 1993).
15. 'Rowen predicts democracy for China in 20 years', *Stanford News*, Stanford University, 15 November 1996. news.stanford.edu.
16. Andrew J. Nathan, 'China's Changing of the Guard: Authoritarian Resilience', *Journal of Democracy*, Volume 14, Number 1, January 2003, pp. 6–7.
17. It is ironic that the term 'barbarians' was used because the Chinese themselves were using the same concept when referring to non-Chinese or specifically non-Han.
18. Quoted in WW2 People's War, BBC Home, 15 October 2014. https://www.bbc.co.uk stories.
19. Both terms used in Brian Parritt, *Chinese Hordes and Human Waves: A Personal Perspective of the Korean War, 1950–1953* (Barnsley, S. Yorkshire: Pen and Sword Military, 2011).
20. Rana Mitter and Elsbeth Johnson, 'What the West Gets Wrong About China', *Harvard Business Review*, May–June 2021.
21. Xi Jinping, 'Achieving Rejuvenation Is the Dream of the Chinese People'; Speech made when visiting the exhibition 'The Road to Rejuvenation', in Xi Jinping, *The Governance of China* (Beijing: Foreign Language Press, 2014), p. 37.
22. Yue Hu, 'Refocusing democracy: the Chinese government's framing strategy in political language', *Democratization*, Vol. 27, 2020, pp. 302–320.
23. *People's Daily Online*, 19 September 2009.
24. Ibid.
25. Cheng Li, 'Intra-Party Democracy in China: Should We Take It Seriously?', *China Leadership Monitor*, No. 30, November 2009, https://www.brookings.edu, pp. 1–14.
26. Quoted in ibid., p. 4.
27. Quoted in ibid., p. 4.
28. Quoted in ibid., pp. 4–5.
29. Ibid., p. 5.
30. Quoted in ibid., p. 6.
31. Ibid., p. 6.
32. Daniel A. Bell, op cit.
33. Ibid., p. ix.
34. Ibid., p. ix.

35. David Runciman, *How Democracy Ends* (London: Profile Books, 2019), p. 1.
36. *The Guardian*, 1 July 2019.
37. Full text: China's new party chief Xi Jinping's speech, 15 November 2012, www.bbc.com.
38. Full text: Speech by Xi Jinping at a ceremony marking the centenary of the CPC, Xinhua, 2021-07-01, www.xinhuanet.com.
39. Elizabeth C. Economy, *The Third Revolution: Xi Jinping and the New Chinese State* (Oxford: Oxford University Press, 2018).
40. See Michael A. Peters, *The Chinese Dream: Educating the Future* (Oxford: Routledge, 2021).
41. Elizabeth C. Economy, op. cit., p. 10.
42. Kerry Brown, op. cit., p. 30.
43. Elizabeth C. Economy, op. cit., pp. 18–19.
44. Full text: Speech by Xi Jinping at a ceremony marking the centenary of the CPC, op. cit.
45. 'China says poverty alleviation always at the top of President Xi's work agenda', CGTN, 06-Apr-2021, news.cgtn.com.
46. 'Xi declares "complete victory" in eradicating absolute poverty in China', 2021-02-25. Xinhuanet, www.xinhuanet.com). Interestingly, the Chinese Embassy in Kuala Lumpur, and elsewhere around the world, released on its website an article entitled 'How Does China Eliminate Poverty', authored by Ambassador Ouyang Yujing himself, 2021/05/03, my.china-embassy.org.
47. 'China claims to have eliminated poverty, but the figures mask harsh challenges', *The Washington Post*, 25 February 2021, www.washingtonpost.com.
48. *Time*, 19 October 2015, time.com.
49. Graham Allison, 'What Xi Jinping Wants', *The Atlantic*, 1 June 2017, www.theatlantic.com.
50. David Shambaugh, 'Return to the Middle Kingdom?: China and Asia in the Early Twenty-First Century', in David Shambaugh (ed.), *Power Shift: China and Asia's New Dynamics* (Berkeley and Los Angeles, California: University of California Press, 2005), p. 23.
51. Full text: Speech by Xi Jinping at a ceremony marking the centenary of the CPC, op. cit.
52. In the novel dramatised by Hollywood, *Hunt for Red October*, Clancy even went to the extent of humiliating the Soviets with the storyline of a captain of the biggest Soviet Typhoon-class nuclear submarine wanting to defect. There were many such negative portrayals of the good guy fighting the bad guy Hollywood-style—reminiscent of the simplistic wild west scenario. In addition to the more sophisticated CIA agent and academic Jack Ryan

character, there was also the famous *Rambo* series—with its Vietnamese and then the Russians in Afghanistan sequels. Even in the boxing series *Rocky*, Hollywood capitalised on the Soviet threat when in *Rocky IV* the main character took on a Russian opponent who was portrayed as almost being in the image of Frankenstein's monster.

53. Ling Wei, 'Developmental peace in east Asia and its implications for the Indo-Pacific', *International Affairs* 96:1 (2020), p. 192.
54. Ibid., p. 193.
55. Ibid., p. 195.
56. Wang Xuejun, 'Development Peace: Understanding China's Africa Policy in Peace and Security' in C. Alden, A. Alao, Chun, Z, and L. Barber (eds.), *China and Africa: Building Peace and Security Cooperation on the Continent* (London: Palgrave Macmillan, 2018), p. 68.
57. Quoted in ibid., p. 70
58. For a background on the setting up of FPDA, see Chin Kin Wah, *The Defence of Malaysia and Singapore: The Transformation of a Security System 1957–1971* (Cambridge: Cambridge University Press, 1983).
59. George Allison, 'UK warship enters South China Sea despite Chinese warnings', 24 July 2021, ukdefencejournal.org.uk.
60. This became the basis of a Netflix documentary, *The Great Hack* (2019).
61. One humorous T-shirt reads, 'GCHQ: We always listen to our customers'.
62. Lord Acton Quote Archive, Acton Institute, acton.org.

CHAPTER 2

Examining China's History: Bringing the Past into the Future

When he addressed the celebration to mark the 100th anniversary of the founding of the Communist Party of China, President Xi Jinping gave an overview of Chinese history that spans more than 5000 years.[1] He declared that 'China has made indelible contributions to the progress of human civilization' and highlighted the 'courageous fight' of the Chinese people, focusing on the genesis of the Party, from its victory in October 1949 and beyond. What is abundantly clear in Xi's speech, which resonated throughout the country, is this sense of pride in its long history and the need to 'rejuvenate' to reclaim its past glory days, when it was once the Middle Kingdom, which, to the Chinese, means to be at the centre of the world. After all, the Mandarin term for China remains precisely that—*Zhong Guo*—middle kingdom.

President Xi's brief and selective history lesson, which now seems to be the standard template for his speeches, does illustrate the country's glorious past but also the period often referred to as the humiliation era. However, for the purpose of reinforcing his notion of the China Dream—which is being used as a rally point to instil and inculcate nationalist sentiments—much of the country's history has conveniently been buried or forgotten. In this respect, Bill Hayton, in his seminal work,[2] argues that much of China's history, which is being projected publicly, is actually the product of its own invention. To Hayton, the tendency to categorise dynasties in convenient time frames 'demonstrates how every group that chooses to see itself as a nation constructs myths around itself and, if they are successful, reconstructs the same around those myths…. they sought

© The Author(s), under exclusive license to Springer Nature Switzerland AG 2021
A. R. Baginda, *The Global Rise of China and Asia*,
https://doi.org/10.1007/978-3-030-91806-4_2

to present themselves as the legitimate successors to their discredited predecessors. The Communists, like the Nationalists before them, are no different.'[3] The glorification of China, seen as a coherent entity over millennia, has brushed aside the fact that *Zhong Guo* was far from being as powerful as it has been made out to be. Nonetheless, the official history as promulgated by the Chinese Communist Party (CCP) was to whip up nationalism amongst a population that is fast becoming more confident than ever. However, China is certainly not unique in the re-writing of its own history, as many countries do the same, for a variety of reasons, such as to justify their present policies or, like China, to appeal to nationalist sentiments. One can think of China's neighbour Japan, which has to deal with its past aggression. Japan does it to help justify, for instance, its invasion of China and its attack on Pearl Harbour in December 1941, which sparked the outbreak of the Pacific War. The glaring difference in the re-writing of history between China and most other countries is that, in the case of the former, there seems to be an absence of critical thinking and discussion over such issues within the country. Nonetheless, President Xi's re-interpretation of China's history has a specific purpose which appears to resonate amongst his countrymen. This chapter will briefly examine China's history with a broad brush—highlighting the salient periods of the country's past.

The Return of Chinese Civilisation

The Chinese rank among the great civilisations of the world, alongside the Egyptians, Persians, Greeks and Romans. However, the Chinese, unlike most other civilisations, had an uninterrupted imperial line governed by dynastic rulers, from their early history to the Xia dynasty beginning in 2205 BCE and then through the Qin dynasty (from when Qin Huangdi crowned himself as the first emperor of a unified China in 221 BCE) to that dynasty's collapse in 1911. The Middle Kingdom, so-named because the Chinese saw themselves as being at the centre of the world, was an imperial system which, though more inward-looking, had ambitions, designs and strategic reach.

While most empires declined or disappeared, relegated to the history books with just the archaeological ruins beloved of tourists, China did not. It could be argued that, alongside the re-emergence of the Middle Kingdom, today's China, Russia and to a lesser degree Iran,[4] also once great powers, also have the potential to make a comeback.

While many refer today to the emergence of China, it is probably more accurate to call it a re-emergence after a period of hibernation. One cannot imagine any of the other great empires making a return. Even the British, with their 'sun never sets' notion, have declined since 'Britannia ruled the waves' and face an uncertain future in a post-Brexit world. The Greeks or the Romans perhaps? Almost impossible. Gibbon's monumental work on the collapse of the Roman Empire delivered a definitive conclusion on the fate of that once great and feared imperial power.[5] All empires experienced what Paul Kennedy refers to as strategic or imperial over-reach.[6] Having expanded their empires, in some instances across vast territories, control from the centre becomes increasingly weak. The imposition of rules, including the collection of taxes which is forced upon the locals, leads to injustices and in turn rebellion, which, mainly due to the great distances, the centre is unable to quash. This is often compounded by all sorts of political machinations and challenges to the leadership. Such scenarios often beset empires, leading to their eventual fall and leaving them doomed never again to rise. To a large extent, China's return is a first in history. However, it is interesting to note that within the intellectual community in China, there have been discussions as to whether China itself is undergoing this perhaps inevitable path of strategic over-reach. In a study undertaken to explore the intellectual discourse amongst Chinese scholars, the conclusion drawn was that 'most Chinese scholars agree that the debate over strategic overstretch is valuable for China's foreign policy community. They disagree on the extent to which China already has such a problem. Some feel that strategic overstretch is primarily applicable in the context of hegemonic power, empire or established power, and that for China, as a rising power, the expansion of power and influence is inevitable: indeed, that by definition a rising power will expand its power and influence… For a rising China, the key danger is not the scope or direction of its expanding influence, but the speed of its rise.'[7] Following from this, the concern is that China—especially under President Xi who has been pushing the country to take the world's centre stage and to declare itself as the greatest—will invite a backlash and pressure and as such 'some Chinese thinkers are calling for a moderation of Chinese "triumphalism"'.[8]

The Making of the Middle Kingdom

The Raison D'être of the Middle Kingdom

The Chinese empire draws mainly from its long-lasting civilisation and its own sense of grandeur. According to Jonathan Fenby, 'China's rulers drew on a national self-confidence, based on the early evolution of Chinese Civilization.'[9] Unlike the British Empire, for instance, which stretched across many oceans, including to the far-flung South Atlantic islands,[10] China boasted no overseas colonies. Instead, its influence was not so much territory-based as its own sense of greatness. Although it saw itself as the centre of a world around which all others orbited, the kingdom's physical expansion was very much confined to adjacent areas despite its enormous size and ever-growing population. This was in great contrast to other colonial powers, such as Belgium and Portugal and even Britain, whose own landmass was greatly surpassed by the size of the colonies or lands they managed to 'conquer'. Belgium's King Leopold II, for example, who reigned from 1865 to 1909, came to control and exploit the Congo, during what became known infamously as the 'Scramble for Africa'—in which European powers divided the spoils of conflict and rapacity.[11]

This is not to suggest that China never expanded its borders. On the contrary, like other imperial powers, through the various dynasties, China grew in size, conquering lands belonging to its neighbours. For instance, the Tang dynasty brought about one of the most extensive expansions of China's real estate and influence, extending its physical empire to include parts of Annam (modern-day Vietnam), the northern Turkic peoples of Central Asia, the Korean Peninsula and parts of Japan.

To some extent, some of the Chinese emperors would be the equivalent of the Muslim Caliphs Umar and Othman, who, through conquest, expanded the Islamic empire beyond the Arabian Peninsula and overran neighbouring areas that once belonged to Sasanian and Byzantine rulers.

Nonetheless, China did not venture beyond its border areas. One of the reasons for China's lack of overseas appetite was its perception of itself. It saw itself as self-sufficient, needing nothing from the outside world. In essence, it saw the world as needing China rather than the other way around. After all, early inventions and sought-after products, which had attracted emissaries and traders from all over the world, reinforced this enormous superiority complex in the minds of Chinese rulers and bureaucrats.

Imperial China was operating a 'tributary' system whereby it exercised enormous influence over others, to the extent that states had to recognise its greatness and, in so doing, pay homage to the Middle Kingdom. To a large extent, this system was self-serving and based on China's perception of its greatness and its sense of self-aggrandisement. The following extract from the ancient Book of Odes, written during the Zhou dynasty (1046–256 BCE), speaks volumes about China's self-centred mentality.

> Everywhere under vast Heaven
> There is no land that is not the King's.
> To the borders of those lands
> There are none who are not the King's servants.[12]

As a demonstration of its superiority, Chinese emperors often boasted that China did not require anything from the rest of the world. During the first British trade mission to China in the summer of 1793, Lord Macartney, the leader of the delegation, who had brought the best Britain could offer in terms of technological prowess, received a lukewarm response from Emperor Qianlong and the imperial household. According to Julia Lovell, the trade mission was doomed long before it reached its destination. She quotes the emperor: 'We have never valued ingenious articles… nor do we have the slightest need of your country's manufactures.'[13] The emperor's words proved to be wide of the mark, as the following decades witnessed the beginning of the end of the Middle Kingdom as its doors were forced open. In retrospect, Chinese insularity was to prove fatal, for it shut itself off from the enormous technological advances which were taking place in Europe in the eighteenth and nineteenth centuries, including in the area of weaponry development.

Today's China still displays some elements of this sense of grandeur, epitomised by President Xi's global agenda for the Belt and Road Initiative (BRI). A statement by the Chinese leader, who said that 'those opposing the BRI or China–Pakistan Economic Corridor (CPEC) will never succeed as the multi-billion-dollar trade and transit projects are aimed at developing the region',[14] reinforced Beijing's central position.

In addition to this sense of greatness was the prominence of the emperors, beginning with the early ones such as Zhou and Shang (during a period known as the Warring States) and continuing through the unified dynasty of Qin beginning in 221 BCE and on to the time of the Qing emperors from 1644 to 1911. Chinese emperors were shrouded in much mythology. They were regarded as divine rulers and known as Sons of Heaven. Before China was unified by the first Emperor Qin, the Zhou dynasty postulated the rather self-serving concept of the Mandate of Heaven, in which rulers had the gods on their side until such time as they angered them, causing their own downfall. When this occurred, it was understood that Heaven's mandate had been withdrawn. This cosmic nexus between the ruler and the divine provided legitimacy for their power base.

Some dynastic rulers tried to enhance their 'connectivity' with Heaven, while others attempted to pacify the divine. For example, the Han retained the Mandate of Heaven by an imperial cult of ritual observances which were devoted to Heaven.[15] This included the construction of splendid edifices devoted to the Heavens, chief of which is the must-see tourist spot, the Temple of Heaven built by Ming Emperor Yongle in 1420. This temple was a physical embodiment of the concept of the Mandate of Heaven and was where emperors would perform rituals which illustrated their subservience to 'the above', which could grant and conversely withdraw its 'blessings' on the rulers. The annual rituals would include fasting and donning special robes, then ascending alone to the open altar and prostrating nine times. There, the emperor would offer his report and seek help and blessings for his reign. This epitomised the concept of the emperor's raison d'être in the Mandate of Heaven. It is interesting to note that the last performance of such a ritual was during the years following the collapse of imperial China. It involved the one-time warlord president of the Republic of China, Yuan Shikai, in 1915, who, aside from his sense of self-worth and somewhat misplaced imperial ambition, wanted to legitimise his rule by making his connection with Heaven.[16] Strangely, and even ironically, he even envisaged himself as the new emperor.

The Pinnacle of Imperial Power

Like most imperial powers, all the emperors experienced various periods of ups and downs, highs and lows. Imperial China's long history witnessed the fall of various dynasties and the rise of new ones. It even saw the kingdom being invaded by foreign entities such as the Mongols and the Manchus, but the invaders soon adapted themselves to Chinese ways. Notwithstanding such changes in the dynastic lineage, the Middle Kingdom survived and flourished.

Given its longevity, it is debatable which of the dynasties and emperors could be hailed as reaching the pinnacle of power and influence. All empires have their great leaders, be they Ramses II of Ancient Egypt, Darius of Persia, Alexander the Great in Ancient Greece and even Britain's Queen Victoria, who presided over the largest empire the country has ever known.

There are several candidates, who, arguably, can be seen as the Middle Kingdom's most successful and influential emperor. Obviously, much depends on the criteria used to identify and judge them, which could include their conquests and their enlightenment, which led to the flourishing of the arts, culture and education, and the great physical edifices they left, at which tourists from all over the world now marvel. Interestingly, they all share a common trait—they were often ruthless towards their enemies, including those from within. As the saying goes, 'you cannot make omelettes without breaking eggs'. In this case, 'you cannot build an empire without death and destruction'.

While many achieved greatness to a varying degree, a number of emperors have been identified as outstanding rulers. Chief among them was the second Tang emperor, Taizong, who ruled from 626 to 649. He has been touted by many as the greatest of all. According to one scholar, 'Taizong's era has been traditionally singled out as the one truly successful reign in what has been conventionally regarded as the most powerful dynasty in China.'[17] To another observer, 'under Taizong's leadership, China became the world's largest and strongest country. The emperor's reign was marked by a number of savvy, innovative, and bold accomplishments, setting a high standard for all leaders who would come after.'[18] He was an all-round achiever; he expanded the Kingdom's territory and influence and engaged in the flourishing of the arts and culture and in the fields of administration, education and religion. He was seen as a benevolent emperor, which is typified by the following quote attributed to him: 'The ruler depends on the state, and the state depends on its people. Oppressing the people to make them serve the ruler is like someone cutting off his own flesh to fill his stomach. The stomach is filled but the body is injured: the ruler is wealthy but the state is destroyed.'[19]

Another Chinese ruler who would certainly be near the top of the list was Emperor Yongle of the Ming Dynasty[20] who ruled from 1403 to 1424. He is best remembered as the builder of the splendid Forbidden City, which is perhaps equivalent to Louis XIV's Palace of Versailles—the most tangible symbol of the Sun King's glory. It was Emperor Yongle who moved the capital city from Nanjing to Beijing. He changed the city's name to 'Obedient to Heaven', to symbolise the heavenly ties to his mandate. *Inter alia*, security was one of the reasons behind the move to Beijing. He had identified himself as a warrior and was naturally preoccupied with the vulnerability of the northern borders. By being in close proximity to the area exposed to the steppe, 'he could at all times oversee its problems and take immediate action against them'.[21]

Undeniably, Emperor Yongle is highly regarded in retrospect, for this period also saw Chinse culture and education flourish. In line with the Confucius sage-king tradition,[22] Yongle promoted Confucian moral education, sponsored imperial publications and followed prescribed ritual proceedings that his father had established.[23] Posthumously, Emperor Yongle was given the highest accolade for a Chinese emperor, that of 'Emperor of Culture'. Another lasting legacy of this Ming emperor was the deployment of the large expeditionary ships led by Admiral Zheng He.[24]

However, according to his biographer, Yongle is seen as something of a paradox, displaying the best and worst of imperial China. He has been lionised as being the best of imperial China because he was a tireless and restless monarch who set the agenda not only for fifteenth-century China but for most of Asia during the early modern era. At the same time he has been criticised because he committed an act of *lèse-majesté* by killing his nephew and seizing the throne. By keeping a large part of the population under severe strain for more than 20 years, he personified imperial tyranny.[25]

During the long period of the Qing dynasty, which lasted for nearly three centuries, a number of emperors could be hailed as luminaries. Among them is the second Qing emperor, Kangxi, whose reign title was 'unalterable peace'. According to one biographer, during his rule, which spanned from 1662 to 1722, 'he governed his vast empire with wisdom and foresight, he expanded its borders and brought a measure of prosperity to the Chinese people'.[26] He was also known to be a patron of the arts and of learning, and 'magnificent porcelain vases bearing his name are to be found in all the museums of the world'.[27]

Another notable Qing emperor was Qianlong, who ruled from 1735 to 1799 and whose most important achievement was 'the conquest and integration of huge areas of western territory—the region later known as Xinjiang, the "New Territories"—into the Chinese state'.[28] This reign can be seen both 'as the culmination of dynastic greatness and as the forerunner of an era of deep troubles'.[29] It was Qianlong who welcomed with great courtesy, in the summer of 1793, the first British official, Lord Macartney, to the Middle Kingdom. Even though Macartney did not achieve the main objective of his mission, to negotiate trade and diplomatic agreements, he was 'remarkably successful in piercing the veils of mystery and misconception that had hitherto prevented Europeans from grasping the nature of Qing China'.[30] The lukewarm imperial response to the British request for commercial arrangements proved to be a harbinger of what was to come over the next few decades.

It was during the long Qing dynasty that China expanded its territories far beyond its predecessors' achievements, more than doubling the geographic expanse of the Ming Empire.[31] This was also a non-Han dynasty and catapulted the Manchus to the helm of political power. The Qing era was a paradox of sorts: while it would receive accolades as being the high point of China's imperial past, it would also oversee the collapse of the dynastic system. It was the Qing dynasty that opened up the inward-looking, isolationist Middle Kingdom to the West and which, in the end, proved unable to resist the might of the Western powers, in particular the British, who resorted to the use of opium and force to subdue the Chinese.

The strength and longevity of such imperial power were often tempered by internal rebellions—often ruthlessly quashed—and by outside threats from non-Han neighbours. On several occasions neighbouring states successfully violated the Middle Kingdom's sovereignty, such as when the Mongols took over as the new Chinese rulers and when the Manchus witnessed the final demise of the imperial system. Just as it could be argued that internal factors were the main cause of disruptions to imperial rule in the era of the Middle Kingdom, it is also likely that these, too, will be the greatest threat to present-day China's overall stability. The issue of a domestic threat within China is a recurring theme in assessing China—past, present and future. Given its enormous population size, with its vast diversity, the internal dynamics of the country will prove to be a critical factor in assessing China's future. This is the invaluable lesson we learn from China's often tumultuous past. As will be discussed later, it takes some reckoning to accept the enormous challenge of managing a population of around 1.4 billion people, a population that is growing every day.

The Beginning of the End for the Middle Kingdom

Tourists and locals alike flock to Yuanmingyuan, northeast of Beijing, to see the ruins of the Summer Palace. It is easy to get there nowadays, as it can be reached via the Beijing metro, on line 4, just one stop after Peking University. The ruinous destruction of what was once the imperial splendour of the emperors is deliberately preserved as a constant reminder of Chinese humiliation at the hands of European powers. To the Chinese, this destruction only confirmed what they had always known—that the Europeans were ferocious, ignorant and utterly devoid of cultural values.[32] They were barbarians according to the Chinese. The huge compound, which was home to the Qing emperors, was destroyed by a combined French and British force, under the command of generals Charles Cousin-Montauban and James Hope Grant, in reprisal for the imprisonment of a number of British military personnel. Many of the treasures found in the palace were looted by the French prior to its destruction. Interestingly, before General Gordon was immortalised by his presence in Sudan, as Gordon of Khartum,[33] he played a small role in the destruction of the Summer Palace.[34]

Although imperial history is not looked upon favourably in post-1949 China, as illustrated by the constant debate over the excesses of the rulers,[35] this humiliating period of Chinese history does resonate in today's China. Perhaps it reminds the populace of the notion of Western efforts to ensure that China will never be superior to the West and even to subjugate it.

The eventual end of imperial China was brought about, ironically, by its own somewhat misplaced determination to be self-sufficient and isolationist, coupled with its economic success. Imperial China felt that it required little from the outside world and was worried about the consequences of opening up. Due to its mentality of 'greatness'—after all, it was the Middle Kingdom, to which vassal states paid tribute to the emperors as a sign of their submission—it became blind to the growing popularity of the notion of free trade, espoused by the European states. Its continued closed-door policy became an anachronism in an era of open trade.[36] There were several negotiations between, for instance, the British and the Chinese over trade concessions, and limited access was granted to the area surrounding Canton. However, with a growing and insatiable appetite for trade, championed by the East India Company and other burgeoning trading houses, the push for more trade openings made a clash with the Chinese inevitable. The trade imbalance had produced a large trade deficit for Britain in its commercial dealings with China. The British were importing from China products such as tea, which became a national obsession, and other sought-after luxuries such as silk (the fashion for Chinese products in Europe even coined a new word—'chinoiserie'). The Chinese, on the other hand, were importing little from Britain other than Indian cotton and other materials. This resulted in the British trying to seek ways to tilt the trade balance in their favour and curtail the drain of silver bullion required to purchase, in particular, the vast amounts of tea needed to meet demand.

The British eventually found opium, which was mostly produced in India, with which they could flood the Chinese market and earn huge profits, thereby recalibrating the balance of trade. Opium, though illegal, was already used in China, mainly for medicinal purposes, but it was the British who brought in huge quantities and it soon became a widespread addiction in the wider population. Between 1820 and 1825, 9708 opium crates were brought into China and between 1830 and 1835 that figure rose to 35,445 crates.[37] Opium was being imported by British trading companies led by two Scotsmen, William Jardine and James Matheson, who were the nineteenth-century equivalent of the Columbian Pablo Escobar, the biggest drug dealer the world has ever seen. The difference between the Scotsmen and Escobar is that the former were officially sanctioned, while the latter was officially hunted down.

According to an official Chinese version of the Opium War, the British 'found opium was a profitable commodity, with a good sale in China among its extravagant, empty-headed aristocrats, bureaucrats, landlords and rich merchants'.[38]

The Anglo–Chinese War, often referred to as the Opium War, broke out in 1840 as a result of Chinese retaliation against the officially sanctioned importation of opium into China. The Chinese suffered a humiliating defeat at the hands of far superior British forces and strategy. However, the Treaty of Nanjing in 1842 did not go as far as the British wanted, which was the opening up of more trading ports. With a divided Qing court and unwillingness to compromise, force was again employed by the British, this time with the French, leading to the outbreak of the Second Opium War, from 1856 to 1860, in which the Chinese were again defeated. These defeats at the hands of Western powers continue to resonate in China today, inculcated by the state through education and socialisation as a constant reminder that the more powerful are always out to get China.

Even President Xi in his speeches often cites the Opium war to illustrate the humiliation period of the country's history. This 'them versus us' mentality is engrained in the minds of many Chinese to this day. To some extent, the ruling power structure uses this as a way to reinforce the fear of the outside world and, at the same time, to enable China to build its own strength for its own prosperity and survival.

China's lowest point must be those two defeats and the associated humiliation, which forced its long-guarded doors open. Unlike Japan, where the doors opened relatively peacefully following the arrival of American Commodore Perry's ships,[39] China fought and, after the defeats, Britain unashamedly used opium as a tool to subjugate the Chinese people. European colonisers flooded in, each power trying to carve out bits of Chinese territory to bring under their control. It was reminiscent of the Scramble for Africa. Shanghai's Bund, with its iconic Peace Hotel, was symbolic of how international the city became. Various European powers had concessions and established their respective enclaves; even the Japanese had one.[40]

China had to accept the presence of foreign troops on its territory. Even the attempt to oust the European powers, taking advantage of the anti-Christian origins of the Boxer Rebellion in 1900, ended in failure.[41] If there was any doubt that the days of imperial China were coming to an end, this failure to curtail Western incursions and the trading presence of Western countries confirmed what was to become a reality in the following decade. The fragility of imperial China was seized upon by the growing discontent among Western- and Japanese-influenced intellectuals. This came to a head with the ascendancy of the May Fourth Movement,[42] which started the process that ultimately led to the final collapse of imperial China.

With the forced opening up of China by Western powers and its outright defeat during the Anglo–Chinese wars, the once feared kingdom rapidly declined. The leasing of Hong Kong to the British for 100 years epitomised this humiliation at the hands of foreign devils or barbarians, terms the Chinese gave to Westerners.

It is interesting to see how the sense of humiliation affected the pride of the Chinese. To some extent, there exists a degree of paradox: on the one hand, China is proud of its glorious past, but on the other, its humiliation at the hands of Western powers and Japan has become part of the Chinese psyche.

Following the forced opening up of China, with imperial prestige experiencing free fall, the time was ripe for democratic forces to surface. With the emergence of the charismatic leader Sun Yat-sen, the stage was set for the eventual demise of rule by the Mandate of Heaven and its replacement by a mandate of the mere mortal.

The Chinese revolution of 1911[43] was the final nail that sealed the fate of the imperial system forever. The last Chinese Emperor Puyi's exile was, in a way, a saving grace, for he lived to tell the tale of his amazing life during a tumultuous and tempestuous period. His life was immortalised in Bertolucci's film *The Last Emperor*, which won numerous academy awards and which traced, sometimes inaccurately, Puyi's early days living in the Forbidden City, his subsequent confinement within its walls and finally his departure from the forbidding edifice.[44] He then effectively led the life of a football, being kicked around by the various parties, all jousting for power and influence in the chaotic years that accompanied the demise of imperial China—from the warlord years to the short-lived dominance of Chiang Kai-shek's nationalist forces and, eventually, the coming to power of Mao's Communist Party in 1949.

The years following the collapse of the millennia-old imperial power were bound to be chaotic and the country descended into anarchy as various warlords emerged with no consensus on who was the paramount ruler. After a provisional government was formed in January 1912, with Sun Yat-sen as its president, Prime Minister General Yuan Shikai forced Emperor Puyi to abdicate. Immediately, President Sun resigned, as he had earlier promised he would in the event of an abdication. This put an end to dynastic China. Sun's resignation and General Yuan's appointment as the new president[45] had the disastrous consequence of bringing instability, as China descended into years of internal wars and a period of Japanese intervention. To some extent, China had gone full circle, returning to the days of the Warring States period before Qin Shi Huangdi unified the country. It was only when Mao Zedong triumphantly marched into Beijing in October 1949 and established the People's Republic of China (PRC) that the country was united once more. One could argue that uniting China under one rule, that of the Communist Party of China, was Mao's single greatest achievement, given that many of his subsequent domestic policies had disastrous consequences. These included the Great Leap Forward in 1958, which resulted in the country moving backwards. Mao's bold economic plan, which required mass mobilisation of the population, had the objective of transforming an essentially agrarian economy into the higher stages of socialist economic development, through increases in production in the agricultural and industrial sectors. The upheaval in the labour market and production led to famine, as grain output was severely disrupted. It would appear that mere revolutionary enthusiasm was insufficient to bring about economic development, especially when the starting point was low to begin with. The utopian fervour and expectations of 1958 were accompanied by a distinctive Maoist theory of economic development, which even on strictly economic grounds now seems illogical and irrational when viewed in the light of concrete Chinese socio-economic realities.[46]

The death of Mao in September 1976 spelt further uncertainty, as the new leadership had to work gingerly through the mess he had left behind.[47] Even prior to his passing, China was experiencing political forces jousting for control, including a coup attempt by the Gang of Four,[48] for whom Jiang Qing, aka Madam Mao, was arguably the *primus inter pares*. She rose to political prominence during the Cultural Revolution, but her power soon waned, especially after her husband died, leaving her at the mercy of the new leadership of Hua Guofeng, the designated successor to Mao. Revenge for her ruthlessness was exacted when she was publicly tried for her crimes and sentenced to death, subsequently commuted to life imprisonment.[49]

The immediate post-Mao era did not help China economically, although it did shift the country away from communist orthodoxy. Most importantly, it paved the way for the return of Deng Xiaoping and the opening up of China to the world. Known as paramount leader, Deng secured his place in the history books as the man who made China 'great again'.[50]

Notes

1. Full text: Speech by Xi Jinping at a ceremony marking the centenary of the CPC, Xinhua, 2021-07-01, www.xinhuanet.com
2. Bill Hayton, *The Invention of China* (New Haven: Yale University Press, 2020).
3. Ibid., p. 244.
4. Before the Islamic Revolution of 1979, the Pahlavi dynasty was very keen to show its links to the old empire. For example, during Mohammad Reza Shah's reign, Iran celebrated the 2500th anniversary of the foundation of the Persian Empire with much pomp. Reza Shah envisaged himself as a modern Cyrus the Great, famously declaring in front of the ancient tomb

at Persepolis, 'Sleep well, Cyrus, for we are awake.' See Homa Katouzian, *The Persians: Ancient, Medieval and Modern Iran* (New Haven: Yale University Press, 2010), p. 263. In contemporary times, Iran sees itself as representing Shia Muslims, potentially challenging the dominance of the Sunnis in the Islamic world. Its involvement in the Syrian and Yemeni internal conflicts are indicative of this.
5. Edward Gibbon, *The History of the Decline and Fall of the Roman Empire* (New York: Random House, 2006).
6. Paul Kennedy, *The Rise and Fall of the Great Powers: Economic Change and Military Conflict from 1500 to 2000* (London: Unwin Hyman, 1988).
7. Xiaoyu Pu and Chengli Wang, 'Rethinking China's rise: Chinese scholars debate strategic overstretch', *International Affairs*, Vol. 94, No. 5, September 2018, pp. 1034–1035.
8. Ibid., p. 1035.
9. Jonathan Fenby, *The Dragon Throne: China's Emperors, From the Qin to the Manchu* (London: Quercus Publishing, 2015), p. vii.
10. Islands such as St Helena, where Napoleon Bonaparte was exiled after his defeat at the hands of the British at the Battle of Waterloo, as well as the Falklands, where, in 1982, a major war erupted between the British and Argentinians, after the latter invaded the islands.
11. The Scramble for Africa was even regulated by the 1884 Berlin Conference, at which leading European powers sat down to manage the emerging rivalries between them. See Thomas Pakenham, *The Scramble for Africa* (London: Abacus, 1992).
12. Quoted in Howard W. French, *Everything Under the Heavens: How the Past Helps Shape China's Push for Global Power* (New York: Vintage Books, 2017).
13. Julia Lovell, *The Great Wall: China Against the World, 1000 BC–AD 2000* (London: Atlantic Books, 2006), p. 3.
14. Quoted in *Hindustan Times*, 21 September 2018.
15. John King Fairbank and Merle Goldman, *China: A New History* (Cambridge, Massachusetts, The Belknap Press, 2006), p. 63.
16. For his visit to the Temple of Heaven, see Jerome Ch'en, *Yuan Shih-K'ai* (Stanford: Stanford University Press, 1972), pp. 162–163.
17. Mark Edward Lewis, *China's Cosmopolitan Empire: The Tang Dynasty* (Cambridge, Massachusetts: The Belknap Press of Harvard University Press, 2009), p. 34.
18. Chinghua Tang, *The Ruler's Guide: China's Greatest Emperor and His Timeless Secrets of Success* (New York: Scribner, 2017), p. 1.
19. Quoted in Ann Paludan, *Chronicle of the Chinese Emperors: The Reign-by-Reign Record of the Rulers of Imperial China* (London: Thames and Hudson, 1998), p. 89.

20. For a good background on the Ming period, see John W. Dardess, *Ming China 1368–1644: A Concise history of a resilient empire* (Lanham, Maryland: Rowman & Littlefield Publishers, Inc., 2012).
21. F.W. Mote, *Imperial China, 900–1800* (Cambridge, Massachusetts, Harvard University Press, 1999), p. 619.
22. This Confucius' notion of an ideal leader combines the virtue and wisdom of a sage with that of the King's power.
23. Shih-Shan Henry Tsai, *Perpetual Happiness: The Ming Emperor Yongle* (Seattle: University of Washington Press, 2001), pp. 129–130.
24. There have been several notable sources on Zheng He. See Edward L. Dreyer, *Zheng He: China and the Oceans in the Early Ming Dynasty, 1405–1433* (London: Pearson Longman).
25. Ibid., p. xiii.
26. Eloise Talcott Hibbert, *K'ang Hsi: Emperor of China* (London: Kegan Paul, Trench, Trubner and Co Ltd., 1940), p. ix.
27. Ibid., p. ix.
28. Jonathan D. Spence, *The Search for Modern China* (New York: W.W. Norton and Company, 1999), pp. 96–97.
29. F.W. Mote, *Imperial China, 900–1800*, op. cit., p. 912.
30. Pei-Kai Cheng and Michael Lestz (eds.), *The Search for Modern China: A Documentary Collection* (New York: W.W. Norton & Co., 1999), p. 98.
31. William T. Rowe, *China's Last Empire: The Great Qing* (Cambridge, Massachusetts: The Belknap Press of Harvard University Press, 2009), p. 1.
32. Erik Ringmar, *Liberal Barbarism: The European Destruction of the Palace of the Emperor of China* (New York: Palgrave Macmillan, 2013), p. 5.
33. His fame was further accentuated by Hollywood's blockbuster, *Khartoum*, in which Charleston Heston played the role of General Gordon.
34. For an early description of Gordon's adventure in China, see Bernard M. Allen, *Gordon in China* (London: Macmillan and Co. Limited, 1933).
35. A renowned Chinese historian, writing in 1980, described the Qing government as being successful in 'converting all the Manchus into parasites living on other people's toil'. See Hu Sheng, *From the Opium War to the May Fourth Movement* (Beijing: Foreign Language Press, 1991), p. 2.
36. Similarly, in the late twentieth century, powerful states were using the International Monetary Fund as a vehicle to force open some countries that were practising protectionism, especially in the area of services.
37. Jean Chesneaux, Marianne Bastid and Marie-Claire Bergere, *China from the Opium Wars to the 1911 Revolution* (New York: Random House, 1976), p. 54.
38. *The Opium War* (Peking: Foreign Languages Press, 1976), p. 8. It is interesting that the official arm of the Chinese Communist Party specified the bourgeois class to be the addicts. Perhaps not surprisingly, the war was

officially referred to as the start of the Chinese people's bourgeois-democratic revolution against imperialism and feudalism. Ibid., p. 1.
39. There was no real resistance at that time, although it planted the seeds of discontent among the samurais who felt that Japanese tradition and cultural roots were being compromised. Discontentment was also brought about by the Meiji restoration when the balance of power shifted to the Emperor from the Shogun. These culminated in a civil war, known as the Boshin War, 1868–1869. For an excellent background, see Romulus Hillsborough, *Samurai Revolution: The Dawn of Modern Japan Seen Through the Eyes of the Shogun's Last Samurai* (Tokyo: Tuttle Publishing 2018).
40. The Hong Kong-produced film of the early 1970s, *Fist of Fury*, starring the legendary Bruce Lee, had this as its backdrop. It was clearly an anti-Japanese movie, with the Japanese suppressing Chinese martial arts and being seen as the enemy.
41. This episode was used by Hollywood in the 1963 film *55 Days in Peking*, which had a cast of famous actors including Caucasians playing key Chinese roles, such as the powerful Dowager and prominent members of her court. For an eyewitness account of the siege of Peking by the Boxers, see Rev. Roland Allen, *The Siege of the Peking Legations* (London: Smith, Elder, and Co., 1901). For background on the Boxer rebellion, see Lanxin Xiang, *The Origins of the Boxer War: A Multinational Study* (London: RoutledgeCurzon, 2003), and Joseph W. Esherick, *The Origins of the Boxer Uprising* (Berkeley: University of California Press, 1987).
42. For background on the May Fourth Movement, see Chow Tse-tsung, *The May Fourth Movement: Intellectual Revolution in Modern China* (Cambridge, Massachusetts: Harvard University Press, 1960).
43. Much has been written on this subject. For an official Communist party version, see Lu Bowei and Wang Guoping, *The Revolution of 1911: Turning Point in Modern Chinese History* (Beijing: Foreign Language Press, 1991).
44. The inaccuracies are not surprising given Hollywood's penchant for the sensational. The ending, with Puyi collapsing as a gardener, is not correct, as he lived a comfortable life once Chairman Mao and Premier Zhou Enlai had recognised the important role he could play. He was feted by the communist leadership and even provided encouragement to write his memoirs, which, for the first time, revealed to the world his fascinating and rather tragic life. See *From Emperor to Citizen: The Autobiography of Aisin-Gioro Pu Yi* (Beijing: Foreign Languages Press, 1989).
45. When Yuan Shikai became president, a controversy arose over whether his inauguration should be held in Nanjing, the revolutionaries' provisional capital, or in Beijing. This led to a larger debate over where the new Republic should locate its capital, to make a clean break from the imperial

past. For this fascinating controversy, see Shang Xiaoming, 'Yuan Shikai and the February 1912 "Beijing Mutiny"', in Joseph W. Esherick and C.X. George Wei (eds.), *China: How the Empire Fell* (London: Routledge, 2014), pp. 233–246.
46. Maurice Meisner, *Mao's China: A History of the People's Republic* (New York: The Free Press, 1977), p. 217.
47. It is always a challenge for a new leader who emerges after a strong predecessor who has been propped up by a personality cult. Nikita Khrushchev, who replaced Stalin's successor Malenkov, vilified the man of steel in his so-called secret speech and in one masterly stroke helped crumble the Stalin edifice.
48. The Gang of Four was essentially a group of four prominent members of the Communist Party, who became prominent during the later stages of the Cultural Revolution.
49. For her biography, see Ross Terrill, *Madam Mao: The White-Boned Demon* (Stanford: Stanford University Press, 2000).
50. Much has been written about this period and Deng Xiaoping. For an excellent biography, see Ezra F Vogel, *Deng Xiaoping and the Transformation of China* (Massachusetts: Harvard University Press, 2013), and Benjamin Yang, *Deng: A Political Biography* (Armonk, New York: M.E. Sharpe, Inc., 1998).

CHAPTER 3

The Multidimensional Elements of Chinese Power: An Assessment

Exactly when China's comeback began is a moot point, but the rise of Deng Xiaoping to the helm of the Chinese political apparatus is a good starting point. Even prior to this, his liberal economic thinking was already recognised, so much so that he fell victim to the purges of the Cultural Revolution led by the fanatical Red Guards. He was accused of being China's 'second biggest capitalist roader', the first being the disgraced Liu Shaoqi, one-time heir apparent to Mao. Perhaps it came as no surprise when Deng emerged during the post-Mao years as the leader who would abandon the orthodoxy of the socialist economic model and replace it with a much more liberal and open economy, thereby setting the scene for China to transform itself into an economic powerhouse some four decades later.

It is interesting to note that in 1975, then Premier Zhou Enlai proposed a two-stage plan for economic development. During the first stage, from 1975 to 1980, the country was to concentrate on industrialisation, while in the second, from 1980 to 2000, it would pursue modernisation in four areas—agriculture, industry, defence and technology.[1] Deng was already associated with such reforms. However, after Zhou's death in January 1976, Mao appointed Hua Guofeng as Acting Premier, then officially as Premier in April, and finally he became Chairman of the Party on Mao's death in September. Between Zhou's and Mao's death, Deng, who was seen as a potential rival to the Gang of Four, who were the 'power behind the throne' during the last years of Mao's life, was purged. Nonetheless, as Chairman and Mao's successor, Hua Guofeng

© The Author(s), under exclusive license to Springer Nature Switzerland AG 2021
A. R. Baginda, *The Global Rise of China and Asia*,
https://doi.org/10.1007/978-3-030-91806-4_3

championed the Four Modernisations programme.[2] Then, following the fall of the Gang of Four after Mao died, Deng emerged as Paramount Leader, while his protégés and followers held official positions, such as Zhao Ziyang as Premier and Hu Yaobang as Party Chairman. Deng had essentially taken up the reins and pushed Zhou's plans forward posthumously.

Deng Xiaoping and the Chinese Economic Revolution

Despite his diminutive physical appearance, Deng Xiaoping is immortalised as the man behind China's economic miracle. In reality, China's economic transformation was no miracle but due primarily to Deng's pragmatism. As the adage goes, 'timing is everything'. Deng's rise to the top of China's political hierarchy and his ability to bring about real economic reform were helped by the changing times that followed the death of Mao Zedong in September 1976. According to Gregory Chow, there were a few reasons why the time for reform was ripe.[3] Firstly, the unpopularity of the Cultural Revolution meant that the Party and the government had not only to distance themselves from the past but also to undertake changes in order to win back the support of the people. Secondly, due to the economic failures of the Mao period, officials came to realise the shortcomings of a centrally planned system. Thirdly, following from this, the success of a number of Asian economies, namely, South Korea, Taiwan, Hong Kong and Singapore, showed Chinese officials and the people alike that an economy driven by market forces works better than a planned one. And fourthly, the mood of the Chinese people was already changing, and they were ready to support reforms, which should bring them a better standard of living.

It was clear that Deng seized the moment. Hailed as the wizard[4] and the world's greatest economist,[5] Deng was neither, for he was essentially a pragmatist. He recognised that the Chinese economy had to adopt a much more open strategy, integrated with the world's, in order for it to climb out of the existing economic morass. Decades of a centrally planned economy, with wholesale plagiarism from the standard textbook socialist prescription, as practised by almost all such states, including the Soviet Union, which led to China's economic ills, was clearly not working and it needed a fresh look at how the country could truly embark on the road to reform.

According to the World Bank, in 1978, with a GDP per capita of around US$200, China was one of the poorest countries in Asia.[6] To Deng, which such low levels, reform had to be dramatic, something revolutionary. In retrospect, Deng chose a hybrid system—one that accepts market forces, but still relies on state intervention and direction, for the Chinese Communist Party (CCP) has to remain supreme. Hence, Deng introduced 'Socialism with Chinese characteristics', as the new system that was to build the Chinese economy into a global power house.[7]

Essentially, Deng juxtaposed a market economy—with its emphasis on the principle of supply and demand—with the existing centrally planned economic system. In doing so, he was able to improve the system, rather than replacing it entirely, which would unnecessarily create a system vacuum, especially after decades of reliance on the state. In other words, Deng placed a market economy within the context of a socialist, state-driven economic structure. After all, it was no easy task to open up the economy to ill-prepared and inexperienced so-called private entrepreneurs as well as officials. What was needed, therefore, was to ease the control on private commercial ventures in order to allow 'market' forces to play their part. This recalibration of the economy was music to the ears of an already increasingly dissatisfied Chinese population, who for years had to tolerate a rigid system that was producing failure after failure. Their patience was running thin, and this was clearly recognised by Deng and his supporters.

Deng unveiled his reform-driven agenda during the 3rd Plenum of the 11th Central Committee of the CCP, in December 1978. As stated, his open-door policy led to the burgeoning of privatisation in the country. This, in turn, led to the development of private entrepreneurs and an overall increase in productivity. In addition, Deng also emphasised an export-led economic strategy. Taking advantage of low-cost domestic labour while labour costs were rising elsewhere in the developed world, the opening up of China presented a golden opportunity for foreign investment to pour in, turning China into what could be dubbed the world's factory. To facilitate this, the state created Special Economic Zones[8] (SEZs), with the first such 'experiment' being the four areas of Shenzhen, Zhuhai, Shantou and Xiamen. These SEZs were given special status meant to attract foreign investment. Dextrously, these four zones were selected due to their proximity to China's booming economic neighbours, namely, Hong Kong, Macao and Taiwan, which could greatly facilitate the SEZs' development. In fact, Shenzhen became the showcase of the vibrancy of Deng's reform, which helped to transform this once unknown backwater into a modern city full of skyscrapers.⁹ It is no surprise that a statute of Deng Xiaoping was erected in Lianhuashan Park, in Shenzhen, to commemorate his profound contribution to the prosperity of the city and the country in general. Following the success of these initial 4 SEZs, 14 more were opened along the coasts, followed by other initiatives, such as the 'open city' concept, such as in Shanghai, where special concessions were given to attract foreign direct investment. This coastal city was to be transformed from being famous historically as a divided city with its foreign concessions, into a modern metropole, with Pudong being a showcase of how a city could be transformed. The skyline of Pudong with the iconic Oriental Pearl Tower is certainly impressive.

These special zones and cities provided the much-needed impetus for the economy to grow. The government probably saw these special areas like locomotives, which would pull the rest of the country forward. However, like every fast-paced development, there were downsides, such as the rise in corruption and the widening income gap between the haves and have-nots as well as regional imbalances. As we have seen, more recently, the Chinese leadership are taking cognizance of these contradictions and addressing them. President Xi's drive against corruption is a case in point.

Deng recognised that as China was venturing into unchartered economic waters, the political system must remain intact and strong, but at the same time, it too had to undergo some adjustments. Deng needed to ensure that liberal-minded officials and those that shared his aspirations were incorporated into Party and government structures. It would be disastrous if the economic reforms were 'sabotaged' by officials, who were stuck in the Maoist era of communist orthodoxy. What he did was to bring back to the fold those who were purged during the Cultural Revolution, and they became the bulwark of Deng's reforms. After all, Deng was more a politician than an economist, for it was his pragmatism that carried the day.

Deng's vision and his pragmatism can be hailed as the beginning of the re-emergence of China. He forced open the country's closed doors which made China much more amenable to the outside world. His pragmatic adage, 'it does not matter whether the cat is black or white, so long as it catches mice',¹⁰ was music to the ears of global entrepreneurs, from neighbouring Asia to Europe and the United States. Despite of the Tiananmen Square episode in 1989, the trajectory was still heading in the right direction, although the open protests had sent shock waves through the leadership.[11]

Although China experienced a slow but steady rise under Deng, with several economic adjustments, it was only in the 1990s that we saw China blasting off into orbit. This transition was much needed after decades of communist economic experimental adventures. The early communist leaders, to a large extent, were trying to make sense of what their philosophical guru Karl Marx had prescribed in his seminal but voluminous and not easily comprehended work, *Das Kapital*.[12] Unfortunately, the only prevailing point of reference for the Chinese was the Soviet Union, whose economy was already moribund.

When China decided to concentrate on economic development it had to confront a number of critical issues, namely, whether political reforms were needed as a prelude to economic development and whether it could learn the lessons of the past so that there would not be a repeat of the years of economic stagnation. It was to reconcile the notion that with economic liberalisation, there will be added pressures on the political system to allow for a much-liberalised political environment. However, as we have seen in the first chapter, the Chinese leadership had their own approach—the China Dream, among other things, was meant to meet the aspirations of the growing prosperous middle-class population.

Nonetheless, the leadership still had to address the above questions. Regarding the first, there is little doubt that those who advocated any form of political reform would have been deterred and discouraged and that any such thoughts would have been crushed; the suppression of the Tiananmen Square protests in 1989 was the clearest possible indication of the zero tolerance of dissenting views within the country. In retrospect, the spontaneous protest around Tiananmen Square was a forerunner of the Arab Spring that saw the end of a number of dictatorships and autocratic regimes in the Middle East, although the Arab Spring has caused more hardship and instability than had existed before. Scholars and observers alike generally view the Tiananmen Square protests as a turning point in China. To Jean-Philippe Beja, it was a watershed in Chinese contemporary history, arguing that the protests (or massacre as he refers to them) still cast a long shadow over the CCP, despite attempts to wipe out any information or reminder of the episode.[13] According to Professor Zheng Wang of the Washington D.C.-based Woodrow Wilson International Center for Scholars, the CCP 'abandoned their approach of balancing economic reform and political reform that had been in practice since the first decade of China's reform and opening up. For economic reform, they went to extreme "liberal" and radical; for political reform, they went to the extreme "conservative" and rigid.'[14] To the Chinese government and the people, the Tiananmen Square protests could well be regarded as a turning point as it showed, beyond doubt, that despite economic liberalisation, the former will not tolerate any political dissent towards its rule and will use whatever steps, including force, to crush any opposition. Any inkling that economic openness will eventually lead to political freedom was seriously diminished with the Tiananmen episode.

In addition, the episode had an international impact. As events were brought to audiences all over the world in real time, through international news networks, such poignant images resonated with many, resulting in the reinforcement of negativity on China. This was compounded by the fact that many of the demonstrators were students and from the younger generation. The effigy of the Statute of Liberty—a symbol of freedom—being paraded amongst the protesters, ignited enormous sympathy amongst many, for it conjures up images of their own fight for a greater say in government policies, for example, during the prolonged protests over American intervention in Vietnam. The violent suppression of the protesters created an instant 'hate China' global audience. This was something that China had to live with in the years following this episode. Subsequent leaders have tried to relegate this public protest to the pages of history. For instance, according to Ezra F. Vogel, 'within two decades after the crackdown, many of those imprisoned were released and the opprobrium of having taken part was gradually reduced as events first called a "counterrevolutionary rebellion" (*fangeming baoluan*), became a "riot" (*Baoluan*), then "political turmoil" (*zhengzhi dongluan*), and finally, the "1989 storm" (*fengbo*)'.[15]

To some extent, contemporary China's emphasis on the 'Dream' of the Chinese middle class—to enjoy a much higher standard of living and be part of the burgeoning consumer society—is to deter the younger generation from having any inclination to protest against the government. To the Chinese leadership, to focus on economic benefits would override any hunger for political freedom.

The protests also had an immediate impact on China, as the United States and its allies, namely members of the European community, began to impose a series of diplomatic and economic sanctions against it. Among other measures, Western-based and -backed financial institutions, such as the World Bank and the Asian Development Bank, halted loans to China.

However, this sanction, like many others, proved to be futile as it did not lead to any change in Beijing's attitude towards dissenting views within the country. Besides, the sanctions were not really tied to any real demands, as it was merely a kneejerk reaction from the United States and other Western countries, in response to what was seen as an anti-democracy move by China. According to Harry Harding of Brooking Institution, despite intense debate by Chinese leaders and officials, from hardliners and reformers to what he refers to as 'tough internationalists', Chinese foreign policy since the Tiananmen protests, has, on balance, seen 'a shift over time toward a more moderate foreign policy, with hard-line positions giving way to policies associated with the "tough internationalists", and with elements of the reformers' proposals increasingly apparent in China's policy toward the United States'.[16]

The Chinese must also have learnt a valuable lesson from Gorbachev's *glasnost* and *perestroika*, the Soviet leader's simultaneous implementation of political and economic reforms. With Gorbachev's openness policy, the lid on dissent was lifted overnight, releasing the long-kept genie, which until then had been starved of freedom of expression. This twin policy overwhelmed the political leadership, which was struggling to crank up the engine of economic reform, itself a gargantuan task, with no point of reference as to how to transform a highly controlled economy into one that would be more liberally orientated. The result was that Gorbachev was overthrown and replaced by Boris Yeltsin, a crude and less sophisticated politician. For the Chinese, the Soviet experience was a lesson in how not to emulate their communist brothers. In fact, the nightmare of potential collapse in China was worsened by the demise of the USSR, which led to the break-up of a union of 15 republics into independent nations, with all its positive and negative consequences.

The second thread was to not pursue the often overzealous and ambitious past policies of socialism and communism, as interpreted by Chinese orthodoxy. The conclusion Chinese leaders reached relatively early was that socialism had to be modified—or at least viewed from a much broader perspective. Hence, the idea of socialism with Chinese characteristics emerged, although it remained a nebulous concept. Plainly interpreted, for China to be economically developed it could no longer adhere to orthodox socialist thinking. However, while retaining the term 'socialism', which essentially means that the state has a role to play in economic development, the brake on free enterprise must be slowly released. The pace of liberalisation must be determined by the political leadership, constantly gauging how the economy is developing, how wealth is being created and in turn distributed. At the heart of this 'liberalisation' in China was the once strictly controlled and highly regulated foreign investment. The controls over Foreign Direct Investments (FDIs), which had proved such a stumbling block to economic development, were removed, paving the way for a tidal wave of foreign investment, and by the beginning of the twenty-first century China was the world's largest FDI recipient and had around US$400 billion in accumulated investments.[17]

At the same time, private land ownership and private enterprise and business, which were taboos in Marxist thinking, were slowly accepted, providing a much-needed engine to help push the economy forward. When China finally joined the World Trade Organisation in 2001, the final obstacle that had prevented economic development in China was removed. China was now a global player, with its people doing business in every corner of the world. As we shall see, the Belt and Road Initiative (BRI) is the crown that China wears to show off its global economic empire—and all of its ubiquitous tentacles.

China: Towards a Multidimensional Global Power

Many people today are focused on the rise of China. Interpretations vary widely, from treating it as a threat or with indifference, to seeing it as a power that should be embraced. As the once popular saying went during the Cold War, 'better red than dead', although in the case of the Chinese today, the red probably only denotes the colour of the 100 Renminbi (RMB) notes.

This book seeks to view the phenomenal rise of China as part of a long historical continuum. It is not that China has just risen up, but simply that it has woken from a deep slumber. Due to imperial or strategic overstretch, coupled with internal contradictions, the mighty Chinese empire fell and the whole edifice came tumbling down. With such a sense of imperial history, one can imagine the long-term effect this has had on the Chinese psyche and mentality. It is this sense of historical longevity in China that we must recognise as a significant and influential factor in its current strategic thinking. Time and history are on China's side. It is perhaps not surprising, then, that when referring to the disputed territories in the South China Sea, the chief architect of the opening of China, Deng Xiaoping, advised that the matter should be left to the next generation. While one could argue that this was just a tactical move by the Chinese leader to skirt round the sensitive issue of sovereignty, it also illustrates China's long sense of history and time.

One of the main factors placing China at the centre of the global radar is the nature of its power. Not only is it an ascending power, but its nature is multidimensional. To a large extent, it is a complete superpower, compared to the Soviet Union, which Paul Dibb once dubbed an 'Incomplete Superpower'[18] because its power base was concentrated in the military dimension but was fundamentally weak in the economic sense. While its military reach was global and had the capability to bring a nuclear Armageddon, its economic presence was limited and confined to its ideological partners. Its economy was moribund.

In another case, several decades ago, Japan was seen to be a rising power with a global presence that would have far-reaching consequences. Threat scenarios, including from the American perspective, were emerging. However, with the economic bubble bursting, Japan's potential began to deflate. Besides, its close alliance with the United States, originating since the American occupation of Japan at the end of the Pacific War, became a natural harness on any ambitions Tokyo might harbour on the world stage. Although there have been discussions in the 1990s about it becoming a permanent member of the UN Security Council, Japan has never been a serious contender. For Japan to join, all five permanent members would have to unanimously agree and this was almost certainly a non-starter. Any such review would inevitably lead to awkward questions about the continued permanent membership of both Britain and France, both of which have lost their 'victorious power status' since the end of World War II. Tokyo has been unable to convert its global economic reach into any kind of political leverage or influence. However, this is because of domestic constraints within Japan rather than any notion of altruism.

Given its multidimensional power, it is no surprise that China finds itself in the spotlight, with all the negativity and criticism that comes with it. As this chapter will illustrate many of the vociferous attacks on China have been hypocritical. It would appear that it is fine if others, such as the United States, would act internationally, but if China does it, then that's bad. And in addition to these double standards, some arguments appear to border on racism or ethnocentrism and, to a lesser degree, contain sanctimonious undertones. Put simply, anything Western is good and acceptable and anything else is bad and unacceptable.

Underpinning the way China is viewed and portrayed is the fact that, for the first time in modern history, a non-Western power is challenging the supremacy of the Western world headed by the United States. This book proposes that this is at the heart of the way China is treated today.

Epitome of China's Global Economic Power: The Belt and Road Initiative

In June 2021, President Xi expressed China's willingness to work with all parties to develop a closer Belt and Road partnership, in the Silk Road spirit, and jointly build an open cooperation platform to provide new impetus for the cooperation and development of all countries.[19]

Never before has there been such an ambitious global programme as the BRI. It is a twenty-first-century version of the ancient Silk Road,[20] only on a greater scale. Its basic concept of inter-regional connectivity is derived from the famous Silk Road route, which linked the commercial centres of the ancient world. While Europe had the Marshall Plan, a US initiative for post-war reconstruction in Europe, the scale and reach of the BRI is unprecedented and perhaps befits a country like China, which already has a global presence. It could be argued that ever since China's economy took off in the 1980s its trajectory has lacked any sense of a master plan. When President Xi Jinping announced the BRI in September 2013 in Kazakhstan, China's global economic presence gained a sense of direction and was placed in a conceptual and more structured framework. The BRI projects an inclusive approach which brings economic growth and prosperity to all its trading partners. It is open-ended and covers a whole host of countries and regions that have natural resources in abundance, in particular oil and gas, as well as one of the most fertile agricultural fields in the world. Within it lies some of the most vibrant and, potentially, commercial areas of the world. Clearly a renewal of the fabled ancient Silk Road was not picked out at random from a hat. As it was centuries ago, this new Silk Road will be the world's economic, trade and commercial hub.

In retrospect, one wonders whether Xi anticipated the enormous global impact his 2013 speech would make. Certainly that speech is devoid of any spectacular words and is even disjointed, as the idea of the BRI only became clear when Xi made a second speech in Jakarta a month later. Nonetheless, the BRI has caught the imagination of states, leaders and entrepreneurs, especially since the Chinese began to talk of how it would be financed. It must be noted that prior to Xi's initiative there were several official statements from the United States, including from the then Secretary of State, Hillary Clinton, who drew on the analogy of the Silk Road and talked of developing the areas that had surrounded it, especially the Central Asian countries. However, as one observer remarks, the contents of such speeches were more visionary than substantial in nature, and 'Like many visions, however, [Clinton's] was more about hope than substance.'[21]

An Overview of BRI

Every leader, in China or elsewhere, aspires to leave a legacy and secure their place in the history books. Very few achieve that and some are remembered only for the wrong reasons. In China, for example, Premier Li Peng will go down in history as the leader who mishandled the Tiananmen Square protests. Every year, on the anniversary of the protests, events are organised across the West to remind the world of the way the Chinese repressed the apparent cry for democracy.

President Xi Jinping's mammoth initiative to launch the BRI, initially known as One Belt One Road, will be his legacy and will secure his place in the history books; the BRI will be synonymous with Xi Jinping. The province of Shaanxi was the starting point of the ancient Silk Road and is coincidentally also Xi's home province, and in his speech launching this initiative he said, 'More than 2100 years ago during the Han dynasty [206 BC–220 AD] a Chinese envoy named Zhang Qian was twice sent to Central Asia on missions of peace and friendship. His journeys opened the door to friendly contacts between China and Central Asian countries and started the Silk Road linking the East and West, Asia and Europe.'[22]

While the ancient Silk Road was conceived first and foremost as a trade route linking Asia and Europe, Xi's BRI is going to surpass this. It will link China with the rest of the world through the Silk Road Economic Belt, which was announced in Kazakhstan in September 2013, and through the Maritime Silk Road, which was articulated a month later in Indonesia. It is interesting to note that the latter is clearly meant to have greater geographical connectivity, far beyond what a land mass can offer, including to the African continent. After all, China's economic reach is global in nature, and it has to provide some sense of economic grand strategy to include its economic ties with Africa and elsewhere.

Notwithstanding official pronouncements, it is clear that the BRI has several purposes. The first is to provide some form of an overarching strategy to China's global economic presence. To some extent, the BRI was conceived as an after-thought, and prior to its conception China's economic reach seemed to lack any sense of direction. The BRI provides a global structural framework through which China's bilateral and multilateral projects can be weaved into one big, connected map. In addition, it will provide legitimacy for China's foreign economic policies that are reaching many corners of the world. In other words, the BRI will provide a sense of global connectivity and belonging. In addition, the idea of BRI came about the same time of Xi's China Dream. To a large extent, this massive initiative was to provide 'meat' to the aspiration of the Chinese president and people. What better way to epitomise the sense of grandeur, inherent in the China Dream, than this mammoth project.

The second purpose is more personal to President Xi: securing his place in the history books not only of China but of the world. It is perhaps not surprising that in March 2018 Xi moved to amend the constitution in order to provide legislative legitimacy for an extension of the presidency, which since the 1980s had been limited to two terms. The often-used excuse of 'unfinished work' as a way to perpetuate a leader's political tenure was used to great effect by Xi. The extension was sanctioned by the country's highest legislative body, the National People's Congress, allowing Xi to seek a third term.

Thirdly, there is an element of competition with the United States. It is clear to most that the current and future clash of the titans will be between the dragon and the eagle. It is perhaps no surprise, then, that even the BRI had an element of trying to put the United States down and project China as the world's saviour. China's return to the world stage has come at a time of global economic malaise and stagnation. The feeling is that capitalism is on its last legs and that an alternative is being desperately sought. Some believe that the West has come to the end of the road and that we are seeing the worst of the Western style of government surfacing with little hope of exit at the other end.[23] To one Chinese scholar, the BRI was initiated because the world needs a clear direction, especially with 'US-style globalisation seemingly unsustainable'.[24] To the Chinese, the non-Western world is theirs for the taking, especially with the West seemingly in a state of decline. As we shall see, this Western decline is confined to not only economic concerns but also political and social dominance. The United Kingdom, for instance, has been paralysed by the Brexit morass. This has come at a time when society is probably at its lowest ebb since the end of the war, when the Beveridge Report created the welfare state as part of a post-war development formula. In a 2016 Organisation for Economic Co-operation and Development (OECD) study of basic skills, England ranked the lowest in the developed world, with some 20 per cent of 16–19 years old classified as having low literacy levels.[25] It is almost unthinkable that a country that boasts some of the best public schools[26] in the world and is the home of both Oxford and Cambridge universities has such a low literacy rate.

In addition, the BRI brings benefits to the Chinese economy, by providing a strategic framework for its economic development domestically and internationally. For decades, Chinese conglomerates have been encouraged to extend their tentacles abroad. The BRI provides greater impetus for this. Following the extension of China's economic reach we could expect an increase in Chinese political influence. Whether Beijing will exercise this new-found power is yet to be seen. Even the US Secretary of Commerce, Wilbur Ross, has admitted the great benefits the BRI will bring to China, saying, 'By pouring money into Africa, China has seen an opportunity to both gain political influence and to reap future rewards in a continent whose economies are predicted to boom in the coming decades.'[27] With a seemingly disinterested Washington in the continent of Africa, the increasing influence of China will be seen as disadvantageous to American strategic interests.

What Is the BRI?

As already stated, the BRI consists of two giant links—'belt' is land-based and 'road' refers to the maritime link. The overall concept is fairly straightforward: to establish links between Asia and Europe that pass through vast areas such as the Middle East and Africa. To one scholar, 'This glorious idea achieves the seemingly impossible: it dresses up straightforward material and commercial interests into something pioneering, ennobling and romantic.'[28]

One officially sanctioned statement encapsulates what the BRI is about. According to Professor Wang Yiwei of Renmin University of China, 'The Belt and Road is, essentially, a Eurasian transport network, an integrated, three-dimensional and interconnected system that is composed of railways, aviation, navigation, oil and gas pipelines, transmission lines and communication networks.'[29] It envisages huge development spin-offs which will benefit surrounding areas, and 'Along these lines there will gradually form industrial clusters serving these networks. Thus, through the industrial effects of agglomeration and radiation, an economic corridor featuring the comprehensive development of construction, metallurgy, energy, finance, communications, information, logistics and tourism will be established.'[30] The BRI has been presented as an economic and social vision for the world that could bring progress and prosperity to areas that have been isolated and undeveloped. Simply put, the claim is that China is bringing light to these dark and isolated areas.

For the land-based economic belt, there are three routes—the Northern Route with the Eurasian land bridge linking Beijing, Russia, Germany and Northern Europe; the Middle Route with oil and gas pipelines running from Beijing to Xi'an, Urumqi, Afghanistan, Kazakhstan, Hungary and Paris; and the Southern Route with transnational highways linking Beijing, Southern Xinjiang, Pakistan, Iran, Iraq, Turkey, Italy and Spain. Within these three mammoth routes there are several corridors: the China–Pakistan Economic Corridor, the Bangladesh–China–India–Burma Economic Corridor, the New Eurasian Land Bridge, and the China–Mongolia–Russia Economic Corridor. These corridors provide the parameters of the BRI on land.

Then there is the maritime component, which links China, through its coastal ports such as Quanzhou, across the vast span of oceans from the Pacific and Indian Oceans, traversing the critical sea lanes of the South China Sea, the narrow Straits of Malacca, the Bay of Bengal and the Arabian Sea, the Gulf of Aden and the strategically important Persian Gulf. These maritime routes will connect the littoral states of this vast area.

Collectively, both the land and maritime components of the BRI will form an intricate and comprehensive line linking China with Europe via Asia, the Middle East and Africa. Effectively, all roads will lead to Beijing.

The BRI official map, when it was first released, illustrated the extent of BRI connectivity. It is a vivid expression of China's grand design. However, this map has been conspicuously less visible lately in Chinese official circles, as it is believed that the illustration has negative, unintended consequences and conjures images of the dragon spreading its claws over half the world.

Apart from its geographical reach, the main thrust of the BRI is twofold—infrastructure development and the joint exploitation of resources. During President Xi's visit to Kazakhstan, where he announced the first leg of the BRI, he witnessed the signing of a number of huge deals involving oil worth US$15 billion. These agreements will bring about the construction of a 1300 km pipeline linking the two countries. Both Sinopec, one of China's state-owned corporations, and the China National Petroleum Corporation are involved in this project.

It is projected that this initiative will see many spin-offs and provide the impetus for many different levels of cooperation among countries along the route, which may not necessarily involve China. One can just imagine that, enabled by an intricate railroad system cutting across this vast area, and pipelines and telecommunication networks, regional countries could be further encouraged to embark on their own bilateral and multilateral arrangements and agreements. For example, the three Central Asian states of Turkmenistan, Azerbaijan and Uzbekistan, through their respective state-owned oil corporations, have agreed to jointly develop fields in the Caspian Sea.[31]

Financing BRI: Some Misconceptions

Given the scale of the BRI, one of the key questions is finance. Who will pay the rumoured trillion dollar bill? The answer is the participating countries themselves, with a helping hand from China. To this end, Beijing has established a number of financial institutions dedicated to providing the enormous funding that will be required to fulfil the strategic objectives of the BRI. They are the Asian Infrastructure Investment Bank and the Silk Road Fund, both led by China; all participating countries are members of both. In addition, most of China's state-owned financial institutions, such as the EXIM Bank of China and the Development Bank of China, have promised to put aside enormous funds to help pay for these projects. China is putting its money where its mouth is.

When various deals are announced, there is much talk of participating countries being caught in a debt trap. There are several misconceptions here. Firstly, there is the perception that countries are forced to undertake these projects and that these loans will put recipient countries at the mercy of the Chinese. There are also those who believe that BRI money comes in the form of Chinese aid to the region.

Here we must quote Chinese leaders and officials who, on several occasions, have stated categorically that BRI is essentially a mutually agreed business venture financed on a commercial basis; it is not an aid package. Thus, the BRI is sustainable because the stakes are high for both China and participating countries. This is not to suggest that China will not benefit. On the contrary, the BRI will catapult China into the heart of Asia and Europe and will be a primary engine that helps those areas develop.

When the BRI was launched, regional states saw it as a great opportunity to jump on the Chinese bandwagon and, through relatively easy access to funds, embark on projects that otherwise would not be possible. Very few global financial institutions would fund projects that some countries would like to launch, due to their lack of qualifying financial credentials. China, however, is providing loan packages which appear to be too attractive to resist. Like all loan packages there are terms and conditions, and those loans will have to be repaid, in one form or another.

When debt-trap arguments are levied at countries that participate in the BRI, there appear to be elements of condescension and racism—it is implied that these countries are too ignorant or blind in the face of the Chinese proposals. To put it bluntly such criticism suggests that the leaders of Asian and African countries are stupid and corrupt and easily conned by the Chinese. Despite the fact that we are not talking of aid here, commentators still refer to the BRI as initiated aid. According to the co-founder and research director at J Capital Research, 'China does not have a very competent international bureaucracy in foreign aid, in expansion of soft power.... As the RMB becomes weaker, and China is perceived internationally as a more ambiguous partner, it is more likely that the countries will take a more jaundiced view of these projects.'[32] Another US-based think tank, the Center for Global Development, has said it has 'serious concerns' about the sustainability of the sovereign debt in eight countries receiving BRI funds. The eight countries identified are Pakistan, Djibouti, Maldives, Mongolia, Laos, Montenegro, Tajikistan and Kyrgyzstan.[33] In combating such negative views, Foreign Ministry spokeswoman, Hua Chunying, denied that Beijing was saddling its partners with onerous debt, saying that its loans to Sri Lanka and Pakistan were only a small part of those countries' overall foreign debt. She hit the nail on the head when she said, 'It's unreasonable that money coming out of Western countries is praised as good and sweet, while coming out of China it's sinister and a trap.'[34]

The debt-trap issue should be discussed within the context of other types of loans that countries provide, as well as those that are associated with Western-based international financial institutions such as the Asian Development Bank, the World Bank and the International Monetary Fund (IMF). During the heyday of Japan's global economic presence, yen loans were given to help states engage in infrastructure projects. They were loans and not aid packages and they all had to be paid back. In fact, when the yen appreciated in value, yen loan debts ballooned and increased the debt burden of those countries that had taken on such facilities. Even the IMF, which provides rescue packages to distressed economies, enforces all sorts of conditions on recipients, such as requiring countries to open domestic markets to foreign investors. In these instances and in the name of free and open trade, locally protected industries are forced open to allow much more experienced and bigger international players to participate; in most cases domestic players are elbowed out by these large global conglomerates. The world witnessed this during the Asian financial crisis of the late 1990s when the IMF stepped in supposedly to rescue the economies of the region from disaster. Instead, the stringent conditions imposed by the IMF led to a considerable political backlash. In the case of Indonesia, it directly led to regime change, creating a widely held belief that behind the veil of an economic rescue package lies a much more sinister US-led political agenda. The graphic picture of the arms-folded IMF managing director, Michel Camdessus, standing over the seated President Suharto of Indonesia while he signed the IMF package went viral around the world and was said to depict the victor forcing the vanquished to submit to their will.

There is also the example of the Greeks being at the mercy of Western-based financial institutions. During a severe economic crisis in 2015, the then Greek finance minister, Yanis Varoufakis, spoke of a possible coup which would bring down the whole country. He was referring not to tanks rolling along the streets but to global financial institutions forcing his country to take dramatic steps, such as shutting down banks, which would almost certainly halt economic activity and result in untold panic. In his memoirs, Varoufakis called it this possibility the 'Cyprus coup', as this was what happened to neighbouring Cyprus when the troika, made up of representatives of the IMF, European Commission and the European Central Bank, forced Cypriot banks to close and dictated terms for their re-opening to the newly elected president. The latter had no choice but to agree.[35] Western financial institutions have themselves proven merciless when it comes to forcing their clients' hands. There is no such thing as a free lunch, despite rhetoric to the contrary.

A case has already been made by Western observers that recipient countries are beginning to see the debt trap and are reviewing or indeed cancelling BRI projects. Malaysia and Pakistan have been cited as examples. However, much of the criticism in these countries appeared to come from members of the opposition who seized the opportunity to take pot shots at the government as part of election campaigning. Concerns such as corruption and high prices as well as the debt trap were music to the ears of their electorates. In both cases, new governments replaced those which had signed with the Chinese. Dr Mahathir became the new Malaysian prime minister in May 2018, while the charismatic Imran Khan became Pakistan's leader in August the same year. Having won the elections both now have to make good their criticism of the deals involving the Chinese. This criticism must have been embarrassing to the Chinese because inherent in the arguments were issues involving high prices and corruption. However, it takes two to tango as far as corruption goes and the implication was that the Chinese were colluding in corruption and the high prices. As it turned out such statements proved to be much more rhetorical in nature, as both new governments became more conciliatory in their dealings with China.

When Imran Khan took office, he promised more transparency, amid fears that the country would be unable to repay Chinese loans related to the multibillion-dollar China–Pakistan Economic Corridor.[36] However, after just three months in office, Prime Minister Khan paid an official visit to Beijing to reaffirm the two countries' close bilateral ties and to negotiate a bailout from Beijing to tackle Pakistan's fiscal crisis.[37] Irrespective of the legitimate concerns of the new government over its commercial deals with Beijing, Islamabad has to view its ties with Beijing within its strategic and security needs. China has been Pakistan's closest security partner for decades, especially in its rivalry with India, which is backed by Russia. Further, there appears to be a convergence of interests between China and Pakistan over India, which has helped to bind the two states together. Over the years, Beijing, too, has had concerns about India.

After forming his new government, Dr Mahathir talked of cancelling the much-discussed East Coast Rail Link (ECRL) scheme and two other Chinese-backed projects, and in August 2018, during a visit to Beijing a few months after becoming prime minister, he cautioned against the rise of neo-colonialism. The reference to new forms of colonisation must have been quite uncomfortable for his host. Dr Mahathir said, 'We do not want a situation where there is a new version of colonialism, happening because poor countries are unable to compete with rich countries in terms of just, open free trade; it must also be fair trade.'[38] Although traditionally new colonisation refers to the rich North, there are severe trade imbalances between China and many developing countries. Notwithstanding the discomfort Dr Mahathir's statement could have given Beijing, China was fully aware that it could not afford to overreact because other countries were watching and because Dr Mahathir is a highly respected leader; China was smart enough to know that it had to demonstrate a levelheaded response to such statements.

However, a few months later, Dr Mahathir's government was dancing to a new tune—one that was more sympathetic to Beijing and not dissimilar to the previous government's line; things were moving forward with the Chinese. A former finance minister, Tun Daim Zainuddin, was deployed to Beijing to re-negotiate the ECRL deal. He returned and announced that the project was back on track. Under the new agreement, construction of Phases 1 and 2 will be resumed at a cost of RM44 billion, a reduction of RM21.5 billion from the original projected cost of RM65.5 billion. However, this new price is based on a much-reduced scope of work, including a shortening of the distance. We can almost certainly expect increases in the price, which will probably not be made public. As any project manager knows, it is no mean feat to reduce the cost of infrastructure projects because this has an impact on the scope of work. In addition to the ECRL project, the new government was clamouring to woo more Chinese investors, as could be seen by numerous announcements made by ministers and officials including the finance minister's report on his discussions with the Chinese about the possibility of the issuance of Panda bonds by the China Construction Bank to ease the government's financial distress.[39] In another announcement, the Malaysian finance minister said he would visit Shenzhen to attempt to attract more Chinese investment to the country.[40] One of the main reasons why Dr Mahathir's government made a 360-degree turn, despite earlier strong criticism of Chinese investments, was the economic reality. This realism was bear out again with the new government which was formed in May 2020, after Dr Mahathir's resignation, thereby leading to the fall of his fragile coalition. In the main, one cannot ignore the Chinese nor can one afford to turn the Chinese away. Doing so would be to lose out to other countries that are only too willing to dance with the dragon. It seems clear that governments have to be realistic when dealing with China. They know that Beijing is in a position to assist them without necessarily having to adhere too much to the stringent conditions imposed by other global financial institutions.

Timeframe

Interestingly, the completion of the BRI will coincide with the 100th anniversary of the founding of the People's Republic. By stretching the BRI timetable to mark a significant milestone of communist China's existence, Xi Jinping will be remembered in 2049 as an iconic leader with a vision for a global China. It is, perhaps, no surprise that it was Xi himself who came up with the idea of the BRI.

BRI detractors argue that this will be the moment when China becomes the new global supremo, when all the participating countries will fall under its control. They believe it will surpass the United States and the rest of the Western world and that the completion of the BRI will mark the end of Western dominance. The BRI is a watershed plan for it marks the beginning of the end of US global pre-eminence with China taking its place. This is the alarmists' narrative.

What Can We Make of the BRI?

The BRI is a work in progress. Since its launch in 2013 various elements have been added—what could be conveniently regarded as adjustments. Despite most countries jumping on the BRI bandwagon in the early stages, and with various projects announced, the direction is still unclear, as some participating countries either appear to have stalled or are in the process of downsizing the scale of certain projects. There are huge projects that have been announced and even agreements signed, but obviously it is still early days.

It must be recognised, however, that there were doubts about how regional countries would respond to such an initiative and, because of this, details were deliberately omitted; only the broad concept was introduced. The actual implementation will depend on bilateral, trilateral and multilateral negotiations involving not only state-to-state talks but also discussions and negotiations involving countries' respective corporate sectors. After all, the business of government is not business. The actual projects will have to be undertaken by commercial organisations, although in the case of the Chinese there is a definite blurring of lines as many businesses are state-owned. One observer remarked that in the first few years of the initiative, 'the great asset of the new Silk Road is that, like the old, it is marvellously vague… But it puts to the fore the primacy of mutually beneficial trade relations, and appeals to self-interest in the softest, most indirect way.'[41]

The BRI is a massive undertaking by China involving almost all countries as well as international organisations. President Xi had announced in June 2021 that to date, China has signed cooperation agreements with a total of 140 countries under the BRI in eight years.[42] That is certainly an impressive feat. Several versions of the total cost have been bandied about, reaching mind-boggling trillions. The majority of the world is participating. One of the reasons why most countries have signed up for the project is fear of being left behind. Although some rival states, like India, have tried to launch an equivalent initiative, albeit on a smaller scale, most believe that the BRI does bring benefits to their own economic development.

Ever since the BRI was announced, the Chinese have been both enthusiastic and cautious, especially in not wanting to be seen as new colonisers. They are mindful of the sensitivities of their partners and the possible backlash that attempts at 'colonisation' may cause. Indeed there is already a body of opinion that has couched the BRI in negative terms. Phrases like 'debt trap' and 'new colonisation' have appeared prominently in the literature. The BRI has also become an issue in the domestic political context of some countries and has forced governments onto the defensive when confronted with such negativity from opposition groups and non-governmental organisations.

As a result, Chinese officials will try at any opportunity to allay the fears of participating countries, by reassuring them that the BRI is a win-win scheme. During the anniversary of the fifth year of the BRI, in September 2018, President Xi declared that 'it is not a China club' but an '"open and inclusive" project'.[43] In another instance, Foreign Minister Wang Yi said that the initiative is 'neither a "Marshall Plan" nor a geopolitical strategy' and that since it was proposed, it 'has adhered to the principle of extensive consultation, joint contribution and shared benefits'.[44] In addressing nuances over possible intervention in the domestic affairs of others, President Xi defended the initiative: 'China neither attaches political strings to its investments… nor intervenes in the internal affairs of other countries, nor does it come up with demands that are against the will of others.'[45] Such statements reflect Chinese consciousness and sensitivity over the BRI and the impact it is having on the world's perception of its growing power. It must be pointed out that, hitherto, China has had no experience of handling any such undertaking at such massive multilateral levels. On the bilateral front, Beijing has helped many countries over the years. Never before, though, has it done so at this magnitude or dealt with such a range of issues, many of which appear not to have been anticipated. In addition, as will be discussed later, public relations do not appear to be one of China's great strengths. This is one department which needs special attention. As we shall see, efforts are being made but much more needs to be done.

Not surprisingly, given the significance of the BRI within the context of China's economic expansion around the world, it has been much discussed and written about. It would appear that politicians, journalists, academics and pundits all have their own take on the BRI and there is a great deal of literature. While taking cognisance of the numerous ongoing projects along the extended routes, the countless debates, as well as the evolving materials on the BRI, this book will try to make some sense of the various schools of thought.

In considering the various opinions and positions on the BRI, it is best to look in the broad sense, like a weather barometer with three identifying points: two at the extremes and one right in the middle.

The first two schools take diametrically opposing sides. The first view mainly comes from the various mouthpieces of the Chinese government, ranging from the leadership, government officials and those who echo and tow the Party line. For instance, to this group, the BRI is seen as China's gift to the world, at a time when pessimism seems to run supreme about the prospects for the global economy. This initiative opens new areas that, hitherto, were isolated and cut off from the world and development. Communities that lie along the new Silk Road will, they claim, be able to prosper, though mainly indirectly. To this school of thought the BRI is the saviour of peripheral economies and societies.

In attracting African countries to join the initiative President Xi talked of achieving 'common prosperity', of being ready to seek 'synergies' and of 'equality and win-win outcomes'.[46] This first school of thought is the official pro-Chinese line which is useful in providing us with the thinking of the leadership and how it addresses some of the emerging issues and concerns. The constant reminders of the positive aspects of the initiative, as expressed by the leadership, reveal the sensitivities and sensibilities of the Chinese. However, we need to go beyond officialdom and examine the nuances behind such statements. In the case of China, the absence of differing opinions among legislators, officials and the leadership makes the interpretation of such latent messages more challenging.

At the other extreme is the school of thought that argues that the BRI is nothing more than a trojan horse—in this case a 'Made in China' gigantic wooden dragon—a way to send Chinese 'soldiers', in the guise of engineers, technicians and other supporting personnel across the world as part of a master plan to dominate the world. This borders on the fiction that the Chinese will subjugate and enslave the peoples living in BRI regions. A similar concern prompted the saying, 'beware of Greeks bearing gifts'; in this case it is 'beware Chinese bearing loans'. This line of thinking is obviously anti-Chinese and often bordering on racist; we should be wary of such extreme views. One of the many flaws of such an argument is that it downgrades the participating countries to the position of willing 'victims'—quite ready and prepared to be enslaved and dominated. Such a condescending view suggests that those countries that are part of the BRI (non-Western, non-white) are not too clever. As stated earlier, there seems to be a high dose of racism in such a school of thought.

The third school is made up of two groups: the first belongs to those who have subscribed to the BRI by signing various agreements with the Chinese. If we see the BRI as a club, then the subscribers to this school are full members. Although these countries have talked about reviewing projects they previously agreed on, many of them have retracted their earlier concerns and have decided to embrace the Chinese dragon. This may stem from a reality check—while they might be critical and move cautiously, there remains an acknowledgement that it is better to be part of the BRI than to be out of it. If there are concerns, then they should be addressed and the necessary adjustments be made.

The second group is those that have remained cautious while keeping their options open. This stems mainly from a sense of rivalry with China rather than from economic or commercial concerns. India is one such country. According to Darshana Baruah of Carnegie India, the Indian arm of the US-based think tank Carnegie Endowment for International Peace, New Delhi should be wary of China's geopolitical ambitions, which are being channelled through the BRI, in particular its investments in ports alongside the Indian Ocean. These will enable China to secure passage of energy imports from West Asia, which raises concerns in India that these ports could be converted into naval bases.[47]

As stated above, as the timeframe for the BRI is spread over a number of decades, the initiative is still very much in its early days. While there appears to be a rush by all parties to start negotiations on various BRI projects, some sense of rationalisation is bound to arise given the initiative's long-term perspective. Economies will experience the vigour of cycles and there will be times when participating countries will not be able to service their loans, leading to the re-structuring of the loans and debts. We have already seen this in the case of Sri Lanka and its inability to maintain its loan repayments to China. Like all commercial financial institutions which provide loans to corporations or countries, any lapse in debt servicing will invariably lead to some form of penalty. When Colombo was unable to repay China loans amounting to US$1.4 billion, taken out to build the strategic port of Hambantota, it was forced to grant China a 99-year lease for port management. To the detractors of the BRI this is a prime example of the punitive measures taken by Beijing in the event of loan default and therefore reveals the true strategic objective behind the BRI.

However, it is interesting to note a report by the Hong Kong-based *South China Morning Post* which argued that to blame China for Sri Lanka's debt woes is wrong, as a large proportion of Sri Lanka's overall external debt is mainly from American and other Western entities, including high-interest loans from commercial banks. The port lease is held jointly by the Hong Kong-based China Merchants Port and the Sri Lanka Ports Authority and was negotiated in the period 2016–2017. Payments of the principal and interest for the port loans comprised only about 1.5 per cent of the country's external debt repayment obligations. The port authority paid on time, using revenue from Colombo port, which includes a successful container terminal run by China Merchants Port.[48] Based on this report it would appear that we have all been victims of much exaggeration and disinformation or at the very least of not assessing the issue fairly.

Notwithstanding the Sri Lankan example, a few observations can be made. Firstly, although the BRI is Chinese-backed and -initiated, it is a commercial enterprise. All the negotiations over projects are conducted on a commercial basis, although many on the Chinese side are huge state-owned conglomerates and some are Fortune Global 500 companies.[49] As already mentioned, there seems to be a misconception that the BRI is aid-related, that China is dishing out a huge amount of aid and assistance to countries along the BRI's vast route. It is not aid and it does not remotely resemble the friendship treaties that countries signed with the then Soviet Union, which poured aid into those same countries. Even Mao Zedong signed a Treaty of Alliance and Mutual Assistance with Moscow, just four months after coming to power, in February 1950.[50]

Whether this is a deliberate attempt to put the initiative in a bad light is a moot point. Nonetheless, since they are commercially driven, the agreements should abide by what the Japanese are keen to refer to as international standards, which means that before projects are undertaken, they should go through a vigorous process of due diligence and feasibility study by both the host countries and the Chinese. Adherence to such stringent processes would help countries be in a better position to make decisions on whether to embark on such projects. Countries should not jump on the bandwagon and think up projects that could generate Chinese loans rather than judging the merits of those projects in terms of their necessity and utility. If not, they could become vanity projects.

The BRI provides enormous opportunities for countries to build up their infrastructure and their economies. However, host countries are in the best position to ascertain whether such projects are feasible, especially in the financial sense. The problem is that several countries see the BRI as a case of the bank giving you a loan without you applying for one. Unfortunately, some see the BRI as giving easy access to Chinese loans, which they can pass on to future generations which may not necessarily benefit from the project. Such funds could well end up in the pockets of the ruling elites. Some countries do not even have the expertise to assess the viability of projects or have the capacity to engage internationally reputable consultants to do the necessary due diligence and ensure that such projects make economic sense.

From the Chinese side, any opportunities to develop host countries and at the same time assist their own companies to venture into such areas will be seen in a positive light. We need to consider the BRI from both perspectives—that of the hosts and that of China. The former see the BRI mainly from a domestic angle, whereas the latter see it in regional and global terms. These perspectives do not always coincide, which may lead to difficulties and financial strains.

Secondly, the BRI is not a panacea for developing economies and no country is being forced to undertake these projects. The Chinese are clearly interested in infrastructure projects that fit into the BRI's often open-ended scope and reach. The responsibility primarily rests with recipient states.

However, the Chinese also have to be prudent when engaging with various countries. Its modus operandi is different to that of Western countries. The Chinese tend to retain the lion's share of work done, including importing its own labour force from China, often to the chagrin of locals.

When there is an influx of foreign labour, there is bound to be some form of local backlash. This was certainly the case in Sri Lanka, as well as elsewhere in Africa. Unfortunately, the Chinese have been known to be somewhat insensitive to local customs and this has led to a number of negative incidents resulting in an adverse perception of the Chinese. To some extent, the Chinese government has acknowledged this issue and is addressing it by stressing the need for Chinese nationals to be sensitive to local customs and practices, through public education and through companies' operating practices.

In addition, the Chinese should also do their own evaluation of the projects they are engaged in, even to the point of advising recipients to reject a scheme because of its non-viability. Some countries are in no position to have extravagant projects because they lack even basic infrastructure. China should be much more circumspect about those it is dealing with, as money could end up in the wrong hands. President Xi is at the forefront of fighting corruption in his country and China has extremely harsh punishments for such practices. In line with this, Beijing should also try to combat corruption when it involves Chinese companies operating internationally.

It is acknowledged that the BRI brings enormous benefits to China. Given its insatiable appetite for economic growth, the country needs an enormous gastronomical menu in order to satisfy its hunger. The BRI provides China with the potential growth trajectory to fuel its economy for decades to come. Alongside this, it is seeking new markets as well as new production lines, for it has become a victim of its own success. China's production costs have increased exponentially and, in turn, reduced its competitiveness, so Chinese companies are looking beyond their shores in a quest to find cheaper sources of production, especially labour. Decades ago, many Western companies shifted their factories and production lines to China, as costs were much lower there. However, due to its success, Chinese companies are now moving out; the BRI provides China with vast opportunities elsewhere.

Another critical question is whether the BRI is part of a larger Chinese grand design going beyond economics. Is this initiative Beijing's answer to global dominance? With many countries being strategic economic partners with China, it is possible that these countries will be dependent on, or at least beholden to, China—more compliant with Beijing's wishes and interests. A pertinent question is whether China could translate its global economic power into world political power. This will be addressed later.

It is axiomatic that the BRI is the world's largest economic undertaking ever. BRI projects just keep rising. The number of zeros is just mind-boggling. With this scale of development, China's economy is not immune to the rigours of the various gigantic projects. Using the analogy of a bank again, it could be the case that if a debtor is unable to repay a loan of US$1 million, it will be ruined; when a debtor cannot repay a US$1 billion loan, the bank is ruined. Such a scenario is unlikely, as China's economic strength goes way beyond the BRI, but it could still lead to problems within China itself and with host countries, in the event of them being unable to catch up financially. It would be prudent for Beijing to manage such issues carefully, not least because of the potential social and political backlash.

Nonetheless, China continues to push forward with its BRI juggernaut, despite hiccups, including the COVID-19 pandemic. President Xi reassured the world that 'facing the Covid-19 outbreak that caught us all by surprise, we have been supporting and assisting each other in the most difficult times and pushed forward the construction of the BRI, conveying confidence and strength to the international community and making an important contribution to global cooperation against the pandemic and economic recovery.'[51]

Towards a Global Military Power

'Bad News: China is building three huge helicopter aircraft carriers.' This was the headline of a July 2019 article in the conservative US online magazine *National Interest*.[52] According to the article, these platforms are currently under construction. However, at the time, China had only one fully operational aircraft carrier, the *Liaoning*, which it had acquired from the Soviet Union, under whose ownership it was called the *Varyag*.[53] After undergoing major refitting and sea trials in September 2012, the *Liaoning* was commissioned and it was only after another four years that it became combat-ready. The *Liaoning* now has a full complement of carrier-based fixed wings, such as the Shenyang J-15 fighter jets, and helicopters of various capabilities, including anti-submarine and airborne early warning and rescue. Interestingly, in 2014, the Chinese navy released a promotional video of its carrier-based jet, the J-15 Flying Shark, presumably in order to burnish its new-found prestige. The video is certainly most impressive and inspiring to some.[54] Alongside the *Liaoning*, in 2019, is the *Shandong*, China's first indigenously built carrier, which was launched from the

Dalian shipyard in 2017. A second China-built carrier is currently under construction. More recently, there was excitement amongst defence experts when photographs of this carrier (designated as Type-003), which is being built in Jiangnan Shipyard in Shanghai, were leaked, with some concluding that it will be the largest ship that has ever served in the Chinese fleet and it will mark another leap forward in China's advance as a naval power.[55] In another report, this new Chinese carrier has already been dubbed a 'super carrier', due to its comparable size to the latest American Ford-class carriers, though somewhat smaller and less capable, as well as being a less-experienced carrier operator.[56]

Before one gets too excited or alarmist, we should be reminded that this Chinese carrier programme cannot be seen in isolation. While China has only two combat-ready conventionally powered carriers at present, the United States could boast ten carrier-strike groups—all operational and ready to be deployed anytime, anywhere. The groups consist of nuclear-powered carriers, each with a full complement of an air wing of around 70 aircraft and an array of escorting naval assets that include submarines and surface warships such as destroyers and frigates. The latest carrier is the Ford-class, USS *Gerald R. Ford*. Against this, Chinese naval plans appear Lilliputian compared to those of the United States. Although alarmists have pointed out that the Chinese are vigorously pursuing an active carrier construction programme, the same can be said of the US Navy, which is in the process of replacing ageing ships. Other Western powers have their own carrier forces, including Britain's Royal Navy, which has two Queen Elizabeth class carriers, HMS *Queen Elizabeth* and HMS *Prince of Wales*.[57] And let us not forget the French, with their latest nuclear-powered *Charles de Gaulle* carrier.

However, it is interesting to remember the rationale used by the Chinese military some 35 years ago for aircraft carriers for the People's Liberation Army—Navy (PLAN). The Chinese naval commander Admiral Liu Huaqing, in 1986, justified the acquisition as 'safeguarding the country's maritime interests, including the recovery of the Nansha (Spratly Islands) and the reunification of Taiwan'.[58]

In assessing China's military capability, it is essential to put it into proper context and not view China in isolation. It is, after all, a competing power. However, when it comes to military power, China is still behind that of its main rival. Nonetheless, the time China has taken to build its military power is impressive, though this has not been done as quickly as its economy has grown.

In considering China's military power, we will not go through its order of battle nor assess each of the services and their capabilities. There is an enormous body of literature[59] on this subject and, not surprisingly, we get the full spectrum of assessments—from alarmist to apologist. This section will be highly selective and is confined to China's ability to project power beyond its shores. In modern warfare, it is sea power that forms the best platform to achieve this. Land and air power play second fiddle and are most relevant when it comes to defending the motherland against invasion or for limited offensive operations, which, given their track record, is likely to be limited to Taiwan. China will never relinquish its dream of reuniting Taiwan with the mainland. It may even resort to the use of force if necessary. For example, in July 2019, China's maritime safety agency announced that its military had held exercises in waters near Taiwan only days after Beijing reiterated it was ready to fight if there was any move towards independence on the self-ruled island.[60]

Power Projection

Every student attending military or naval academies, or for that matter students of strategic or security studies, irrespective of origin, would have been exposed to advocates of sea power, such as Mahan (American) and Corbett (British). Collectively, a number of principles have emerged. Chief among them is the notion that sea power is an essential ingredient in the development of a country's sense of greatness, whether in peace or wartime. In his seminal work, *The Influence of Sea Power upon History*, Alfred Thayer Mahan concluded that nations that control the seas would control all. Mahan's book is essentially a historical study focused on the Royal Navy.[61] According to Geoffrey Till, Mahan 'explained Britain's success by developing a simple deduction: greatness and strength are the product of wealth derived from trade; navies protect trade'.[62] Within this context, China's development of its navy could be said to be such an approach—the necessity of building its naval power in order to control the seas, as much of its trade is sea-bound. Although sea power is also about denial—the ability to deny the enemy the use of the sea—this is obviously only applicable during wartime. During peacetime, it is more a question of ensuring access to the seas.

Concomitant to Mahan's naval thinking is 'the fact that secure bases constituted the necessary foundation for power upon the sea'.[63] Advocates of sea power would argue that to project power a country needs either its own overseas bases or access to bases and facilities abroad, in order to operate far beyond its shores. In this regard, the construction of China's first overseas base in Djibouti has caught the attention and imagination of so many—policy makers, academics, media and enthusiasts alike. In addition to this African base, China is gaining access to other ports and facilities, such as in Myanmar, where military ties are strong.

As a footnote to history, it is interesting to note that imperial China was never a sea power despite the fact that, during the Ming dynasty, it had the largest fleet in the world and deployed it far beyond its shores—including on the seven voyages led by Admiral Zheng He. The problem then was that, even though China had the capability, it did not regard itself as a sea power. To the naval strategist Mahan, this mindset is essential to becoming one. It is safe to assume that today's China has embraced Mahan's analysis, consciously or unconsciously. While China's military might is still far behind that of the United States, it is becoming more powerful. China has invested in technology and this has found its way into its military industrial complex. This is not unique and we have seen this in the development of Western powers. After all, for centuries, the major conflicts have involved European powers, with the French having fought with the English over the centuries in famous battles like Agincourt and Crécy. Throughout history, technology has, paradoxically, brought progress as well as death and destruction to mankind; it is often referred to as the dual use of technology—to build and to kill. The splitting of the atom, which contributed to the production of the atom bombs that were dropped on Hiroshima and Nagasaki in August 1945, also assisted in the development of nuclear power.

Given China's growing power it is expected that we will continue to see a steady growth in its naval, air and ground forces. Apart from China's aircraft carrier plans, within the PLAN (People's Liberation Army—Navy) it has a whole range of assets, including nuclear-powered submarines carrying nuclear weapons that are undergoing various stages for upgrading and modernisation. For example, according to a recent report, China is developing conventional diesel-powered submarines, the Type 039A, which features 'an unusual sail, which appears to increase its agility and stealth', that could well assist the Navy in 'a possible war for Taiwan reunification and territorial conflicts in the East and South China seas'.[64]

Within the air force, the People's Liberation Army—Air Force (PLAAF) has an impressive military aviation force headed by its newly developed Chengdu J-20, officially named *Weilong* or 'Powerful Dragon' and with stealth technology comparable to that of the American F-22 Raptor.[65] This illustrates China's ability to match America's advance in fighter jets, although the latter may still have the advantage in numbers.

Ground forces are also advancing technologically—from the standard assault rifles to a more robust and agile armoured force, including Armoured Fighting Vehicles (AFVs) and Main Battle Tanks (MBTs), and sophisticated air wing with greater battlefield mobility. As with the other two services, we can expect greater technology advancement in land forces, the most senior of the services, especially with an increasing budget allocation.

Military Diplomacy

The Prussian strategist, Clausewitz, famously said, 'War is an extension of policy by other means.'[66] Today China is engaged in military diplomacy, for it sees this as an extension of policy, by other means. This is a far cry from the era prior to the 1980s when the People's Liberation Army (PLA) was still regarded as a highly secretive organisation. To some extent, the opening up of the military ran in tandem with economic openness, albeit at a different pace. Nonetheless, today, defence attachés[67] are part of most major Chinese embassies around the world and foreign military personnel can be found in various military, educational and training institutions in China.

There are several levels of military-to-military tie, each reflecting the closeness of the relationship. The most basic is an exchange of visits which could be referred to as the 'getting to know' phase. In most cases it is the Chinese who would make the first move, for the onus mainly rests with Beijing. This is so because most countries are eager to establish some form of military tie with the Chinese, especially when good diplomatic relations have been established. It could be at general staff level or even an invitation from military colleges to visit China.[68] The exchange of defence attachés could be the next level, followed by the deployment of observers during military exercises and even participating in such manoeuvres. Arms acquisition followed by joint production and technology transfer could all be developed and would be regarded as reaching a high level of military partnership. This is all part of normal military diplomacy in today's world.

To Beijing, engaging in military diplomacy brings enormous benefits, especially in putting countries at ease when they are looking at China. It also demonstrates China's willingness to be much more open in sensitive areas like defence forces. If China is still seen as the outsider, the military establishment is perhaps the last hindrance to overcoming that, and with the military veil being slowly lifted, much more comprehensive ties could be developed. As China's strength grows, and with it its confidence, we can expect Beijing to be much more enthusiastic and engaged in military diplomacy as it recognises that for China to be seen in a positive light any barriers to this must be removed.

Military Power and Potential Conflicts

Despite the various conflict scenarios involving China and the United States, including those that have become fiction bestsellers, there are two possible, and even likely, areas of potential conflict—over Taiwan and the South China Sea.

Taiwan

When the defeated Kuomintang forces crossed the Taiwan straits in September 1949 to establish a government in exile, many anticipated that this was going to be a major problem for both Taiwan and China as well as for the wider international community. The status of the newly created states—the People's Republic of China (PRC) and the Republic of China (ROC)—proved to be a diplomatic quagmire. Then, in 1971, the UN finally resolved this issue once and for all by expelling Taiwan, which resulted in most countries recognising Beijing as the legitimate holder of the UN seat. Nonetheless, Beijing still dreams of a final solution—of Taiwan uniting with the motherland to establish one China. The Taiwan question is fundamentally different from the cases of Hong Kong and Macau, which were Chinese territories 'lost' to colonial powers on long-lease agreements. They were returned to the mainland in 1997 and 1999 respectively. In these cases, there were specific agreements, and when the time was up, the leased territories were returned to the Chinese. As the systems in these areas have adopted different political, economic and social structures over the centuries, both are in transition, with the designated status of Special Administrative Region. Taiwan, however, can be regarded as a renegade territory—seized by the nationalists when they fled the mainland after losing the civil war to the communists.

Ever since the creation of the ROC, the mainland's position has been consistent—it seeks to reunite the island with the People's Republic. As a result, tensions have periodically erupted and there have been occasional clashes and skirmishes. Both sides have flexed their muscles in order to demonstrate their resolve and commitment to their sovereignty. For instance, while the Chinese navy was conducting military drills near Dongshan Island and Zhoushan Island in July 2019, the Taiwanese staged a live-fire exercise involving the launching of over 100 missiles of various types, including anti-ship missiles, from their Kidd-class destroyers, as well as the deployment of F-16 fighter jets armed with AGM-84 Harpoon missiles.[69]

There is a general consensus that Taiwan will be the issue on which China will resort to the use of force in the future, in order to take it back. Chinese leaders have no qualms in stating that they will fight for Taiwan. However, such provocative statements are often qualified by phrases along the lines of 'should Taiwan push for independence'. China vacillates between threats of peaceful and forceful unification.

There are two key issues here. The first is whether China has the military capability to seize Taiwan; does it have the wherewithal to carry out large-scale operations across the straits? This requires, *inter alia*, a large amphibious force with sufficient air support. The narrowest point between the southeast coast of China and Taiwan is around 130 km. This would require an impressive invading force made up of both sea-borne and air-borne components. According to a US-based news report, China is consciously focusing on building its amphibious assault capability; for Beijing, 'a well-developed amphibious capability is vital to one of China's most cherished political and military goals, the incorporation of Taiwan under mainland control'.[70] There are three components to such a capability: large landing ships, which are troop carriers as well as military assets, including MBTs; amphibious transport docks, which have a greater survivability rate and flexibility of deployment, as they can offload troops and assets without having to land on a beachhead; and helicopter carriers, designated as Type 075, to provide air support for the amphibious troops.

Notwithstanding China's ambitious plans to acquire a greater invading force, it is still highly contentious whether China has sufficient power to mount such a massive deployment of troops and assets. Perhaps a bigger question is what Beijing is going to do after having invaded Taiwan. Does it have the capability and capacity to hold it? Invading is one thing; occupation and reintegration is a different ball game altogether. But there is a much larger consideration for Beijing before it makes real the threat of resorting to force, which leads us to the second issue—the role of the

United States in the event of a major conflict erupting between the two Chinas.

Any country, most of all the United States, has to tread gingerly in its ties with Taiwan in order not to upset China, which does not recognise the legitimacy of the island. Over the decades, countries have been able to strike a good balance, focusing mainly on commercial links with Taiwan and steering clear of any sensitive political issues. However, as the United States once had a mutual defence treaty with Taiwan, which was abrogated in 1979 as a pre-condition to the establishment of full diplomatic relations with the PRC, the level of sensitivity is often heightened. Washington's ties with Taipei are governed by the Taiwan Relations Act of 1979, which, interestingly, according to Article 3(c), maintains its continued interest in Taiwan's security, albeit with a more ambiguous commitment in the event of a threat to that security. The provision calls for the US president 'to inform Congress promptly of any threat to the security or the social or economic system of the people on Taiwan and any danger to the interests of the United States arising therefrom. The President and Congress shall determine, in accordance with constitutional process, appropriate action by the United States in response to any such danger.'[71]

Despite this Act, it is for the US president to decide the level of response to the Chinese when it impinges on security matters with Taiwan. On the one hand, the United States knows its priority is to maintain a stable relationship with the PRC, but on the other, it has to demonstrate its continued interest in the security of its long-term friend and ally, Taiwan. It is safe to assume that policy makers are constantly reminded of the wrong signal the Americans gave over their commitment to the Korean Peninsula, just before the North crossed the 38th Parallel and invaded the South in June 1950. Prior to this first major conflict of the Cold War, Washington stated that it would not necessarily adhere to the 'swing strategy' or the 'trip-wire concept'. The swing strategy was the approach of moving troops from the Western European theatre to Asia in the event that South Korea was invaded, and the trip-wire concept called for an immediate military response when such a situation arose. Creating ambiguity over these two key issues gave the impression that the United States had experienced a change of heart over its defence commitment to South Korea. The then North Korean Great Leader, Kim Il Sung took this as a signal that the United States would not come to the South's rescue, prompting his decision to invade.

In addition, US presidents can also show Beijing their unhappiness by cosying up to the islanders. For instance, in July 2019 the United States, under President Trump, announced that it would sell weapons to Taiwan, worth some US$2.2 billion, including M1A2T Abrams MBTs and handheld Stinger missiles, much to the anger of Beijing. It is difficult to know what was behind this decision, as the timing was not the best. The announcement came at a time of heightened tension between China and the United States, driven by the ongoing trade war started by a maverick American president. Trump's style was most intriguing as it often mixed personal feelings with matters of state. While some might admire his 'guts', others cringe whenever he appeared at public events. Trump's often erratic behaviour did cause unnecessary tense and unpredictable situations. As he was seen as someone who came from outside the establishment and who had no experience in government or the legislature, his tenure was seen as an aberration rather than any permanent shift. Thus, with regard to Taiwan over the longer term, Washington may exercise more caution and steer away from highly sensitive issues involving security and military matters.

The key question here is whether the United States would come to Taiwan's assistance in the event of China launching what could be interpreted as an invading force. While the United States will always provide the umbrella of an indirect deterrent over Taiwan, one thing is for sure: it will not sit idle in the event of any serious tensions erupting. It is a matter of American global prestige as well as the raison d'être for its global military presence to maintain peace and security. Besides, any conflict in the area will lead to serious disruption of sea lines of communication, which would be a sufficient pretext for American intervention. To what extent the United States will defend the island is open to debate, conjecture and speculation.

As far as the United States and China are concerned the status quo is the preferred option, although what seems worrisome is domestic Taiwanese politics, in particular any push for independence, for which Beijing will show zero tolerance.

South China Sea

Whoever named this vast span of water, with its strategic sea lines of communication, must be turning in his grave, for the name has given the Chinese the best possible claim.[72] Without going into all the intricacies of the various positions of the claimants, suffice to say some countries, such as Malaysia and Brunei, have taken a much less confrontational stance towards China, while others, like the Philippines and Vietnam, have tended to be more aggressive in stating their claims.[73] China's position has been consistent: the South China Sea has been part of Chinese territory for the last two millennia. This history-based claim is disputed by all the other claimants. The Philippines took the matter to UN arbitration and in July 2016 an international tribunal in The Hague rejected China's argument that it enjoys historic rights over most of the South China Sea. It also found that China had violated international law by causing 'irreparable harm' to the marine environment, endangering Philippine ships and interfering with Philippine fishing and oil exploration.[74] This is the first time that a ruling has been made on China's claims by the UN-appointed international tribunal. Despite the ruling being legally binding, there is no mechanism to enforce the decision. Not unexpectedly, China rejected the ruling, with President Xi himself stating that China's territorial sovereignty and maritime interests in the waters would not, under any circumstances, be affected by the verdict.[75] In this respect it is foolhardy to suggest that China will ever entertain any claims—legitimate or otherwise—on what it regards as part of its territory. Chinese leaders have consistently reinforced this belief and have never been remotely open to any idea of negotiation. Beijing recognises no other claims on this vast span of water. Any such recognition could legitimise the various claims, which mostly stem from the adoption of the 1982 UN Convention on Law of the Sea, which enshrines the rights of states to claim some 200 nautical miles around their coasts as their legitimate exclusive economic zone.

Despite its non-recognition of the various claims and earlier reluctance to accept an Association of Southeast Asian Nations (ASEAN) initiative for a code of conduct over the South China Sea, China seems to be increasingly open to the idea of at least sitting down and talking about such issues. For example, in July 2019, after a meeting with all his ASEAN counterparts in Bangkok, Chinese Foreign Minister Wang Yi announced that the ASEAN delegates had completed the first reading of the text to negotiate the code of conduct which would form the basis of future discussions on a system to manage and resolve disputes in the South China Sea.[76] Despite this positive development, one can expect many issues and difficulties to surface. And despite agreement to the code of conduct, enforcement will be the biggest challenge, as there exists an asymmetrical power balance between China and the rest of ASEAN and, specifically, other claimants. Perhaps it is no coincidence that at the same meeting the Chinese foreign minister warned outside nations against any attempt to sow discord between Beijing and Southeast Asian countries by playing up disputes over the South China Sea, saying that differences could be resolved peacefully between the affected parties themselves.[77] There have been many occasions during which the United States has deployed its carrier-strike group to patrol the area as a show of force and conducted naval exercises in the area, often jointly with other countries. For instance, in June 2019 the US Navy Nimitz-class nuclear-powered aircraft carrier USS *Ronald Reagan* and the Japan Maritime Self-Defense Force's largest flattop, the first-of-class JS *Izumo*, jointly held a naval exercise in the South China Sea.

A potential conflict over the South China Sea can be viewed from several perspectives. This highly sensitive area can be seen within the context of China's rivalry with the United States and the dynamics of this relationship. It must also be considered in the context of Beijing's relations with its neighbours, especially with other claimants. What it does and how it behaves will have an impact on perceptions of China in these countries. Negative perceptions will play into the hands of Washington, enhancing the United States' global pre-eminence. To be positive towards the claimants will improve goodwill, which could benefit China. Here lies China's dilemma over the disputed South China Sea: to exercise the arrogance of power or to show a degree of magnanimity. Beijing has chosen to play the soft card, which appears to be reaping benefits, as some of the claimants view this as positive. China's acquiescence in the ASEAN-initiated code of conduct is a case in point.

On the strategic rivalry with the United States, a Japanese official report summarised the situation thus: 'China has created artificial islands in the South China Sea and constructed military bases there, steadily building up its maritime military presence. In doing so, it has restrained the actions of the US military, which has heretofore served as the linchpin of the region's security order, and is overtly acting in a way aimed at weakening the US military presence.'[78] Given Japan's own military alliance with the United States, it is in Tokyo's interests to see the latter's continued presence and supremacy and to ensure that China's growing military power remains checked. Nonetheless, to suggest that China's military activity in the area has somehow restrained the US military is overstating the case. The reinforcement of China's claims through the militarisation of the area has not hindered the ability of the US navy to operate in and around the region.

Indeed, China is not alone in building up bases and enhancing its presence in the area. Other Western forces also patrol the area and various claimants have reinforced their claims by either re-claiming land in order to build concrete bases or facilities or deploying their own military force as a show of force and to re-instate their claims. Countries such as Malaysia have been doing this incrementally over decades, so much so that Malaysia now has a substantial presence in the area it claims, specifically Layang-Layang Island (it was originally a mere atoll but through reclamation has become a man-made island).

On the whole, all the claimants know the limits of what they can do in the disputed territories. They are fully aware of where the sensitive buttons are and which ones to push and when. Each disputant will need to gauge the advantages and costs it will have to bear when it comes to asserting its claims. The overall state of relations between China and the claimants will be the critical determinant in their respective decision-making processes.

An Assessment of China's Military Power

With President Xi Jinping's notion of 'great power-ness', it is perhaps no surprise that China is pursuing military modernisation to protect its core interests. After all, the very essence of a sovereign state is the enhancement of national interests. Over centuries, countries have gone to war to secure their interests—it is the most common *casus belli*. According to a Japan-based think tank, the National Institute for Defense Studies, 'China is embroiled in confrontation with some of its neighbours, chiefly over its maritime core interests, with the Xi Jinping administration bolstering actions to change the status quo by coercion in a way advantageous to itself, intimidating its opponents through the exercise of military power and its maritime law-enforcement capacity.'[79] While this is put rather bluntly, it is no surprise coming from an official Japanese source. With rising confidence, stemming from its economic global presence and strength, coupled with impressive military capability, we can expect to see a much more assertive China on the world stage. To those who feel rather claustrophobic under US dominance this is welcome news, while those who cherish the continued supremacy of this long-time superpower will want to deny the emergence of a potential challenger.

With China becoming more global, it is reasonable to expect that its military will grow correspondingly. Like all interests it needs to be protected, a responsibility that rests solely on the shoulders of the PLA. This was explicitly stated in a Chinese national defence white paper, in which the military was described as taking on the strategic duty of the 'protection of the security of overseas interest'.[80]

The notion of the protection of the motherland is as sacrosanct to China as it is to all sovereign nations. The challenge, however, is to make sense of what constitutes the protection of interests. How far is a country willing to go towards meeting this national goal? How far would China go, even if it meant resorting to the use of force, in order to protect its interests, which are already global in nature?

There is no doubt that China draws a clear line when it comes to what it regards as its territory, namely all the disputed areas. For every Chinese leader, stretching back to the emperors, uniting the country has been a fixation. Conversely, to lose any real estate to the 'enemy' would be unthinkable. We should expect no compromise from China on this key national interest.

Extrapolating this idea of real estate to include Chinese nationals abroad makes the discussion much fuzzier. We have seen how the United States protects its citizens in distress overseas, at times using such cases as a pretext to intervene more than it should,[81] and we should expect the Chinese to do the same. After all, why should we regard the Chinese as different from the United States or any country that extends the same protection to its citizens abroad, guaranteed by international laws and conventions? The big question is whether China will go beyond diplomacy and resort to the use of force in order to secure the safety of its citizens abroad. Would the Chinese follow the negative example of the United States by invading countries deemed to be acting against its interests, using the same pretext Washington has used? Worse, would Beijing follow Washington's example of mendacity over its past invasions. After all, if Washington has done it, with the collusion of some Western powers and with no serious legal consequences, Beijing could follow suit.

As China is a great power and increasingly a superpower, one should not dismiss such a possibility. Much will depend on the circumstances and perhaps more importantly on China's capacity to undertake such an operation. Projecting power is one thing; invading and occupying require a separate strategy and approach. While outright disproportionate use of force in order to protect its citizens in danger abroad, as the United States has done, may not be the first option, the Mekong incident of 2011, described below, suggests that China will exert pressure and force to ensure its citizens are protected and to ensure that justice is seen to be done in its eyes.

The Mekong River connects Southern China with mainland Southeast Asia and has become a major waterway for the transportation of goods, including contraband such as drugs. The area is notorious for being one of the world's major sources of drugs and is dubbed the Golden Triangle. In October 2011, on Thai territory, two Chinese-crewed barges were attacked and all 13 crew members killed. Their bodies were badly mutilated, apparently by the drug gangs controlling the trade along the waterway. This sparked a major cyber-storm among Chinese netizens, pressuring the government to take action.[82] As a result of the slowness of investigations by the Thai, Laotian and Myanmar governments, Beijing decided to take the lead in solving this crime perpetrated against its citizens, put diplomatic pressure on the leaders of those three countries and dispatched an investigative team consisting of officials from various agencies, including Public Security. After effort and intrigue worthy of a movie production the Burmese national drug lord Naw Kham was caught and taken to Southern China to stand trial. More than two years after the incident Naw Kam was executed, to the satisfaction of the Chinese public. His arrest and what followed is reminiscent of the case of the notorious Mexican drug lord, Joaquin Guzman, better known as 'El Chapo', who, having escaped twice, was finally captured and brought to trial in the United States, found guilty in July 2019 and sentenced to life imprisonment. The US Drug Enforcement Agency was heavily involved in the whole process.

At the same time, discussions to establish some kind of broader multilateral security mechanism for the Mekong waterway began, resulting in joint patrols which have improved security along this vital transportation link. This whole episode suggests that we can expect more of the same from the Chinese if its citizens' well-being is threatened. As Chinese nationals, tourists as well as workers become ubiquitous in many countries, the risks increase, which is going to keep China busy.

Perhaps it is no surprise that several Western observers and media saw the Mekong incident, and its impact on China, as negative and requiring caution. For instance, the *New York Times* described China's role as 'a hard-nosed display of the government's political and economic clout across Laos, Myanmar and Thailand...' and that 'the capture shows how China's law-enforcement tentacles reach far beyond its borders into a region now drawn by investment and trade into China's orbit, and where the United States' influence is being challenged'.[83] The article was clearly biased against the Chinese as it even suggested that Beijing had 'pressured the countries to participate in Chinese-led river patrols'.

What can we make of this Chinese action over the Mekong incident? It is precisely this: with growing confidence in its power, China is behaving like any great power, extending its interests to protect its citizens abroad. China has come of age as a major power, if not a superpower. We can certainly expect more such of the same if similar situations surface.

One of the ongoing debates about China's military power is 'How strong is it?' To answer this question one must look at its strength in relation to two factors: what it takes to protect its core interests and its ability to challenge the supremacy of the United States. Both are open to subjective assessment. On the latter, a US Department of Defense report published in May 2019 stated that the Chinese military was expanding at a rate that could soon 'contest US military superiority' and that it would try to transform its military into a major global power by any means necessary, including 'a variety of methods to acquire foreign military and dual-use technologies, including targeted foreign direct investment, cyber theft, and exploitation of private Chinese nationals' access to these technologies, as well as harnessing its intelligence service, computer intrusions, and other illicit approaches'.[84]

Interestingly, one basis for comparison is to look purely at numbers when considering Chinese and American military forces. Such an approach, looking at the order of battles, is flawed as there are many other factors that need to be taken into account, namely the technology and the 'human' factor. Some scholars have pointed to factors that would tilt the balance in favour of the United States. According to a Chinese military expert based at the International Institute for Strategic Studies in London, 'The greatest advantage that the US has at the moment over the PLA is that the US has been working on doctrine, training, professionalisation for a lot longer than the PLA, with actual experience to back it up.'[85]

There have been similar reports, emanating mainly from the United States and other Western-based media. Reuters ran a series of reports focusing on China's military capability, in particular under Xi, preferring to substitute his title of president with that of marshal. In one such report, it argued that 'the rapid and disruptive advance of Chinese hard power on Xi Jinping's watch has ended the era of unquestioned US supremacy in Asia.'[86] Such an alarmist report fits with and reinforces the official American narrative on the potential threat that China poses. The Reuters reports appear not to take into consideration the broader US military presence in

Asia—it has permanent bases and facilities throughout the Asia–Pacific region, such as in Japan, South Korea and Singapore. The US Indo–Pacific Command, which is a unified combatant command, is based in Hawaii and has impressive assets at its disposal, including five carrier-strike groups. Surely this enormous capability alone cannot be matched by the two Chinese combat-ready carriers. Even when it comes to a second-strike capability, the US nuclear submarine (SSBN) fleet traverses the oceans of the world. It has one of the largest fleets of SSBNs, alongside the Russians. Such an invulnerable capability in large numbers will surely keep the US nuclear arsenal in a far superior place to that the Chinese could ever muster.

Another rather more sober report in the *South China Morning Post* questioned the notion that China is fast outperforming the United States. It argued that, despite the broadening of 'its reach from an inshore defence force to an offshore presence, meaning it can now protect the Chinese Sea Lines of Communication', China's rise 'as a credible global military force remains a work in progress, and overall is still far from being able to challenge US supremacy'.[87]

One of the much-quoted sayings of Mao Zedong is that 'political power grows out of the barrel of the gun'.[88] However, there is a corollary to this quote which is 'the Party must control the gun'.[89] This reinforces the supremacy of the Communist Party and the unambiguous subordination of the military to it. This is further confirmed by the Party structure, where the chairman of the Central Military Commission of the CCP, the supreme military policy and decision-making body, is the president himself. This is a central theme of Chinese politics and the Party has always maintained it, hence reducing, though not eliminating entirely, the possibility of a military coup. While it is safe to assume that there has been much surreptitious political machination and intrigue within the Party, open conflicts have been the exception rather than the rule. There was, of course, the rather intriguing case of Marshal Lin Biao, the powerful and one-time heir apparent to Mao, whose plane is believed to have been shot down as he tried to flee to the Soviet Union in September 1971. He was accused by the Party of leaving the country after attempting to stage a coup, although another version is that Lin fled before being purged, as ties between him and other senior Party leaders had soured.[90]

While the possibility of a military coup in China is extremely low, if not non-existent, this does not mean that only the military can appeal to nationalism or militarism. While we have seen how the rise of militarism has led to warmongering, such as in Japan and Germany in the 1930s, the possibility of the PLA pushing the country to take such a course seems improbable. One scenario that has been painted points to the Chinese military gaining the upper hand in decision-making and opting for a much more aggressive stance towards issues such as Taiwan and the South China Sea. This follows a favourite scenario involving what was the Soviet Union and leading to a confrontation with the United States.[91] As stated earlier, China does not need the military to push the leadership to take a more belligerent attitude. It will remain steadfast in exerting its sovereignty over the disputed areas.

Another aspect of China's military power is its increasing contribution towards peacekeeping operations, in terms of both personnel and finance. Such contributions have been publicly acknowledged by the UN. According to one UN senior official, 'China is in a unique position of not only being the largest contributor among permanent members of the Security Council, but also being one of the 10 top contributors of uniformed personnel.'[92] By 2019, China had dispatched more than 39,000 peacekeeping military personnel, participated in 24 missions and contributed significant amounts of infrastructure and support. This included the building of 13,000 km of roads in the peacekeeping operation area, the provision of medical treatment for more than 170,000 patients and the provision of more than 300 armed escorts and patrols, such as in the Gulf of Aden, to protect Chinese and other foreign vessels.[93] This came at a time when President Trump was seen to be disengaging from activities and commitments towards the UN, preferring to undertake unilateral operations, much to the chagrin of the international community. In contrast, China's continued commitment is hailed as an exemplar of a responsible great power and permanent member of the UN Security Council. This view is echoed by an official Chinese publication: 'As permanent members of the Security Council, China shoulders responsibilities of a big power for a series of major issues concerning the peace and security of mankind. Active participation in the UN peacekeeping operations embodies the responsibilities of China as a great power, as well as the support of China towards [the] UN peace cause.'[94] Beijing's motives are clear in this regard. It wants not only to be seen as a responsible permanent member but also to ensure that as China goes global, especially in economic terms, its international commitments do as well. Besides, almost all the UN missions China has been involved with, including in Cambodia, the Democratic Republic of Congo, Liberia, Sudan and Mali, have been in countries where China has some interest, economic or otherwise. Goodwill can only help China's image in these countries and in the wider international community.

All things considered, there is no doubt that China is fast becoming a global military power, if it is not already so. With a greater budget being committed to building a credible defence force, we can expect Beijing to reach greater heights and at the same time project power. China's global economic interests must be protected by a global military force and we must prepare to deal with this. China's behaviour is no different to that of other great powers or superpowers and we should not expect otherwise.

Engaging in Soft Power: Challenging Western Cultural and Social Dominance

Joseph S. Nye of Harvard University coined the term 'soft power' and it has become a popular theme within the international relations discipline. Power is about means and ends. Nye says that while soft power shares the same basic goal of affecting or influencing the behaviour of others to get desired results, it 'co-opts people rather than coerces them'.[95] Thus, we cannot ignore China's use of soft power as a means to achieve its objective—which, to quote President Xi, is to secure its 'core interests'. Xi himself has stressed the importance of soft power ever since his ascendancy to power in 2013, as an instrument of the state.

Not surprisingly, the notion of soft power has become a favourite topic within the discussion of China's growing influence globally.[96] While the usage of the term soft power is relatively new, the concept has been discussed extensively amongst academic circles around the world, including in China. As early as 1993, a Chinese academic from Fudan University, writing in Chinese, talked of projecting culture as part of the country's soft power. Writing in the post-Tiananmen era, he argued that national morale manifested in patriotism plays an important role in a country's power and believes that a positive image, which consists of positive impressions about a country's credibility, behaviour, style and so on, would greatly enhance a country's soft power.[97]

Over the years, but more recently, Chinese leaders have also stressed the importance of soft power as part of the state's instruments of power. In 2014, President Xi said, 'We should increase China's soft power, give a good Chinese narrative, and better communicate China's message to the world,' and during the 19th National Congress of the CCP in October

2017, among the 2020–2035 goals, he outlined steps to enhance China's soft power, and the greater appeal of its culture, stating, 'We will improve our capacity for engaging in international communication so as to tell China's stories well, present a true, multi-dimensional and panoramic view of China, and enhance our country's soft power.'[98] Xi's predecessor, Hu Jintao, had also talked of the country's soft power. In his keynote address at the CCP 17th National Congress in October 2007, he announced that 'culture has become a more and more important source of national cohesion and creativity and a factor of growing significance in the competition in overall national strength', and as such China must 'enhance culture as part of the soft power of our country to better guarantee the people's cultural rights and interests'.[99] It was also reported that, during the same Congress, Hu Jintao declared that 'the great rejuvenation of the Chinese nation will definitely be accompanied by the thriving of Chinese culture.... We must enhance culture as part of the soft power of our country.... We will further publicise the fine traditions of Chinese culture and strengthen international cultural exchanges to enhance the influence of Chinese culture worldwide.'[100] It is made abundantly clear, through the speeches of Chinese leaders, that the country has taken soft power as an integral part of its overall power structure, and as such it has been given its due attention and focus. As we shall see, it could be argued that this is a reflection and recognition of China's ability to influence the world towards its thinking.

In the broadest sense, soft power involves the use of a whole range of instruments, including economic and commercial means, to achieve political benefits. Following Nye's interpretation, anything that resembles co-option as opposed to coercion is tantamount to taking a soft approach. Certainly, as far as China is concerned, it has embarked on a broad range of what could be classified as the soft expression of power, from engaging in a much more sophisticated public diplomacy, including in cultural and educational areas, as well as in economic and military diplomacy. The Chinese have resorted to the employment of soft power as a way to help smooth their entry onto the world's centre stage. It wants to be accepted, clearly on its own terms, and not to pander to Western and other influences. China will not kowtow to 'foreign' influence; instead, it not only would like others to understand and even accept it, but also, as we have seen in earlier chapters, Beijing, especially under President Xi, wants to advocate and promote its own brand, its own model, which can be emulated and adopted by other countries, in a challenge to the domination of the Western political–economic development model. Putting it simply, it is about building a softer image of China as it wants to be liked. In June 2021, Xi Jinping's speech to senior CCP officials was covered by the leading Western news media, for the Chinese president said that 'it is important to present an image of a 'credible, loveable and respectable China'.[101] However, interestingly, Xinhua, China's official news agency, did not use the word 'loveable', preferring the much more subtle 'admirable'.[102] As such, much of the discussion of Chinese soft power centres on the country promoting a better image to the world, in what one Chinese scholar based in Southeast Asia refers to as the soft power's 'behavioural approach'.[103]

In essence, when we refer to the employment of Chinese soft power, we are focusing on the projection of a positive image of China, whether regionally, such as in Africa, or on the world's stage. In this respect, Beijing is involved in a whole array of activities, which to one scholar dubs China's tool kit of soft power diplomacy, and includes, firstly, its reassuring political discourse; secondly, its diplomatic conduct including self-restraint over controversial issues; thirdly, cultural and public diplomacy; and fourthly, trade and assistance.[104]

A major theme of this book is that we cannot discuss China in isolation and that China behaves like many other great powers. Many countries are consciously or unconsciously engaged in soft power, especially in the area of public diplomacy. Some social and cultural activities used by China should be viewed in the same light as the activities of the United States and others, including the United Kingdom. One is reminded of President Kennedy's initiative to set up the American Peace Corps, to get young Americans to different parts of the world, engaged in assisting other countries, especially in the developing world, in areas such as education and health. In launching the Peace Corps, Kennedy said, 'This Corps will be a pool of trained American men and women sent overseas by the US Government or through private institutions and organizations to help foreign countries meet their urgent needs for skilled manpower.'[105] Less than half a century later, the Chinese are doing just that, promoting the image of China, while at the same time assisting less well-to-do societies around the world.

The opening of Kong Zi (Confucius) Institutes by the Chinese government in many capital cities has often been cited as an example of China's soft power. Essentially, these institutes, which are overseen by China's Ministry of Education, promote the Chinese language and culture. They offer Mandarin classes and cultural activities and organise exchange visits to promote a better understanding of China within host countries. These institutes are really no different to the United Kingdom's British Council, the French Alliance Française and the German Goethe-Institut. No doubt to China, the Kong Zi Institutes are part of its soft power armoury to promote Chinese culture and language to the world, in the hope that the recipients would not only be exposed to the richness of China's heritage but also gain a better understanding and appreciation of its long civilisation, with the hope that they would be much more 'sympathetic' to the aspirations of the country. This is probably one of the main goals of China's soft power.

In another area that appears successful is the global entry of Chinese 24-hour news media. For many years, the West almost monopolised the airwaves with news channels from CNN to BBC. Most major Western powers have their own channel. The Chinese started their own with CCTV, which was later renamed CGTN, and now reaches many living rooms globally, projecting China's version of the world. In addition, the Chinese have expanded their news agency, Xinhua, globally, increasing its news coverage with its own perspective. Interestingly, the Chinese have also invested heavily on the big screen, with feature films ranging from historical themes to more modern settings. It could be argued that, at a time when there is dwindling investments in such areas, China is pouring in money to project its own image through movies and drama series which also appeal to the public. For instance, action movies, such as the *Wolf Warrior* and its sequels, do project the image of China, in this case, the PLA's Special Operations Forces. No doubt, the Chinese are appealing to the world's younger population, with such action-packed movies. Chinese production houses have also tried to enter into joint productions with US- or Western-based companies. The film *The Great Wall*, released in 2016, is a case in point. It brought together Hollywood's Matt Damon and Willem Dafoe, with Chinese superstar Jing Tian, and Hong Kong's Andy Lau, in a film with a historical setting but a fictional storyline. According to one observer, this movie could be seen as 'an example of a new kind Chinese soft power effort that seeks to place China much more prominently in the public's eye'.[106]

China's Discursive Power

There is an emerging body of opinion that argues it would be more appropriate to refer to Chinese soft power as discursive power. While the reliance on public speeches and official narratives as a way to project a state's power beyond its borders is not new, the term 'discursive power' is relatively new. Often associated with the French post-modernist Michel Foucault,[107] the concept, which is gaining popularity among the intellectual community, rests on the keyword 'discourse'. Foucault essentially challenged the more traditional notions of power, in which the French intellectual famously articulated that power is everywhere and comes from everywhere. Extrapolating from this argument, discursive power has emerged where discourse has been identified as a source of power. In other words, states, using discourse as a platform, are projecting their power in the international arena. However, according to some scholars, 'Understanding discourse as involving the ideal and the material, the linguistic and the non-linguistic, means that discourses are performative. Performative means that discourses constitute the objects of which they speak.'[108] In the case of China, the manifestation of its discursive power could be the Chinese model, which it wants to articulate in the public domain. In other words, discursive power is a manifestation of the use of discourse in the international area, in order to promote and project a positive image of the country.

While China has been broadly engaged in projecting its soft power through various tools, it has also focused on its discursive power.[109] China is competing in the discourse arena, in projecting its image and its own narrative. While Deng and his successors tended to prefer a much lower profile in projecting China, President Xi seeks to take it to new heights. As we have seen in previous chapters, Xi's Chinese Dream, with its international dimensions, has started to push the Chinese narrative to the forefront of its public diplomacy. Today, China is trying to sell its political–economic model to the rest of the world. In this regard, it is employing its discursive power at the global level. They need the public space and are trying to compete and even dominate it. However, as the basis of the Chinese model is fundamentally different from the prevailing Western model—the former rests on a more authoritarian system, with its one-party rule, while the latter is based on a democratic system—the competition between the two would be intense and, arguably, irreconcilable. As Mark Twain wrote, 'East is East, and West is West, and never the twain shall meet.' However, to the Chinese, the battleground is on the plains of the developing world.

Not surprisingly, China's emphasis on soft power has stirred up much discussion, including viewing it through the threat prism. To alarmists, for instance, this is yet more evidence that China wants to dominate the world, and to them there is something sinister in China's use of soft power. There is also a growing number of sceptics that argue China's soft power is not working, but backfiring, as many in the West are either not impressed or not convinced by Chinese methods. For instance, one observer noted, 'Despite extensive investment in cultural promotion, educational exchange, and foreign-language media offerings, Chinese soft power initiatives do not seem to have had a major impact on public opinion toward China.'[110]

One of the challenges facing China's soft power approach may well be the difference between theory and practice as well as different notions of what constitutes outright or subtle forms of propaganda and value systems. While it may want to project a positive image internationally, often something happens in China, and it receives adverse publicity, resulting in its soft power approach taking a step backwards. Such incidents usually involve either human rights or security issues. Recently, the suppression of the Uyghurs of the Xinjiang autonomous region in Northwest China has damaged China's image amongst human rights activists and Muslim groups around the world, although governments, especially Muslim ones, have tended to show more restraint in their open criticism of China's ill treatment of the Uyghurs. China has also shown zero tolerance towards its own dissidents, most of whom have been imprisoned. Some of them are high profile, which obviously has struck a chord amongst human rights groups. For instance, one of China's most prominent human rights and democracy advocates was a Nobel laureate. When Liu Xiaobo died in prison, while serving an 11-year prison sentence, China received significant adverse publicity, reminding people around the world of the nature of the Chinese state. According to a BBC report, Liu played a significant role in the Tiananmen Square student protests of June 1989, where he and other activists negotiated the safe exit of several hundred demonstrators, and has been credited with saving their lives.[111] Throughout his life, he was in and out of prison. To one observer, when Liu died, it was a soft power 'own goal' for China as the world saw how the Nobel Prize-winning activist was treated.[112] Therefore, the Chinese narrative of events is often seen in a different light around the world. One example is that it is quite common to see wrongdoers (according to the Chinese authorities) confessing their crimes on television, while this public charade could well be viewed in a cynical manner elsewhere. However, the Chinese public have become accustomed to such 'confessions' on their television screens, especially those among the older generation, during the Cultural Revolution and post-Mao period.

On the whole, it is perhaps too early to draw any conclusions on the success of China's soft power. Much would depend on the recipients, on how they view China in general. Obviously, in much of the Western world, which emphasises issues such as democracy and human rights, the perception of China would not be that rosy. In a European-based report, assessing China's soft power in Europe, the conclusion they drew was negative. For example, it stated that, 'Over 2018–2019, the EU became an increasingly sceptical receiver of China's soft-power strategy (which was increasingly seen as "sharp power" instead), with more communications pointing to the risks posed by China's geopolitical ambitions.' It went further to conclude that 'China's image projection lacks credibility among part of the EU and EU member states' leadership. The debate over China's image at the EU level is framed in normative, geopolitical and economic terms— that is, it is discussed in terms of its human rights situation, its international standing (or geopolitical ambitions) and fairness in the economic relationship.'[113]

Not surprisingly, China's image seems to be improving in other parts of the world, for example, in Africa and Asia. As argued in earlier chapters, non-democratic states are more inclined to see China positively, for they view what the country can offer as much more attractive and appealing when compared to often rigid doctrinaire-driven Western governments. As argued previously, the double standards of some Western powers only play in the hands of the Chinese, for states that are considered non-democratic are frowned upon by the West. In many parts of Africa, states and their populations tend to receive the Chinese more positively. It is interesting to note, as already been pointed out, that the Chinese government is fully aware of some of the negative behaviour of their own people 'on the ground', either as aid workers, or construction workers, or as tourists, and of the need to address such negativity, which goes to show the seriousness of the state in such matters.

Given the decades of Western influence in much of the world, there tends to be some degree of scepticism when it comes to anything non-Western, especially when there is a choice, cost notwithstanding. For instance, in COVID-19 vaccination programmes, given the choice of Western-based vaccines, such as Pfizer, Astra-Zeneca or Modena, against Chinese ones, such as Sinovac or Sinopharm, many, for instance, in Malaysia, would prefer the former although both types are being administered, without giving a choice to the recipients. This is only due to a bias, inculcated unconsciously over decades, irrespective of the reality. Despite this, many welcomed Chinese vaccines as part of the world's vaccination programme to combat the pandemic. In this regard, China has been active in public diplomacy, by generously donating its vaccines to many countries around the world.

In an age when Chinese products are ubiquitous and their leaders' announcements of great achievements in the area of high technology, including space and artificial intelligence, are plentiful, the world perhaps will slowly view China differently, arguably more positively. This is especially true at a time of asymmetrical emphasis on soft power between the Chinese and the West. While the former is investing heavily in soft power, by stepping up efforts to project and improve China's image, the latter, due mainly to budgetary constraints, is experiencing a decline. In other words, while attempts to improve its image in the Western world may be an uphill battle, doing so in the rest of the world may be relatively easier, though far from a 'walk in the park'.

China Exercising Great Power Status

From economic to military and cultural dimensions, China is indeed a multidimensional power—having achieved superpower status. During the Cold War both the United States and the Soviet Union were locked in a nuclear confrontation, which, if it had materialised, would have led to Armageddon. Only the Soviet Union could rival the United States, but only in military terms (Moscow had the nuclear capability to destroy much of continental America). In economic and commercial fields, however, Soviet influence was extremely limited and confined to its allies, who were invariably highly dependent on Moscow's largesse, political and otherwise. Today, China has replaced the USSR as the power that can challenge US pre-eminence, but unlike the USSR it can now rival the United States in most areas.

While it is clear that China is both an economic and a military power, it is less so in terms of political influence. However, we have not seen Beijing use, on a large scale, these two powerful tools as leverage over other states. This is a much harder issue to debate because it warrants further evidence and not just conjecture. As an example, a study of UN members' voting behaviour, especially on issues important to China, could shed further light on the use of political leverage for political ends. Nonetheless, even if the evidence is staring us in the face, such behaviour is only to be expected of great power. What is the point of having power if you do not exercise it? However, as we have seen due to China's enormous power, countries prefer not to unnecessarily antagonise Beijing. While China may not overtly be using its power as leverage, countries themselves tacitly recognise the reality of power balance. After all, sometimes, you don't need to exercise your power or even flex your muscles in order to achieve your objectives, especially when everyone recognises who is the most powerful. Such is the nature of power.

Notes

1. Alfred K. Ho, *China's Reforms and Reformers* (Westport, Connecticut: Praeger Press, 2004), p. 81.
2. For a discussion on Hua's post-Mao's role, see Frederick C. Teiwes and Warren Sun, 'China's New Economic Policy Under Hua Guofeng: Party Consensus and Party Myths', *The China Journal*, No. 66, July 2011), pp. 1–23.
3. Gregory C. Chow, 'China's 40 Years of Reform and Development: 1978-2018', Australian National University, press-files.anu.edu.au.
4. Patrick E. Tyler, 'Deng Xiaoping: A Political Wizard who put China on the Capitalist Road', *The New York Times*, 20 February 1997, www.nytimes.com.
5. John Ross, 'Deng Xiaoping—the world's greatest economist', Learning from China, www.learningfromchina.net. To the writer, 'by far the greatest economist of the 20th century was not Keynes, Hayek or Friedman but Deng Xiaoping'.
6. World Bank, Databank, World Development Indicators. https://databank.worldbank.org/data/source/world-development-indicators.
7. There are numerous excellent works on the subject of China's economic growth from the open door policy onwards. See, for example, Susan L. Shirk, *How China Opened Its Door: The Political Success of the PRC's Foreign Trade and Investment Reforms* (Washington, D.C.: Brookings Institution Press, 1994); and Linda Yueh, *China's Growth: The Making of an Economic Superpower* (Oxford: Oxford University Press, 2013).
8. For background of the SEZs, see Jung-Dong Park, The Special Economic Zones of China and Their Impact on Its Economic Development (Boulder, Colorado: Praeger, 1997), and Douglas Zhihua Zeng (ed.), *Building Engines for Growth and Competitiveness in China: Experience with Special Economic Zones and Industrial Clusters* (Washington, D.C.: World Bank Publications, 2010).

9. See Mary Ann O'Donnell, Winnie Wong, and Jonathan Bach (eds.), *Learning from Shenzhen: China's Post-Mao Experiment from Special Zone to Model City* (Chicago: University of Chicago Press, 2017).
10. Excerpt from a speech at the Communist Youth League Conference on 7 July 1962, China Daily.com.cn., 2014-08-20.
11. For a journalistic account of the episode, see Nicholas D. Kristof and Sheryl WuDunn, *China Wakes: The Struggle for the Soul of a Rising Power* (London: Nicholas Brealey Publishing, 1994), pp. 77–91.
12. Karl Marx and Frederick Engels' *Das Kapital* is voluminous, in three parts, and is not at all easy to understand. It is something of a paradox that communism has mass appeal and yet its philosophical foundation is too esoteric and impenetrable for the common masses to understand. Lenin was perhaps wise to identify the party as the vanguard of the proletariat and kept it rather elitist, as only discerning members could decipher the works of Marx and Engels.
13. For further discussion, see Jean-Philippe Beja (ed.) *The Impact of China's 1989 Tiananmen Massacre* (London: Routledge, 2010).
14. Zheng Wang, 'Tiananmen as the Turning Point: China's Impossible Balancing Act', *Insight and Analysis*, Wilson Center, 4 June 2014, www.wilsoncenter.org.
15. Ezra F. Vogel, *Deng Xiaoping and the Transformation of China* (Cambridge, Massachusetts: The Belknap Press of Harvard University Press, 2011), p. 634.
16. Harry Harding, 'The Impact of Tiananmen on China's Foreign Policy', *NBR Analysis*, Vol. 1, No. 3, December 1990, www.nbr.org.
17. Peter Nolan, *Transforming China: Globalization, Transition and Development* (London: Anthem Press, 2004), p. 1.
18. See Paul Dibb, *Soviet Union: The Incomplete Superpower* (London: Palgrave Macmillan, 1988).
19. 'Xi Jinping: China welcomes closer "Belt and Road" partnerships', 23 June 2021 https://news.cgtn.com.
20. The Silk Road goes beyond the basic idea of linking trading routes from the East to the West. It conjures up a romantic notion of fabled lands. One cannot escape the Western idea of the exotic East, with images of the famed *Ali Baba and the Forty Thieves* and the swashbuckling adventures of Sinbad.
21. Peter Frankopan, *The New Silk Roads: The Present and Future of the World* (London: Bloomsbury Publishing, 2018), p. 89.
22. 'Work Together to Build the Silk Road Economic Belt', part of the speech at Nazarbayev University, Astana, Kazakhstan, 7 September 2013, in Xi Jinping, *The Governance of China* (Beijing: Foreign Language Press, 2014), p. 315.

23. This has manifested in many ways, including in the rise of extremist politics, especially among white and anti-establishment elements. Numerous books have gained much currency, highlighting the ills of the current state of affairs in the Western world. This is clearly the case in the United Kingdom. See Robert Peston, *WTF* (London: Hodder & Stoughton, 2017), and Stig Abell, *How Britain Really Works: Understanding the Ideas and Institutions of a Nation* (London: John Murray, 2018).
24. Wang Yiwei, *The Belt and Road Initiative: What Will China Offer the World in Its Rise* (Beijing: New World Press, 2016), p. 1. This book was available in the Foreign Language Bookstore in Beijing and only officially sanctioned books are usually found there.
25. *The Spectator*, 29 January 2016.
26. In the United Kingdom, strangely, public schools are actually private and not state schools. The three top public schools are Eton, Harrow and Westminster, which collectively have produced numerous prime ministers and top civil servants. The idea of elitism is alive and kicking in the United Kingdom. For a fascinating look at this aspect of British society, see Andrew Neil's 2011 BBC TV documentary programme, *Posh and Posher: Class Politics in the UK*. It argues that despite enormous economic progress and social mobility, British society has become much more elitist. Oxford University has produced more than half of all British prime ministers. My Oxford college, Trinity, has the distinction of producing three British premiers.
27. https://www.forbes.com/sites/greatspeculations/2018/09/04.
28. Kerry Brown, *CEO, China: The Rise of Xi Jinping* (London: Tauris, 2016), p. 203.
29. Wang Yiwei, op. cit., p. 2.
30. Ibid., p. 3.
31. Peter Frankopan, op. cit., p. 62.
32. 'China's "Silk Road" project runs into debt jam', AFP, 2 September 2018.
33. Ibid.
34. 'China's "New Silk Road": A dead end for some nations?', https://www.japantimes.co.jp/news/2018/09/02.
35. Yanis Varoufakis, *Adults in the Room: My Battle with Europe's Deep Establishment* (London: The Bodley Head, 2017), p. 78. Quoted in David Runciman, *How Democracy Ends* (London: Profile Books, 2019), p. 33.
36. https://www.deccanherald.com/02/09/2018.
37. *South China Morning Post*, 2 November 2018. It must be pointed out that the fiscal crisis was not caused entirely by the loans and project agreements with the Chinese.
38. Reported in www.straitstimes.com, 21 August 2018.

39. Reported in www.theedgemarkets.com, 27 June 2019.
40. Reported in www.theedgemarkets.com, 15 July 2019.
41. Kerry Brown, *CEO, China*, op. cit., p. 202.
42. 'Xi Jinping: China welcomes closer "Belt and Road" partnerships', op. cit.
43. 'China's "Silk Road" project runs into debt jam', AFP, 2 September 2018.
44. Mo Jingxi, 'BRI no Marshall Plan or political strategy', *China Daily*, 25 August 2018.
45. 'Countries welcomed to join in mutual benefits of Belt, Road', chinadaily.com.cn.9/6/2018.
46. 'Countries welcome to join in mutual benefits of Belt, Road', ChinaDaily.com.cn.9/6/2018.
47. https://www.livemint.com/Politics/08/23/2018.
48. Barry Sautman and Yan Hairong, 'The truth about Sri Lanka's Hambantota port, Chinese "debt trap" and "asset seizure"', *South China Morning Post*, 6 May 2019.
49. The Fortune Global 500 list is made up of the biggest corporations in the world. For the first time ever, in 2019, there were more companies from China—129—than from any other country, with the Americans second with 121 companies listed. Walmart of the United States was top for the sixth consecutive year, while China's largest state-owned oil and gas company, Sinopec Group, secured second place. https://fortune.com.global500.
50. Although this treaty deals with a number of bilateral issues, it was also clearly designed to protect China from possible US intervention. The first article in the Treaty stipulates that in 'the event of one of the contracting parties being attacked by Japan or any state allied with it and thus being involved in a state of war, the other contracting party shall immediately render military and other assistance by all means at its disposal'. Quoted in Michael B. Yahuda, *China's Role in World Affairs* (London: Croom Helm, 1978), p. 52.
51. 'Xi Jinping: China welcomes closer "Belt and Road" partnerships', op. cit.
52. https://nationalinterest.org/blog/buzz/bad-news-china-building-three-huge-helicopter-aircraft-carriers-69472.
53. This was not the first ex-Soviet carrier that China had bought. Like most big naval powers, its dream is always to acquire a carrier, for such platforms symbolise all that is great in a nation. Its power projection capability is proven and tested. The Chinese Navy is no exception; to acquire such a capability have existed since the 1970s. It was only in the mid-1980s that concrete steps were taken to bring this about when it acquired the decommissioned Australian HMAS *Melbourne*. Prudently, over the

next decade, the Chinese slowly made further acquisitions of the ex-Soviet *Kiev*-class, the *Minsk* and *Kiev* in 1998 and 2000 respectively. These were all mainly for training purposes.

54. The last non-Western power that deployed any such capability was the Japanese Imperial Navy with its fleet of carriers and Zero fighters, from the 1930s and until 1945.
55. 'China's next aircraft-carrier will be its biggest', 1 July 2021, economist.com.
56. 'China's New Super Carrier: How it compares to the US Navy's Ford Class', 2 July 2021, www.navalnews.com.
57. The Elizabeth here refers to the Virgin Queen, Elizabeth I, rather than Elizabeth II. This is based on a tradition of naming HM ships for posthumous luminaries. Interestingly, another HMS *Prince of Wales* was the infamous RN battleship which was deployed supposedly to provide protection to Malaya but was sunk by the Japanese in December 1941 in the South China Sea. Its wreck still lies somewhere off Kuantan in this highly disputed territory, which some have forecast as the site of a potential naval confrontation involving the various protagonist navies.
58. Quoted in *Financial Times*, 11 August 2021, www.ft.com.
59. See M. Taylor Fravel, *Active Defense: China's Military Strategy since 1949* (Princeton, New Jersey: Princeton University Press, 2019); and David Shambaugh, *Modernizing China's Military: Progress, Problems, and Prospects* (Berkeley and Los Angeles: University of California Press, 2002).
60. 'China to conduct military drills in waters near Taiwan', www.reuters.com. 29 July 2019.
61. For an overview of Mahan, see Margaret Tuttle Sprout, 'Mahan: Evangelist of Sea Power', in Edward Mead Earle (ed.), *Makers of Modern Strategy: Military Thought from Machiavelli to Hitler* (Princeton, N.J.: Princeton University Press, 1971), pp. 415–445.
62. Geoffrey Till, *Maritime Strategy and the Nuclear Age* (London: Macmillan Press, 1984), p. 31.
63. Margaret Tuttle Sprout, 'Mahan: Evangelist of Sea Power', in Edward Mead Earle (ed.), *Makers of Modern Strategy: Military Thought from Machiavelli to Hitler* (Princeton: Princeton University Press, 1971), p. 429.
64. 'New submarine hints at China's search for stealth ahead of potential Taiwan war: analyst', *South China Morning Post*, 8 August 2021, ww.scmp.com.
65. For a comparison between the J-20 and F-22, see *South China Morning Post*, 28 July 2018, https://www.scmp.com.
66. Carl von Clausewitz *On War* (Princeton, New Jersey: Princeton University Press, 1989), p. 87.

67. Defence attachés are often regarded as legitimate and recognised spies. Their role, among other things, is to gather information (intelligence) on the military establishment of their host countries.
68. This was precisely the situation in Malaysia. The first official visit from the Malaysian military establishment to China took place in July 1992 and involved the Armed Forces Defence College, the highest level of military training in the country, with students of lieutenant colonel and full colonel level. The author, then a member of the civilian staff as head of strategic studies and international relations, was part of this one-week visit to China during which the PLA was the host. Apart from visiting their counterparts, the National Defence University, the delegation visited the Foreign Affairs Bureau of the Ministry of National Defence, Shanghai Naval Base, PLAN, and was hosted for dinner by the Deputy Chief of the General Staff, PLA.
69. *Taiwan News*, 2019/07/31. Taiwannews.com.tw.
70. *The National Interest*, 27 July 2019. https://nationalinterest.org.
71. Quoted in Richard Bush, 'The United States Security Partnership with Taiwan', Asian Alliances Working Paper Series, Paper 7, July 2016. https://www.brookings.edu.
72. The name given to a span of water mainly denotes its proximity to its hinterland rather than a right of ownership. For example, the Indian Ocean certainly does not belong to India.
73. Given the prominence of the potential conflict in this area, not surprisingly, there is a large and wide body of literature on this subject. Specifically for China's involvement in the South China Sea, see Humphrey Hawksley, *Asian Waters: The Struggle over the South China Sea and the Strategy of Chinese Expansion* (London: Duckworth Overlook, 2018).
74. Reported in *The New York Times*, 12 July 2016.
75. *South China Morning Post*, 12 July 2016.
76. *South China Morning Post*, 31 July 2019, www.scmp.com.
77. Ibid.
78. *NIDS China Security Report 2019: China's Strategy for Reshaping the Asian Order and Its Ramifications* (Tokyo: The National Institute for Defense Studies, 2019), p. 2.
79. Ibid., p. 2.
80. *People's Daily*, 27 June 2015, quoted in ibid., p. 19.
81. This was the case in Grenada where a group of American medical students studying on the island were rounded up by the authorities. Using the excuse of 'rescuing' the Americans, the United States launched a full-scale invasion of the island, which saw the assassination of the charismatic Prime Minister Maurice Bishop. The tiny island in the Caribbean had

been a thorn in the sides of the United States and Bishop was classified as a pro-Cuban socialist.
82. Not surprisingly, the Chinese film industry capitalised on this high profile incident and came out with a movie, *Operation Mekong*, in 2016, under the directorship of Dante Lam.
83. Jane Perlez and Bree Feng, 'Beijing Flaunts Cross-Border clout in Search for Drug Lord', the *New York Times*, 8 April 2013. cn.nytimes.com.
84. Reported in *International Business Times*, 5 March 2019, www.ibtimes.com.
85. Quoted in *Defense News*, 15 February 2019. www.defensenews.com.
86. 'How China is replacing America as Asia's military titan', 23 April 2019. www.reuters.com.
87. Cary Huang, 'China's military is stronger than ever, but is it strong enough?', *South China Morning Post*, 30 July 2017. https://www.scmp.com.
88. Li Gucheng (ed.), *A Glossary of Political Terms of the People's Republic of China* (Hong Kong: Chinese University Press, 1995), p. 325.
89. Ibid.
90. For background to the Lin Biao affair, see Frederick C. Teiwes, and Warren Sun, *The Tragedy of Lin Biao: Riding the Tiger During the Cultural Revolution, 1966–1971* (Honolulu, Hawaii: University of Hawaii Press, 1996).
91. Such a scenario was popularised by the novelist, Tom Clancy, in his book *Hunt for Red October*, which was subsequently made into a movie. This scenario seems to be a favourite amongst movie makers. A similar theme was the basis of a 2018 movie, *Hunter Killer*, directed by Donovan Marsh.
92. Kong Wenzheng, 'China's peacekeeping efforts lauded at UN', 12 February 2019. www.chinadaily.com.cn.
93. Ibid.
94. Shang Changyi, *Chinese Peacekeepers Overseas* (Beijing: China Intercontinental Press, 2015), p. 213.
95. Joseph S. Nye, Jr., *Soft Power: The Means to Success in World Politics* (New York: Public Affairs, 2004), p. 5.
96. There are many works written on this subject. See Kingsley Edney, et al., (eds.), *Soft Power with Chinese Characteristics: China's Campaign for Hearts and Minds* (Oxford: Routledge, 2019); Hongyi Lai and Yiyi Lu (eds.) *China's Soft Power and International Relations* (Oxford: Routledge, 2012); and Mingjiang Li (ed.), *Soft Power: China's Emerging Strategy in International Politics* (Lanham and Plymouth: Lexington Books, 2011.
97. H. Wang, 'Culture as national power: Soft Power', *Journal of Fudan University*, 3, 1993, pp. 91–96, quoted in Paul S.N. Lee, 'The rise of

China and its contest for discursive power', *Global Media and China*, Vol. 1, 1–2, June 2016, pp. 102–120, journals.sagepub.com.
98. 'China's soft power is on the rise', 2018-02-23, www.chinadaily.com.cn.
99. 'Hu urges enhancing "soft power" of Chinese culture', www.chinadaily.com.cn.
100. Reported in 'China's Big Bet on Soft Power', Council on Foreign Relations, February 9, 2018, www.cfr.org.
101. 'Xi Jinping calls for more "loveable" image for China in bit to make friends', 2 June, www.bbc.com.
102. 'Xi Focus: Xi stresses improving China's international communication capacity', 2021-06-01, Xinhuanet, www.xinhuanet.com.
103. Mingjing Li, 'Soft Power in Chinese Discourse: Popularity and Prospect', in Mingjiang Li (ed.), op cit. pp. 7–10.
104. Hongyi Lai, 'The soft power concept and a rising China', in Hongyi Lai and Yiyi Lu (eds.), op. cit., p. 2.
105. Statement upon signing order establishing the Peace Corps, 1 March 1961, John F Kennedy Presidential Library and Museum, www.jfklibrary.org.
106. Thomas Barker, 'The Real Source of China's Soft Power', *The Diplomat*, 18 November 2017, thediplomat.com).
107. There are many works of Foucault; see, for example, Michel Foucault, *The Foucault Reader*, edited by Paul Rabinow, (New York: Pantheon, 1984).
108. Tim Dunne, Milja Kurki and Steve Smith, *International Relations Theories: Discipline and Diversity* (Oxford: Oxford University Press, 2013), p. 235).
109. For an analysis of this, see Kejin Zhao, 'China's Rise and Its Discursive Power Strategy', *Chinese Political Science Review*, 19 April 2016, pp. 1–25.
110. Robert C. Thomas, 'Why China's Soft Power Solution Lies in its Past', *The Diplomat*, September 22, 2017, thediplomat.com.
111. 'Liu Xiaobo: China's most prominent dissident dies', *BBC News*, 13 July 2017, bbc.com.
112. Thomas Barker, 'The Real Source of China's Soft Power', *The Diplomat*, 18 November 2017, thediplomat.com; see also, Robert C. Thomas, 'Why China's Soft Power Solution Lies in Its Past', *The Diplomat*, 22 September 2017, thediplomat.com.
113. Ties Dams, Xiaoxue Martin and Vera Kranenburg (eds.), *China's Soft Power in Europe: Falling on Hard Times* (Amsterdam: The Netherlands Institute of International Relations, 'Clingendael', April 2021), p. 111.

CHAPTER 4

Evaluating the China Threat: Between Perceived and Real

In the recent trade war between the United States and China, there were those applauding President Trump's attempt to put a stop to what is often referred to as China's 'dominance of the market place'. This narrative even goes to suggest that China's economic expansion has to be stopped given the enormous trade imbalances that exist not only between Beijing and Washington but also between it and many other countries.

President Trump's trade war with the Chinese was aimed not only at correcting the trade deficit that has ballooned over recent years but also at ensuring that China's rise is checked so that the United States maintains its supremacy and dominance. Even his successor, President Biden, who many believed would bring an improvement to the tense relationship between China and the United States during Trump's administration, seemed tempted to play the 'China card'. Referring to the ambivalence of the Biden administration, the president of the US–China Business Council, Craig Allen, stated that, 'Before he came into office, many of us, myself included, expected a calming of the waters and reduction of bilateral tension. Rather, what we've seen is very little change in policy, particularly trade policy, and indeed we've seen a heightening of tensions, and for businesses, increased uncertainty. Biden has changed Trump's policies in so many areas. But why not US-China relations and trade policy?'[1]

The above narrative reflects the current suspicion over China. One of the most intense debates taking place today, in many circles, intellectual or otherwise, is whether China poses a threat or not. Sentiments identifying China as a threat are primarily based on speculation and conjecture, rather than on any track record. They are also based on the need to maintain the status quo of American dominance, albeit in a qualified state, given the United States' decline relative to previous decades.

To some extent, the kind of arguments we hear today regarding the China threat creates a sense of déjà vu. Similar arguments were heard in the 1980s and 1990s in reference to the Japanese and books such as *The Coming War with Japan*[2] symbolised the often emotional and speculative view of what was to come. Similarly titled books[3] echo such fear, only this time it involves China.

This debate is essentially based on perception, whether real or imagined. An important additional ingredient is who is making the arguments. The 'who' may be relatively easy, but it may well prove more challenging to unravel the motive. This chapter will try to make sense of the debate by looking at China's track record and some possible future scenarios.

There have been countless claims that China is a potential threat. While some might argue that concepts such as balance of power[4] are becoming irrelevant in a more globalised world, it would appear that this concept is very much alive and kicking. The apparent rapprochement between the Chinese and Russians[5] could well be seen as an attempt to provide some form of balance against the United States. The good personal ties between Presidents Putin and Xi symbolise this emerging friendship.

In order to examine the so-called China threat, China's record of resorting to the use of force must be considered. After all, we need some basis from which to question whether Beijing poses a danger to the world or not.

A Historical Overview of the Use of China's Military Power

Despite its perceived aggressive stance, China has been rather restrained in the use of force. Its intervention outside its borders has tended to relate either to territorial disputes or to defending what it believes to be its interests. This cautious use of force, limited primarily to border areas, is similar to that of its imperial predecessors. It has employed force around its borders with Korea, India, Russia and Vietnam and in Tibet, and has lent a helping hand to emerging independent movements in the name of international communist solidarity.

Annexation of Tibet

Notwithstanding the debate over China's rightful claim to Tibet as part of its territory, the annexation[6] of Tibet is the first instance of the Chinese employing force to achieve a political objective. When China annexed Tibet, many countries recognised Tibet as an integral part of China predating the establishment of the People's Republic. In fact, imperial China had experienced problematic ties with Tibet as early as the Tang dynasty,[7] when Tibet was regarded as a tributary state and was required to pay some degree of homage to Chinese emperors. For instance, in 1653 the fifth Dalai Lama had an audience with the Qing emperor Shunzhi—a visit to Beijing that could have been interpreted as the Chinese emperor summoning another political leader to his court and as unmistakable evidence of the nominal submission of the Dalai Lama and Tibet's subservience to China.[8] This territorial issue was inherited by the nationalist government of the Republic and the territorial claim over Tibet has been the consistent position of the Chinese.

Like Afghanistan, Tibet was part of the power play of the great powers. The British invaded Tibet in 1904 when it controlled India to secure its boundaries. The Chinese annexation of Tibet could also be seen within a wider context of great power politics. It was, perhaps, no surprise that New Delhi provided sanctuary to the 14th Dalai Lama when he fled his homeland in 1959.

Although military power was used to enforce China's control within a year of the opening of hostilities, the level of force employed in China's annexation of Tibet was minimal—mainly due to the limited resistance shown by the Tibetans. In addition to their strong Buddhist tradition of non-violence, the force available to defend Tibet was rudimentary, especially against a well-prepared and highly motivated neighbour. As far as the communists were concerned, they were unifying this territory with the motherland to bring progress to what they regarded as a backward area.

Chinese hostilities came after a few attempts were made to 'unite' Tibet with China without resorting to the use of force, although contingency plans to invade must have been formulated much earlier, in the event that diplomacy failed. Knowledge of the actual military operations remains patchy even today, mainly due to the polarised nature of sources, which reflects the conflict. Nonetheless, Chinese military operations were limited and confined to the battle of Qamdo, which started on 6 October 1950 with the objective of wresting control from the independent Tibetan government[9] and forcing the Tibetans to submit to Beijing. After their defeat at Qamdo, the Tibetan leadership began negotiations, which led to the eventual incorporation of Tibet into China. The 14th Dalai Lama fled to India and established a government in exile. The Indians feted the Dalai Lama, who was greeted by Indian Premier Nehru. Not surprisingly, this has remained a thorn in Sino–Indian bilateral ties.

China's annexation of Tibet must be seen in the context of the former's attempt to take advantage of its newly established People's Republic to enforce its control over what the country had consistently claimed was part of its territory. It was consistent with declarations on Tibet by the nationalist government in 1949, and they seized their opportunity within a year of the triumphant march into Beijing and the formation of the PRC. It is always difficult to make any judgement about a state's attempt to enforce its sovereignty over what it considers part of its territory. Tibet was not a far-flung territory, unlike the Falklands Islands for Great Britain. When Argentinian troops landed on those islands, which they call the Malvinas, in 1982, British Prime Minister Margaret Thatcher decided to make a stand and to use force to take the islands back, even though the distance from Britain made the campaign difficult. Thatcher's decision was received with enthusiasm and a level of patriotism not seen since England's 1966 World Cup win.

While not necessarily taking sides or being sympathetic to Beijing, the issue of China's annexation of Tibet must be seen in the context of the latter's attempt to reinforce control over its own territorial boundaries. Such an argument, obviously, might be snared in the over-used justification for states to seize territories that they believe, mainly in historical terms, belong to them. However, calling for UN backing in an attempt to justify the use of force, or resorting to the sacrosanct principle of the right to self-defence, is often used by states to justify their actions. In the case of the Falklands, London felt it was essential to get the overwhelming support of the UN Security Council for its actions to reclaim the Falklands from the Argentinians. Whether the Chinese should also have gone to the UN to seek its approval for their actions is highly debatable. Given the hostility of the UN towards communist states at the time of the annexation, it seems highly probable that the Chinese would not have received any support for their subsequent actions.

Crossing the Yalu River

One of the first major uses of military power by the Chinese occurred only a year after the founding of the People's Republic of China (PRC). On 19 October 1950, a Chinese People's Volunteers (CPV) force crossed the Yalu River, which separates China from North Korea, hence entering the Korean War. Earlier suggestions by the US Commander General MacArthur that his force might cross into China, and even warnings of a nuclear strike, may have prompted Beijing to deploy its troops pre-emptively. However, its desire to assist its North Korean communist ally under Kim Il Sung was a *casus belli* for the Chinese. Their decision to intervene in the conflict marked the culmination of a protracted decision-making process, as Beijing was caught by surprise when the Korean People's Army launched a dramatic strike on its southern neighbour.[10] There appeared to be a lack of consensus over the decision to intervene, with opposition coming from within the ruling elite in Beijing. For instance, Peng Dehuai,[11] one of China's top military leaders, was initially opposed to intervention, arguing that the conflict was a Soviet–US one and that while China should be concerned, it should not commit forces. However, he later fell in line as Mao Zedong was strongly supportive of intervention; Mao then made Dehuai the commander of China's forces in Korea. Another military figure who opposed this venture was Lin Biao, who was a veteran of the civil war against Chiang Kai-shek's nationalist forces. He believed that intervention could hurt China and feared the United States' use of nuclear weapons and its superior military power. According to one account, Lin declared, 'The United States is highly modernised. Furthermore, it possesses the atomic bomb. There is no guarantee of achieving victory against the United States. The central leaders should consider this issue with great care.'[12] Despite turning down Mao's request to command the CPV, supposedly due to ill health, Lin rose to become minister of defence in 1959 and was even named as Mao's official successor during the Ninth National Party Congress in 1969. However, his bizarre entanglement in a plot to kill Mao halted his career and he was killed in an accident while trying to flee China.[13]

Chinese intervention in the Korean War, which saved the North Koreans, has been well documented.[14] Suffice to say, this first overseas deployment was remembered, among other things, for its use of 'human wave' tactics—the deployment of huge numbers in frontal assaults to overcome a superior force. Hundreds of thousands of Chinese infantrymen overwhelmed US forces, pushing most of them south. Only the Pusan perimeter was retained. It was from here that MacArthur achieved his bold and successful landing at Incheon and thereafter managed to push the communist forces back to the 38th parallel, where it had all started. The war then got bogged down and it was another two years before an armistice was signed between the two sides and a demilitarised zone established. This border area remains one of the most militarised regions in the world.

In all conflicts, warring states try to learn lessons from their experience. To the Chinese, their costly intervention[15] revealed many inadequacies in their military forces. In 1950, a year after its final victory in the civil war, the Chinese military force was still essentially a people's army. It had grown from a guerrilla into a more conventional force but was still very basic in terms of its organisational structure, doctrine, equipment and training. For instance, its air power was rudimentary at the outbreak of the Korean conflict. However, with sheer determination on the part of Chinese leadership it managed to deploy its quickly augmented force to the battlefield, thanks to arms transfers from the Soviet Union following visits there by both Premier Zhou Enlai and General Lin Biao to appeal for assistance. Although initially reluctant to deploy their limited air force in the early stages, the Chinese eventually sought to establish air superiority over north-western Korea and to extend their air operations to the Pyongyang–Wonsan line.[16]

It is clear that the Chinese intervention in Korea had no overt ambition of gaining control and expanding influence. If anything, it was a matter of honour and solidarity with its communist brother-in-arms. It is also clear that Beijing played no role in the initial decision by Kim Il Sung to invade South Korea, which demonstrates the North's independent policy and the limited, or non-existent, role of China in that country's decision-making. This remains true today and Kim's grandson now sits at the top of the North Korean political hierarchy despite assumptions that Beijing has a degree of influence on Pyongyang.

Fighting the Indians

The October 1962 Sino–Indian border war was a culmination of centuries of disputes between China and India. The clash of these two giant neighbours was perhaps inevitable, given the comparative legacies they both have—two great civilisations, two strong religious personalities (Confucius and Buddha), religions (Taoism and Hinduism), the two most populous places in the world and iconic political leaders (Mao, and Gandhi and Nehru).[17] The list of comparisons goes on and on. Paradoxically, the common ground they share has become a factor in the rivalry that has accumulated over the centuries,[18] and a long common border has led inevitably to disputes, namely over the Himalayan region and Tibet, dating back several centuries.[19]

Prior to the Chinese annexation of Tibet, there had been minor clashes between China and India, for instance, in August 1959 at Longju on the Chinese side of the McMahon Line, the eponymous area drawn by the British in February 1914 as a way 'to limit Chinese authority in Tibet and to commit the Chinese to accept the Himalayan crest—India's vital rampant of defence—rather than the Himalayan southern base as the northeast boundary between India and Tibet'.[20]

In 1962 there were accusations from both sides about violations of their respective territories. For instance, in April 1962 the Chinese Foreign Ministry sent a diplomatic note to its counterpart stating that they had 'discovered that Indian troops have intruded into China's Sinkiang Uighur Autonomous Region and established two new military posts'.[21] As in all such disputes, there were different versions of what took place and both sides accused the other of territorial violations. After several months of rising tension over the border issue, the Chinese decided to launch an attack on 20 October along the Namkha Chu River and in the Khinzemane area.

According to one report, some 20,000 Chinese troops took part in what was described as 'a full scale and obviously well-planned attack, launched skilfully across the world's highest mountain range'.[22] In the official Chinese version, this attack was a strike in self-defence and followed a massive general offensive by Indian forces in both the eastern and western sectors of their common border.[23] However, according to one Indian official position, India was the victim of unabashed aggression.[24] The first phase of hostilities saw a victory for the Chinese People's Liberation Army (PLA), due to their large numbers and superior firepower. The second offensive, launched on 14 November by Beijing, confirmed Chinese superiority. Defeat at the hands of the Chinese shocked the Indians and brought home to them the inadequacies of their own military forces, which led to significant changes in their structure and strategic thinking. This shock was to be experienced by the Chinese themselves 17 years later, when they suffered heavy losses at the hands of the Vietnamese in February 1979.

How does one understand China's move against India? There appears to be a consensus that China's decision to launch a pre-emptive attack on India was both a defensive measure and a deterrent against future military action by the Indians. According to one assessment of the war, 'China behaved more like a reluctant older fighter who in the end relished the chance to throw a knock-out punch.'[25]

China's full-scale invasion of Indian-held territory must be seen as a forward defence approach by Beijing. China felt threatened by India and decided to launch a pre-emptive attack to tilt the balance in its favour. As it transpired, its superiority in both numbers and equipment meant it could then pursue wider and less defensive objectives.[26] It took that initiative to demonstrate to the Indians China's determination to defend its territories and to show that it would resort to the use of force for this purpose—all as a deterrent against future possible Indian incursions or challenges to China's territorial positions in the disputed area.

The war was a victory for the Chinese and its deterrent value was enhanced as a result; there have been no subsequent substantial military clashes between the two since then, although the territorial dispute has not been resolved and the occurrences of small-scale skirmishes, such as the one that took place in May 2020. Ties between the two countries have generally improved, with both sides even engaged in joint military exercises, for example, in 2008 in Belgaum. In 2003 Beijing and New Delhi established the Special Representatives' Meeting as a mechanism to manage their border dispute.[27] Nonetheless, ties between these countries continue to experience ups and downs.

One political lesson the Chinese learnt from their war with India was the support of the Western powers for their opponent, in particular the British—mainly due to historic ties—and also the Americans, for ideological as well as strategic reasons, despite the fact that New Delhi was moving closer to Moscow at that time. Indeed, due primarily to the growing dispute between China and India, the Soviets were cautious in providing military assistance to India despite earlier promises that they would transfer MiG-21 fighters to them. Both Britain and the United States did supply military equipment to India.

In summary, the conclusion drawn by a comprehensive study undertaken on the Chinese use of force against India in October 1962 is most apt and perceptive. Among the points made was that 'the use of force is not a paramount characteristic of Chinese foreign policy as manifested in the behaviour of the People's Republic over the past quarter of a century' and that 'China's past border settlements indicate a willingness to compromise rather than exert the full strength of its powerful bargaining position'.[28] This rather sanguine conclusion may not necessarily predict China's future behaviour, as this study, published in 1975, predates the re-emergence of China as a pre-eminent power in the twenty-first century.

Clashes with the Soviets

The cracks between the Soviets and the Chinese began to surface even before 1949. The rivalry between these two giant neighbours certainly predated the rise of communism in China. As in the case of Sino–Indian ties, relations between China and Russia have involved territorial disputes spanning centuries.[29] The Russians and Chinese had clashed, some half a century before, on the battlefield during the Russo–Chinese war of 1900—at a time of foreign interventions in the Middle Kingdom.[30] The fighting mainly occurred in Manchuria and over Amur, which was also the site of a Soviet–Chinese skirmish 60 years later.

The origins of the Sino–Soviet dispute can be traced back to before the establishment of the PRC. When communist ideology first took root in China the pioneers looked to the Bolsheviks and subsequently the Soviets as their source of inspiration and support. This early ideological position did not resonate entirely with all followers, including a young Mao Zedong. In simple terms, it boiled down to the idea of adhering strictly to the Marxist notion of dialectic materialism and revolution, which the Soviets pursued. Ideological orthodoxy was the crux of the matter. Without dwelling too much on ideological polemics, the heart of the ideological dispute revolved around whether it was the proletariat, as envisaged by Marx and Engels, or the peasants, who should form the dominant group in China and which should lead the revolution. The lack of a strong industrial working class reflected the essentially agrarian nature of Chinese society at the time, but despite China's economic backwardness, the Soviets insisted that it should stick to the Marxist stages of development by first pursuing a bourgeoise revolution and then a proletarian one—following in the footsteps of Russia in 1917 with the February and October revolutions.

The Soviet tendency to want to control the Chinese communists, not only in ideological terms but also in their strategy, became unpalatable to some. Not surprisingly, the Soviets were supportive of Sun Yat-sen's revolution as it fell within its 'interests' in promoting world revolution, although their support went beyond rhetoric. Moscow's somewhat erratic behaviour towards the nationalists and the communists in China, mainly driven by their own interests, remained a strong sticking point even after the latter's triumph. For instance, the formation of the tripartite cooperation in 1920 between the Soviets, nationalists and the communists proved to be problematic and created a complicated web of ties. The idea behind such complex cooperation was 'the result of complex historical factors or forces, as well as decisions made by individuals. In 1920 Soviet Russia was still in chaos, there was no Communist Party of China and the Kuomintang struggled to survive as an influential political movement.'[31] It would appear that the Soviets, especially after the conclusion of their own civil war against the White Army, wanted to keep their options open, as the situation in China itself was fluid and without clear victors. With Comintern (Communist International) representative Borodin's arrival in China in 1923, the Soviets began a relationship with the nationalists that 'proved disastrous to the CCP (Communist Party of China)'[32] and sowed seeds of suspicion towards Moscow. The organisational structure of the communists was fully exposed to the nationalists, and when the so-called united front failed, Kuomintang's Chiang Kai-shek annihilated CCP's organisations in the coastal cities.[33] The memory of Soviet 'betrayal' remained strong among Chinese communists.

After October 1949, Sino–Soviet ties evolved over a number of brief periods—from honeymoon to a cooling of relations to open hostility. When Mao Zedong triumphantly marched into Beijing in October 1949, Moscow welcomed the communist victory. A brief period of cooperation ensued, marked by the signing of the Treaty of Friendship, Alliance and Mutual Assistance on 14 February 1950.[34] However, cracks soon began to appear as Stalin and Mao did not have the chemistry needed to forge a close personal relationship. Neither leader was an easy character and both were feared at home. Both Stalin and Mao have since gone down in history as two of the most repressive leaders ever and responsible for the deaths of millions of their own people.

The Sino–Soviet schism became clear after the death of Stalin when his successor pursued a policy of de-Stalinisation. Nikita Khrushchev, in what became known as the 'secret speech',[35] denounced Stalin to puncture the personality cult that had built up around his predecessor and to enable him to shine instead.

The rivalry between the two communist giants peaked when their armed forces clashed during a period of heightened tension in 1969, over their common border. It started in March in the area of Zhenbao Island (Damansky Island to the Russians) on the Wusuli (Ussuri) River close to Manchuria. Suspicions over each other's intentions spiralled into an increased deployment of military forces to the border area, coupled with belligerent rhetoric emanating from both Beijing and Moscow. Fear that Chinese troops (which by 1969 had reached 1.5 million strong in the area) would cross the border, as they had in the Korean Peninsula and in India, must have been prevalent in the minds of the Soviet leadership. On 2 March a skirmish broke out when Chinese troops attacked Soviet border guards resulting in casualties on both sides. It would appear that, as in the case of the Chinese taking the initiative over their border dispute with India, Beijing decided to initiate the assault against the USSR, probably for the same reasons. Tensions remained high although talks began. The dispute was finally resolved in October 2003, with both sides signing an agreement that divided sovereignty to the satisfaction of both parties.

Chinese Involvements in Wars of National Liberation

As a communist state and as part of its ideological obligation and commitment, China supported various organisations in the fight against colonial powers. This anti-colonialist struggle had been enshrined in proclamations made during the setting up of the Communist International in 1919, and with the proclamation of the PRC in October 1949 Beijing joined the struggle internationally. This aspiration was further reinforced by China's participation in the Afro–Asian conference in Bandung in April 1955. In his conference speech, Chinese Premier Zhou Enlai, while condemning subversive activities, stated that China was prepared to 'establish normal relations with all the Asian and African countries, with all the countries of the world, and first of all, with our neighbouring countries'.[36] The real issue facing China at this time was two-fold. Firstly, the decolonisation process taking place in Asia and Africa provided opportunities for Beijing to play a role and to increase its influence in those regions. At the time of the Bandung Conference, many countries were yet to break the shackles of colonialism and there were many liberation movements seeking outside help.

Secondly, with Sino–Soviet rivalry clouds gathering, there was an element of competition between the Chinese and the Soviets to encourage these movements to adopt their brand of the armed struggle. It was an ideological battle, with the Chinese trying to bring about the growth of Maoism. Indeed, this ideological split led to the fracture of communist movements in many parts of the world and the division deteriorated to such a level that a special gathering was held in Moscow in November 1960 attended by 81 communist parties. The aim was to reconcile the differences that were threatening the solidarity of this large and diverse movement. According to an editorial published in the CCP's theoretical political journal *Red Flag*, which appeared a month after the Moscow meeting, the gathering would 'prove to be one of the most hard-fought and memorable meetings that the movement has ever had.... The meetings demonstrated that communism was beyond the point where the Russian comrade could give orders which the international comrades would automatically and unquestioningly obey.'[37] This ideological divide was to sever the whole edifice of monolithic communism.

As already mentioned, the ideological debate started much earlier, in the 1920s, notably after the establishment of the Communist International under the auspices of Moscow, which wanted to impose its own brand of communist struggle. Moscow was trying to 'control' the Chinese communists and dictate the various stages of their struggle.[38]

Unlike the Soviet Union, however, China's involvement in lending support to independence movements globally was limited—not by its lesser adherence to communist ideals but due to its lack of resources and the struggle internally within China, which diverted attention away from its external fraternal obligations. Nonetheless, given its limited resources the Chinese tended to lend their support to movements that were geographically closer, in particular those in Southeast Asia, where they were in competition with the Soviets who were also eyeing up the chance to increase their influence in the region. Despite Premier Zhou's statement in Bandung condemning subversive activities, China was supporting various independence movements in Asia and Africa.

In Asia, for instance, China's support for revolutionary movements in Southeast Asia can be divided into a number of categories and took a number of forms. The first category applies to the whole Indochinese region consisting of Vietnam, Laos and Cambodia, which saw greater direct participation by the Chinese. China's involvement during the Vietnam wars has been documented elsewhere.[39] Beijing directly supported the Khmer Rouge in its successful quest for power in Cambodia in 1975 and helped sustain its stranglehold on the population, although Beijing was not responsible nor supportive of the regime's genocidal policy of creating a 'new' society from ground zero. As we will see, Beijing was extremely upset when Vietnam-backed Heng Samrin forces ousted the Khmer Rouge from power in December 1978, so much so that a few months later China retaliated with a limited invasion of northern Vietnam.

In a second category were countries in which communist movements were led by ethnic Chinese, such as in Malaya and Thailand, where Beijing played an indirect role in supporting them. This support included propaganda materials and sanctuary for the exiled leaders of local communist parties, such as the chairman and general secretary of the Malayan Communist Party who lived in Beijing for several decades after leaving Malaya following the failed insurrection that began in 1948—a period known as the Emergency (1948–1960). This led the British to deploy military forces alongside the Malayan military and successfully contain the rise of communism in that territory.

In the third category was Indonesia. China had ties to the Communist Party of Indonesia, and at a critical stage, Beijing was believed to have backed a coup plot by the communists to seize power from a weakened President Sukarno.[40] The coup failed because the Indonesian military struck pre-emptively by arresting and subsequently executing hundreds of thousands of plotters and their associates, and anyone remotely connected with the communist movement. Their action was believed to be assisted by the CIA which wanted to prevent the establishment of a communist Indonesia.

The extent to which China was directly involved in the coup attempt is a matter of conjecture. The plot was highly complex, as there were several players including a faction within the Indonesian military made up of several generals. However, one study of China's role categorically concluded that China 'had no direct responsibility for the events of September 30, 1965', although Mao certainly had encouraged the Indonesian communists to undertake an armed struggle, which was consistent with his thinking, and supplied them with weapons.[41]

The other region in which China was actively supporting national liberation movements was Africa, and here its interests were very much influenced by Zhou's wish for China to play a larger role in the developing world. He probably saw these areas as virgin territory that could provide considerable opportunities for China, especially if the movements it backed proved to be successful in transitioning into independent political entities. This was also part of China's attempt to woo such states to their side rather than to the Russians.

The Bandung Conference signalled the beginning of links between China and Africa although of the 29 countries invited only 6 were from Africa—Egypt, Ethiopia, the Gold Coast (Ghana), Liberia, Libya and Sudan.[42] In the post-Bandung years, China became active in extending invitations to African leaders to visit China and in reciprocating with significant trips made by Chinese leaders, including Zhou Enlai, who visited the continent several times. One of the countries China successfully developed ties with was Tanzania and in particular with its leader Julius Nyerere.

Despite China's involvement in these movements, it was not entirely successful in influencing the newly independent states, especially against the Soviets. For instance, towards the end of the 1960s, some of those governing newly independent states who were friendly to China refused to commit themselves to China's world view and in particular to echo Beijing's criticism of the Soviet leadership.[43]

It must be pointed out that China's failures were the result of several factors and not all the groups that the Chinese supported were successful in gaining power. In addition, those regimes that did win power were not always able to hold on to it: some were overthrown in coups, which tended to be the norm rather than the exception. In Ghana, for instance, when the Beijing-backed nationalist Kwame Nkrumah was overthrown in February 1966, China's loss was substantial. Nkrumah's China connection drew the wrath of the new regime in Ghana because it suspected that China subsequently tried to help the former leader regain power. The regime accused Beijing of sending a 'shipment of substantial quantities of arms and other war materials to the Republic of Guinea with a view to assisting Kwame Nkrumah to return to Ghana to stage a counter-revolution'.[44] The Chinese denied this, and it seems likely that the story was either fabricated or a mere rumour. Unlike in Southeast Asia, China faced a dilemma in its policy towards Africa because the various movements and regimes were varied and factious in nature, which provided fertile ground for many parties to interfere including the Soviet Union and the United States. The rivalries continued after the independence of many African countries, and in the case of the Democratic Republic of Congo, its Prime Minister Patrice Lumumba was overthrown and executed by pro-Western forces. China had tried to woo Congolese politicians, but the Soviet Union and Belgium, backed by the United States, were doing so too.

Thus, China's involvement in national liberation movements produced mixed results. Its intervention must be seen within the context of its ideological rivalry with the Soviet Union; it wanted to spread Maoism and be seen as a leader of Marxism–Leninism. Although the Chinese did provide aid to various groups and regimes in the form of propaganda materials, limited arms transfer and fraternal support and solidarity, their success was mixed and there were no lasting results.

Losing to the Vietnamese

China's limited invasion of North Vietnam in February 1979 was one of the first instances in which Beijing had deployed its forces unprovoked; previous military interventions had been the result of either pre-emptive measures or border skirmishes. A few weeks before hostilities broke out, during his visit to Washington in late January 1979, Deng Xiaoping referred to Vietnam's invasion of Cambodia a month earlier and warned that 'if you don't teach them some necessary lessons, it just won't do'.[45] It is interesting that Deng chose his US visit to make such an ominous statement, and it is possible that, given America's own bitter experience in Vietnam, he may have assumed that his remark would not necessarily go down negatively.

Despite the seemingly unprovoked nature of China's military action, it could be argued that its limited invasion of northern Vietnam was intended to help its former ally, the Khmer Rouge, though if so, this action was too little too late. However, the move was neither a full-scale invasion nor a border skirmish. It is unlikely that Beijing wanted to occupy parts of Vietnam, for the preparations for this incursion were limited. In addition, such an operation would have been imprudent and could have bogged down the Chinese in a hostile environment.

The planning was also flawed and Chinese forces were ill-prepared. When military plans are ambiguous—something which is anathema to military planners—the result is often dismal; military objectives must be clearly defined. The overall objective was more political and remained open-ended—it was to teach the Vietnamese a lesson.

The limited operation launched in February 1979 by the PLA was the first since it had clashed with the Soviets almost a decade before. The Chinese military had not undergone any major reform or modernisation for decades, but the Vietnamese were battle-hardened, having fought and defeated first the French and then the Americans and then having invaded neighbouring Cambodia. The Vietnamese also had the Soviet Union as their patron and benefitted from significant arms transfers. At the time of the invasion, while the People's Liberation Army—Air Force (PLAAF) could only muster their ageing MiG-17s and MiG-19s, the Vietnamese had the latest Mig-23s and even MiG-25s. Furthermore, defending one's homeland from invaders lends added patriotic and moral appeal.

Given the asymmetrical nature of the two opposing military powers, the outcome seemed predictable. It was not the Vietnamese who were taught a lesson; instead, the Chinese had to swallow their pride and learn. The whole military operation lasted less than one month, from 17 February, when infantry troops crossed the border in five major spearheads, until 16 March, when all Chinese forces were pulled out.

There were conflicting claims about the number of Chinese troops involved in the operations. According to official reports from Beijing, the attacking force comprised about 100,000 troops with additional units of 120,000 men kept in reserve.[46] However, another source states that 20 main force divisions were used, totalling 300,000 men, with 700–1000 aircraft, 1000 tanks and 1500 pieces of heavy artillery also deployed, although the majority were held in reserve.[47] The rate of casualties was also disputed, with the Vietnamese claiming that 42,000 Chinese soldiers were either killed or wounded, while Beijing declared the figure to be half that number.[48]

There was, however, consensus on the impact of this limited conflict on the Chinese: it was a disaster. But it proved to be a watershed because it showed the political and military leadership the urgent need for the PLA to undergo serious reform; it provided a much-needed impetus for Beijing to undertake a serious military modernisation programme, which is still ongoing.

Keeping Taiwan Under Control

Ever since the Kuomintang lost the civil war and its leadership and the remnants of its military force fled to the island of Taiwan and established the Republic of China, Beijing has remained committed to the reunification of the two unequal territories. In addition to the overarching principle of territorial integrity and of unifying China—an idea that stretches back to the first Chinese emperor—the continued existence of Taiwan, seen as a renegade entity in the eyes of the People's Republic, has been a thorn in the side and an issue which must be resolved at some point. China's continued perceived aggression towards Taiwan must therefore be considered within this context. From the perspective of the Taiwanese, of course, the China threat is a real one. It presents a clear and present danger to their existence. In this respect, Taiwan will do whatever is possible to ensure its territorial integrity is secured—based on both self-reliance and dependence on the United States.[49] Washington must walk a tightrope in order to balance its 'commitments' towards Taiwan on the one hand and, perhaps more critically, its ties with Beijing on the other.

While not wishing to dismiss the China threat towards Taiwan, it is primarily bilateral in nature and the former's ambition remains unification. The challenge is whether Beijing will resort to the use of force or rely on diplomacy and peaceful negotiations. The Chinese have exercised their military options by periodically conducting military exercises and manoeuvres to intimidate Taiwan. In one episode, as a reaction to Washington's invitation to Taiwan's President Lee Teng-hui in the spring of 1995, China launched a total of six M-9 ballistic missiles into the ocean about 100 nautical miles north of Taipei, followed by air and naval exercises including the test-firing of cruise missiles.[50] While such a show of force was a clear demonstration of China's resolve to claim back Taiwan, and to indicate its zero tolerance of any provocation political or otherwise, it was also aimed at the domestic audience, especially within the political establishment. It reinforced the power and willingness of the leadership to stand up to the United States, in particular over Taiwan. Not to do so would have been seen as weak at home.

Other Interventions

The Chinese have also played lesser military roles in other parts of the world. This has taken various forms such as arms transfers to warring factions and sending advisors and, as seen in the previous chapter, participating in the United Nations-led peacekeeping operations, including disaster relief deployments involving military personnel.

Making Sense of the China Threat Narrative

The above overview of instances in which China has resorted to the use of force illustrates that China has been extremely cautious in its military deployments. It has been more than 40 years ago since we have witnessed the deployment of Chinese troops in a hostile manner—the invasion of northern Vietnam in 1979. Since then China has concentrated on its economic well-being and has preferred to focus on establishing trade and commercial links and being seen as a responsible member of the international community, for example, as a permanent member of the UN Security Council. However, these economic ambitions do not prevent China from paying attention to other areas, including the military. As we saw in the previous chapter, China has also been modernising its military by concentrating on technology—its quality rather than quantity.

It is clear that Beijing will not acquiesce to any move that threatens its territorial integrity, including in the disputed South China Sea. If push comes to shove, Beijing will use force, if necessary, over this and other disputed areas. No Chinese leader will want to be remembered as the one who conceded territory. Like their imperial predecessors, Chinese communist leaders are obsessed with the unity of the motherland—something which is sacrosanct to political leaders of any sovereign state.

China's use of force must also be viewed in its historical context. At the time of Mao's triumph in October 1949 and China's first use of force across its borders a year later, most of Asia was directly or indirectly controlled by the West. As such, Chinese intervention was regarded as a threat and as evidence of communist expansionism. It was, after all, at the height of the Cold War and communism was seen as a monolithic ideology geared towards destroying the Western world. The so-called domino theory, espoused by President Truman, was most prevalent in the minds of the Americans. The arrival of communist China on the world stage fed into the frenzy that was already raging. McCarthyism in the United States is a good example particularly with its portrayal of 'the red menace' being in every corner of the country. Such hysteria hit a high point in the United States when the Rosenbergs were found guilty of espionage.[51]

During this post-war period, Japan was still under the tutelage of the Americans, redefining its political institutions and working out its security relations. The Treaty of San Francisco of September 1951 signalled the end of the allied occupation of Japan, establishing its independence but remaining under the American security umbrella.[52] The Korean Peninsula remains a major strategic consideration for Tokyo. The Korean War had a direct impact on Japan as it posed a threat to Japan's security and because its territory was used as a staging post for US forces.

Over and above this, there exists a historic animosity between Japan and China, which has remained a constant factor in their relationship, causing a mutual perception of threat. Atrocities committed by the Japanese military in China during its brutal war in the 1930s cut deep into the Chinese psyche.

With the exception of Thailand, which was never colonised, most of Southeast Asia was under Western control during this period. The process of decolonisation was slowly taking shape. For instance, the Indonesian independence movement against Dutch rule started in 1908, but it was only after the end of World War II, which delivered a devastating blow to the colonial powers, that freedom movements began to take shape—with differing outcomes.

In Indonesia, some independence groups took advantage of the crippling effects of the war on the Dutch and declared unilateral declaration of independence (UDI) in August 1945. They were the first in the region to do so. However, an armed struggle ensued, with much internal fighting and disagreement among the contending parties, and after a military stalemate between the various warring parties, including the Dutch, peace was restored.

The Philippines, though not formally colonised by the Americans, was under considerable American influence after World War II. The close attachment between the Filipinos and the Americans was epitomised by the famous 'I shall return' speech made by General MacArthur when he was forced to withdraw from the Philippines when faced with impending defeat at the hands of the imperial Japanese army in March 1942. As part of the US military alliance system, Manila was anti-communist and viewed the Chinese intervention in the Korean conflict as a threat and a demonstration of communist expansionism.

At the time of the outbreak of the Korean War, the French Indochinese states and Malaya were still under colonial control. It was not until 1954, at the famous battle of Dien Bien Phu, that the French were ousted from Vietnam and subsequently from Cambodia and Laos. Despite the influence of communist ideology, and the involvement of both Russia and China, Vietnam had a high degree of independence. The Vietnamese leader, Ho Chi Minh, was often seen as a nationalist first and a communist second. In this regard, Hanoi's position vacillated between its support for the Soviet Union and wanting to benefit from China, without unnecessarily compromising its independence.

The threat scenario must be considered against today's changing world. Although conflict and war are still very much part of the world we live in (to think otherwise would be naïve), conflicts increasingly do not involve powerful nations outright fighting each other; however, this does not preclude the use of proxies. They are more likely to involve the powerful bullying the weak, as we have seen with the United States.

It has been pointed out that we must not see China in isolation but rather in comparison with other powers, especially the United States. In this regard, the latter's use of force has far outstripped that of the Chinese. This includes both overt and covert actions, and in the latter the US intelligence community has played an active role in deposing regimes that do not see eye to eye with Washington. The list is long and includes the assassination of democratically elected leaders. The military coup in Chile in 1973, which ousted the popular Salvador Allende and installed the dictator, Pinochet, involved the CIA.[53]

While China appears hesitant to threaten the use of force, the United States seems to be gung-ho when flexing its military muscle. Such displays of machismo can be seen over the years when Washington has interfered in the domestic affairs of other countries. In its accusation that Iran was behind the attack on Saudi oil refineries in September 2019, President Trump, reminiscent of the cowboy era in American history, warned that the United States was 'locked and loaded'.[54] The record of the United States speaks for itself—its history has been an egregious record of the blatant use of force.

The China Threat Beyond Force

Is China a threat in non-military terms? Once upon a time it was argued that the ethnic Chinese diaspora in several countries in Southeast Asia could be seen as sympathetic towards its motherland and as a potential fifth column and therefore was a threat in domestic terms. While such perceptions used to be prevalent among the indigenous peoples of the region, such notions are less so today. This is primarily due to the role played by these groups, which have integrated into the economic mainstream of their respective countries. In addition, the so-called motherland has proved to be a more romantic notion, harking back to the ancestors, rather than one which has real political impact. Besides, the communist system in mainland China is anathema to Chinese overseas, so much so that they regard it as an alien system.

As far as economic threats are concerned, we saw in the previous chapter that countries are doing their utmost to attract Chinese investments. If indeed the economic sphere can be considered a threat, then these countries are inviting the threat into their homes. In a globalised and integrated world, the idea of economic aggrandisement is no longer compelling. US leader President Trump had often lamented that the Chinese have taken American jobs. However, it could also be argued that this has been brought about by their own complacency and high costs of production.

We have also looked at the issue of countries taking enormous loans from the Chinese for various infrastructure projects, including those that come under the Belt and Road Initiative. Suffice to say, it is incumbent on states to undertake their own due diligence and make their own assessment of their ability to service such loans before agreeing to them. Loans provided by the Chinese are not in the form of aid but are commercially driven.

If a country feels threatened by China, in military or non-military terms, it should be equally concerned about the United States' ability to start a war or even to control its economy. The United States could pose a threat as it drags its allies and friends into wars it has chosen to start without necessarily consulting them first.

Today, the notion of the China threat seems misplaced. However, this does not guarantee that Beijing would never pose a threat; it will use force when it comes to defending its borders, which would include Taiwan and the South China Sea. Obviously in such a scenario, countries in dispute may well confront the Chinese. However, it must be hoped that those countries would rely on diplomacy and negotiation rather than resorting to the use of force. Let prudence and rational thinking prevail.

Notes

1. Russell Flannery, 'Seven Months In, Biden Uncertainty on China Policy Is Hurting American Business', *Forbes*, 21 August 2021, www.forbes.com
2. George Friedman and Meredith LeBard, *The Coming War with Japan* (New York: St Martin's Press, 1991).
3. See Peter Navarro, *The Coming China Wars: Where They Will Be Fought and How They Can Be Won* (London: Financial Times, 2008), and Jonathan Holslag, *China's Coming War with Asia* (London: Polity Press, 2015).

There is also a fiction about a war with China. See Humphrey Hawksley and Simon Holbertson, *Dragon Strike* (New York: Thomas Dunne Books, 1999).
4. While much has been written about the concept of balance of power, most would start with the seminal work of Hans Morgenthau, *Politics Among Nations* (London: McGraw-Hill Education, 2005).
5. Historical ties between these two giant neighbours, focusing on the period from 1949, have vacillated between friendship and animosity, even leading to border skirmishes, followed by a prolonged period of coolness and the current warming of ties. For a more contemporary analysis, see Alexander Lukin, *China and Russia: The New Rapprochement* (Cambridge: Polity Press, 2018).
6. There have been many examples of states annexing territories which they claim are part of their homeland, for example, Hitler's annexation of the Sudetenland, which was claimed as part of Germany. The deployment of the Wehrmacht across the border was a precursor to its invasion of Poland in September 1939, which sparked World War II. Not surprisingly, China's annexation of Tibet has often been classified as an invasion—but this is dependent on which standpoint one adopts.
7. For a good historical background to the boundary disputes, see Elliot Sperling, *The Tibet-China Conflict: History and Polemics* (Washington, D.C.: East-West Center, 2004).
8. Hsiao-Ting Lin, *Tibet and Nationalist China's Frontier: Intrigues and Ethnopolitics* (Vancouver: University of British Colombia Press, 2006), p. 6.
9. The Chinese invasion of Tibet became the backdrop of Hollywood's *Seven Years in Tibet*, a movie based on the Austrian climber Heinrich Harrer's encounter with the young 14th Dalai Lama. In the full glory of Hollywood action, the Chinese were, not surprisingly, depicted as the bad guys and carrying out acts of cruelty and showing no respect for Tibetan religious practices.
10. Andrew Scobell, *China's Use of Force: Beyond the Great Wall and the Long March* (Cambridge: Cambridge University Press, 2003), p. 80.
11. Like several others within the higher echelons of the communist elite, he was to fall from grace, having openly criticised Mao. For background, see *The Case of Peng Teh-Huai, 1959–1968* (Hong Kong: Union Research Institute, 1968).
12. Quoted in Sergei N. Goncharov, John W. Lewis and Xue Litai, *Uncertain Partners: Stalin, Mao and the Korean War* (Stanford, CA: Stanford University Press, 1993), p. 167.
13. For background on Lin Biao's downfall, see Frederick C. Teiwes and Warren Sun, *The Tragedy of Lin Biao: Riding the Tiger During the Cultural Revolution* (London: C Hurst and Co Publishers, 1996).

14. For a comprehensive analysis of the Chinese intervention, see Xiaobing Li, *China's Battle for Korea: The 1951 Spring Offensive* (Bloomington, Indiana: Indiana University Press, 2014)
15. This Chinese military intervention saw Mao's own son killed in action.
16. Xianming Zhang, *Red Wings over the Yalu: China, the Soviet Union, and the Air War in Korea* (College Station: Texas A&M University Press, 2002), p. 204
17. Jay Taylor, *The Dragon and the Wild Goose: China and India* (Westport, Connecticut, 1987).
18. The rivalry even extends to the origin of China and one Indian author postulates it could be traced to India. See Paramesh Choudhury, *Indian Origin of the Chinese Nation: An Unconventional Challenging Theory About the Origin of the Chinese* (Calcutta: Dasgupta and Co., 1990).
19. For good historical background, though now a little dated, see Alastair Lamb, *The China-India Border: The Origins of the Disputed Boundaries* (London: Oxford University Press, 1964). See also Chih H. Lu, *The Sino-Indian Border Dispute: A Legal Study* (New York: Greenwood Press, 1986).
20. John Rowland, *A History of Sino-Indian Relations: Hostile Co-existence* (Princeton, New Jersey: D. Van Nostrand and Company, 1967), p. 41.
21. *Selected Documents on Sino-Indian Relations, December 1961–May 1962* (Peking: Foreign Language Press, 1962), p. 47.
22. John Rowland, op. cit., p. 166.
23. 'Statement of the Government of the People's Republic of China, October 24, 1962', in *The Sino-Indian Boundary Question* (Peking: Foreign Languages Press, 1962), p. 5.
24. V.B. Karnik, 'The Invasion and After', in V.B. Karnik (ed.), *China Invades India: The Story of Invasion Against the Background of Chinese History and Sino-Indian Relations* (Bombay: Allied Publishers, 1963), p. 224.
25. Gerald Segal, *Defending China* (Oxford: Oxford University Press, 1985), p. 140.
26. Ibid., p.142.
27. See Lu Yang, *China-India Relations in the Contemporary World: Dynamics of National Interest and Identity* (Oxford: Routledge, 2017), p. 39.
28. Allen S. Whiting, *The Chinese Calculus of Deterrence: India and Indochina* (Ann Arbor: The University of Michigan Press, 1975), p. 243 and p. 245.
29. See S.C.M. Paine, *Imperial Rivals: China, Russia, and Their Disputed Frontier* (Armonk, New York: M.E. Sharpe, 1996).
30. For background on this not so well-known conflict, see George Alexander Lensen, *The Russo-Chinese War* (Tallahassee Florida: The Diplomatic Press, 1967).

31. C. Martin Wilbur and Julie Lien-ying How, *Missionaries of Revolution: Soviet Advisers and Nationalist China, 1920–1927* (Cambridge, Massachusetts: Harvard University Press, 1989), p. 18.
32. Sow-Theng Leong, *Sino–Soviet Diplomatic Relations, 1917–1926* (Canberra: Australian National University Press, 1976), p. 237. This is an excellent work on the early period of ties between the Soviets and the Chinese.
33. Klaus Mehnert, *Peking and Moscow* (London: Weidenfeld and Nicolson, 1962), p. 138.
34. For comprehensive background to the period leading to the high-point of ties, see Dieter Heinzig, *The Soviet Union and Communist China, 1945–1950: The Arduous Road to the Alliance* (Armonk, New York: M.E. Sharpe, 2004).
35. This speech revealed the full extent of Stalin's iron rule. See T. H. Rigby, *Stalin Dictatorship: Khrushchev's Secret Speech and Other Documents* (Sydney: Sydney University, 1968).
36. Speech made by Premier Zhou Enlai before the Full Conference of Afro-Asian Countries at Bandung, 19 April 1955, in G.V. Ambekar and V.D. Divekar (eds.), *Documents on China's Relations with South and South-East Asia (1949–1962)* (Bombay: Allied Publishers, 1964), p. 15.
37. 'A Great Anti-Imperialist Call', editorial in *Hung-Ch'i* (*Red Flag*), Peking, 16 December 1960, in Dan N. Jacobs and Hans H. Baerwald (eds.), *Chinese Communism: Selected Documents* (New York: Harper & Row Publishers, 1963), p. 187.
38. For a brief background on the CCP and Comintern, see Richard C. Thornton, *The Comintern and the Chinese Communists, 1928–1931* (Seattle: University of Washington Press, 1969); and Shanti Swarup, *A Study of the Chinese Communist Movement* (Oxford: Clarendon Press, 1966), pp. 202–226.
39. For example, see Qiang Zhai, *China and the Vietnam Wars, 1950–1975* (Chapel Hill: The University of North Carolina Press, 2000).
40. The full extent of the coup is much disputed, especially as to who supported who. For example, see Helen-Louise Hunter, *Sukarno and the Indonesian Coup: The Untold Story* (Boulder, Colorado: Praeger Press, 2007).
41. Jay Taylor, *China and Southeast Asia: Peking's Relations with Revolutionary Movements* (New York: Praeger Publishers, 1976), pp. 117–118.
42. Ian Taylor, *China and Africa: Engagement and Compromise* (Oxford: Routledge, 2006), p. 20.
43. Bruce D. Larkin, *China and Africa, 1949–1970: The Foreign Policy of the People's Republic of China* (Berkeley: University of California Press, 1971), p. 2.

44. Larkin. *Peking Review*, 25 March 1966, pp. 8–9, quoted in ibid., p. 132.
45. *The New York Times*, 31 January 1979, quoted in William J. Duiker, *China and Vietnam: The Roots of Conflict* (Berkeley: University of California, 1986), p. 85.
46. Quoted in Willian J. Duiker, *China and Vietnam: The Roots of Conflict* (Berkeley, University of California, 1986), p. 85.
47. Gerald Segal, *Defending China* (Oxford University Press, 1985), p. 219.
48. King C. Chen, *China's War with Vietnam: Issues, Decisions, Implications* (Stanford, California: Hoover Institution Press, 1987), p. 114.
49. For background on this triangular relationship, see John F. Copper, *China Diplomacy: The Washington-Taipei-Beijing Triangle* (Boulder, Colorado: Westview Press, 1992).
50. See Edward Timperlake and William C. Triplett II, *Red Dragon Rising: Communist China's Military Threat to America* (Washington, D.C.: Regnery Publishing, 1999), p. 154.
51. Husband and wife, Julius and Ethel Rosenberg, were executed in 1953 having been found guilty of spying for the Soviets, although the trial was seen as controversial. See Charles River (ed.), *The Case of Julius and Ethel Rosenberg: The History of America's Most Controversial Espionage Trial* (New York: CreateSpace Independent Publishing Platform, 2015); and Lori Clune, *Executing the Rosenbergs: Death and Diplomacy in Cold War World* (New York: Oxford University Press, 2016).
52. After several revisions, the US–Japan Alliance was formalised by the Treaty of Mutual Cooperation and Security and signed on 19 January 1960.
53. The days following the coup were the backdrop to the poignant Hollywood movie *Missing* (1982), starring Jack Lemon, which portrayed the conservative and patriotic father who went to Santiago to search for his missing son, who was found to have been executed by the military.
54. Widely reported in the world's media. See *The Japan Times*, 16 September 2019, japantimes.co.jp.

CHAPTER 5

Regional Perceptions Towards China: Safeguarding Interests

Perceptions are influenced by many factors, chief of which are history, politics, psychology and ideology. They can be real or imaginary. Perhaps more important is the question of whose perceptions we are referring to—those of state or non-states. We often think of these entities as homogeneous and permanent, but they are not. In the current age, in which political and non-political groups have taken to the streets to protest against democratically elected governments and to express deep unhappiness and frustration with the establishment, it is difficult to discuss the subject of perceptions without clarifying whose perception it is. Without dwelling too much on this, the discussion in this chapter will be based mainly on such factors as geography, history, politics and security.

The geographical factor is one of the realities governing how a country perceives China and proximity influences perception. Often tied to this is the question of territorial disputes. Countries that have either a land or maritime boundary with China will invariably have a dispute over real estate, often relating to some historical hangover from the past or, in the case of conflicting claims over the South China Sea, to legal provisions enshrined in the UN Convention on the Law of the Sea, which overnight legalised the right of states to lay claim beyond their territorial waters, which themselves extend 200 nautical miles from the coast and are part of their exclusive economic zone (EEZ). While this provided states with the right to exploit the riches of the sea, it is also a recipe for political dispute and military conflict.

Not surprisingly, China's neighbours have had mixed historical and contemporary experiences. Any historical animosity with the Middle Kingdom will have a bearing, in part on the psychological dimension of states. Although ties can be improved over time, history is not easily erased from the often-entrenched mentality and psyche of society.

It would appear that much of the threat perception debate over China centres on two interrelated factors—the position of states regarding the Western world, in particular the United States, and their belief that China will become the dominant global power and will subjugate them. While the first of these is based on reality, the second is more uncertain, built on fear of the unknown and based on assumption and conjecture. To some extent, there is an element of the race factor here, which is perhaps the result of decades, if not centuries, of Western domination over others, notwithstanding the fact that most of these countries achieved independence over half a century ago. Despite China being in the East, there is still much negativity towards China, in favour of the West.

The question, therefore, of who is afraid of China is a combination of reality and perception. While the prevalent reality is that most countries maintain reasonable ties with Beijing, predicated mainly on economic and trading interests, underneath this veneer of cordiality lies some lingering suspicion. This is mainly based on the influence of the strong narrative that, in the future, China will be a powerful hegemon that may end up influencing, if not controlling, smaller, weaker states.

For the present, however, regional states are taking a more pragmatic approach to China and will not unnecessarily antagonise Beijing. They are clamouring among themselves to woo Chinese investors. While the Belt and Road Initiative (BRI) provides a strategic framework for China's grand economic plan, China is not confined to this. Its economic expansion goes beyond the BRI; it is economic realism that is driving policies on China. To some extent, it is a zero-sum game: if a country adopts a less friendly attitude towards China, it may end up losing its goodwill. This may explain why states that bear some degree of historical animosity towards China may not be willing to allow the past to become a stumbling block in the development of economic and commercial ties.

This chapter will provide an overview of how a number of Asian countries view China. Many are hedging their bets—on the one hand, trying to derive benefits from China and all that it can offer and, on the other, maintaining close ties with the West, largely as an insurance policy; they want to be reassured of protection if all goes pear-shaped. However, China is the proverbial elephant in the room that no state can ignore. While this chapter conveniently divides up the states in terms of their threat perception regarding China, it is not absolute. There is no longer a them-against-us or better-red-than-dead scenario; rather, it is a prudently cautious optimism that states have come to adopt.

Northeast Asia: Too Close to Call

Japan: Going Beyond Historical Animosity

Japan has enjoyed a mixed historical experience with its close neighbour. Ties can be traced back centuries and much of what we see in Japan today comes from a common heritage.[1] While the historical animosity continues to live in the minds of both sides, in contemporary times, the US factor has become more compelling. However, economic and commercial realities have also become critical in shaping the relationship.

The more recent experience of Japanese military adventures in China from the early 1930s formed an indelible mark on the psyche of the Chinese that went beyond politics. The Marco Polo Bridge incident[2] in the summer of 1937, which the Japanese used as a *casus belli* to invade China, has become a landmark symbol of this negativity towards Japan. The massacre of Nanjing in January 1938 during the Japanese invasion is another factor in shaping Chinese attitudes, although the atrocities in Nanjing have been rebutted by some Japanese commentators who have advanced a much less aggressive account of the episode.[3]

It is interesting to note that, according to an extensive study of the China–Japan relationship between the late nineteenth century and 1937, bilateral ties developed within the context of an unequal treaty system—a concept that was associated mainly with the British and other colonial powers who were attempting to expand their imperial reach.[4] It was employed in situations where entities were too weak to resist but strong or large enough to prevent territorial conquest. For the Japanese, the decade leading to the collapse of dynastic China and the tumultuous years that followed placed it in just such a situation and left China ripe for intervention. This period coincided with the rise of militarism in Japan, which had been preceded by its historic victory against the Russians in 1905, during the Battle of Tsushima. Admiral Togo's brilliant naval manoeuvres against the Russians earned him a special place in the annals of Japan's military history.[5]

The historical dimension cannot simply be dismissed as a mere irritant. It runs deep in the consciousness of the Chinese. Although pragmatism now drives the relationship forwards, this factor remains a constant. However, the US connection, formalised by treaty, has cemented Japan's continuing negative perception of China. Whether this is a price, including its loss of independent thinking, that Tokyo pays for its alliance with Washington is open to debate. Irrespective of this, this threat perception is very much present from the perspective of the establishment.[6]

The Pacific War left a dark stain on the conscience of the Japanese—it is as if the guilty burden is being carried far beyond the generation that was directly responsible for the hostilities beginning with the infamous attack on Pearl Harbour in December 1941.[7] This subject remains highly contentious. Central to the debate is the role of Emperor Hirohito and the degree of his culpability in the decision to go to war.[8] Given the deep reverence in which Japanese people hold the emperor, the subject has proved to be highly emotive.

Japanese views on China take three forms. The first two are more extreme in nature and belong to right-wing conservative forces and pacifists. The third is held by those who vacillate between the two. Attitudes towards China stem from the dynamic interaction between these groups. Linked to this is China's role in perpetuating Japan's war guilt, such as the periodic anti-Japanese—and therefore officially sanctioned—protests in China. In Japan, meanwhile, the ritual visit of leaders to the Yasukuni Shrine in Tokyo has become a symbol of Japan's recognition of its war dead who served in the name of the emperor, including during the Pacific War. Such visits are seen outside Japan as an endorsement by the state of the legitimacy of Japan's aggression in the region, with all the atrocities and exploitation associated with it. It is rarely missed if a Japanese official pays an official visit to the Shrine. Such visits are often accompanied by very public criticism from countries like China. For example, Defence Minister Nobuo Kishi visited the Yasukuni Shrine in August 2021, resulting in both South Korea and China lambasting him. The Chinese Defence Ministry issued a statement, expressing the country's strong dissatisfaction and resolute opposition to the visit, which reflected 'Japan's wrong attitude toward its history of aggression, and its sinister intention to challenge the post-war international order'.[9] Interestingly, the statement also took the opportunity to criticise Japan for smearing China's defence policy and military development in collaboration with countries outside the region while conducting targeted military exercises, intervening in the Taiwan issue and carrying out provocative actions in the South China Sea.[10]

To some extent, the negative perception towards such visits has kept the Japanese at bay and they are constantly reminded of what Japan did during their aggressive action. Indirectly, this puts a check on Japan that serves the interests of countries that view it as a potential threat or rival power.

In addition to the historical dimension, there are two factors that feature in the perception of Japan's attitude towards its once limited 'colony'[11]—military and geographic. The annual government publication *Defense of Japan* reflects the perception of threat of the Japanese establishment. During the Cold War the Soviet threat featured most prominently in the government's threat assessment, with several possible military scenarios of a Soviet attack on Japanese soil highlighted.[12]

However, from the end of the Cold War in the late 1990s, the Soviet threat was watered down and China began to feature more prominently. For example, the 2018 edition highlighted China's rapid modernisation and what it described as 'China's attempts to change the status quo by coercion'.[13] The report also identified Russia as a significant power in the context of Japan's defence.

Geographical proximity will always be a compelling factor in Japan's identification of China as a potential threat. The territorial dispute over the Senkaku/Diaoyu Islands has brought both countries into direct confrontation. Over the years, there have been various incidents at sea that warrant red flags for both sides. For example, according to a Japanese official account of May 2017, 'it was confirmed that an object that appeared to be a small drone was flying above a Chinese government vessel intruding into Japanese territorial waters around the Senkaku Islands. This flight also represents a unilateral escalation of the situation and constitutes an invasion of territorial airspace.'[14] The Japanese subsequently claimed that Chinese vessels had passed through its territorial waters around Tsushima (Nagasaki Prefecture) and Okinoshima Island (Fukuoka Prefecture) and in the Tsugaru Strait in July 2017 and that in the following month they had sailed through Japan's territorial waters from Sata Cape to the Kusagakiguntou Islands (both in Kagoshima Prefecture).[15] For Tokyo, such Chinese incursions, together with their substantial military build-up, are a danger to Japan's national security.

Tokyo also pays attention to the situation in the South China Sea, due to its paramount strategic importance to Japan's economic and trading interests. With regard to the conflicting claims over the South China Sea, Japan is obviously an interested party, not only due to proximity, but it is also concerned with sea lines of communication, which are vital to the country's trade and economic well-being. Tensions have been brewing in that area, involving not only among claimants but also with external powers, especially the United States. In this regard, Tokyo has joined with other countries to mount pressure on China, including protesting China's claims to the United Nations. It has also accused the Chinese of restricting freedom of navigation and overflight.[16] Obviously, this has angered China, as it sees this as Japanese interference in what it regards as its traditional domain. In other words, despite being a non-claimant, Japan has indirectly got involved with this highly disputed area, putting itself in harm's way, with the Chinese. However, it is possible that apart from its own strategic interests to ensure the freedom of the seas, Tokyo might have felt they needed to do something in order to reinforce its interests and concerns, as well as to buttress the United States' involvement in the area.

Japan is also concerned about the situation in the Korean Peninsula and the unification of Taiwan. Clearly, any hostility in that area could lead to a wider conflagration which would inevitably involve the Americans and Japanese. All this highlights the critical importance of the US–Japan alliance; Tokyo will automatically be dragged into any broader military confrontation between Washington and Beijing. After all, Japan still hosts US military forces and the existence of a joint military command makes it indistinguishable from the United States, from China's perspective. Irrespective of whether Japan sees China as a threat, it is not immune to how the United States views China. The alliance could be seen as both a curse and a blessing to Tokyo because its strategic appraisal is necessarily tied to that of the Americans, whether it likes it or not.

Conversely, the Chinese will always view the Japanese in broader strategic terms, as being part of the US-led Western alliance in the region. Japan is an integral part of the United States' Indo-Pacific strategy, and therefore Beijing has to view the former as such. When Biden met the Japanese premier, Suga Yoshihide, in April 2021, the White House issued a statement essentially expressing the two strategic partners' reaffirmation of their dual alliance, with American 'unwavering support for Japan's defense under the US-Japan Treaty of Mutual Cooperation and Security, using its full range of capabilities, including nuclear'.[17] The joint statement also highlighted their common concerns about China, including, firstly, over the East China Sea, opposing 'unilateral attempts to change the status quo in the area', and, secondly, their 'objections to China's unlawful maritime claims and activities in the South China Sea and reaffirmed our strong shared interest in a free and open South China Sea governed by international law, in which freedom of navigation and overflight are guaranteed, consistent with the UN Convention on the Law of the Sea'.[18]

In other words, in Beijing's strategic calculation, Tokyo is inseparable from Washington. According to a report from London-based Chatham House, 'While there is a long history of international partnerships in the Indo-Pacific, many recent forays in the region are in response to China's economic, political and military expansion there.'[19]

In economic terms, China's growth provides vast opportunities for Japan and its corporate sector. Despite the prolonged stagnation of Japan's economy, it remains a substantial contributor to China's foreign direct investment. However, in the economic sphere both Japan and China are rivals in Southeast Asia and beyond, including in Africa, where the latter has stepped up its investments.[20] In terms of infrastructure projects the Japanese are still ahead of the Chinese; according to 2019 figures, Japan's outstanding projects in Southeast Asia are valued at $367 billion; China's are $255 billion.[21]

The economic factor may well prove to be an irritant in bilateral relations between Japan and China, but it is likely that pragmatism will be the driving force for both to move forward, at least for the foreseeable future. Nonetheless, the rise of China will feature prominently within Japan's strategic calculation, which viewed from Tokyo's perspective will converge with the United States' interests.

China in Between North and South Korea

The Korean Peninsula is one of the most militarised areas of the world. The historic meeting in June 2019 between President Trump and Pyongyang leader, Kim Jong Un, technically in North Korea as the former did step across the 38th parallel, has not led to a significant de-escalation in the tensions that have existed since the beginning of the Korean War in 1950. For South Korea, China will always be viewed with this broader context in mind. Seoul sees Beijing as having some degree of influence on North Korea, although the extent of it remains uncertain. As we have seen, Chinese intervention during the war was primarily to protect its own security interests and to bolster communist fraternalism. Nonetheless, it is believed that the China factor will loom large in any strategic calculations made in this area. This is further reinforced by the security alliance between South Korea and the United States. In this regard, for the South, the China threat is a constant factor as its primary preoccupation is to deal with the possibility of a major confrontation. This is part of Seoul's security dilemma.

Relations between South Korea and China have been mired in suspicion, especially given Seoul's perception that Beijing is in cahoots with Pyongyang. There is a convergence of interests between China and North Korea over the position of the United States. China sees the North as part of a broader strategic consideration vis-à-vis Washington. After all, 'the enemy of my enemy is my friend' is one way of looking at North Korea. Pyongyang's constant antagonism with Washington does serve Beijing's interests, although its influence over North Korea is uncertain. However, this does not suggest that China has a trouble-free relationship with North Korea. One of the biggest challenges facing Beijing when dealing with the Democratic People's Republic of Korea (DPRK) is its fierce independence together with the often-unpredictable nature of its leaders' behaviour. For example, even though China and North Korea have both agreed to renew the Treaty of Friendship, Cooperation and Mutual Assistance[22] for another 20 years, Beijing was not at all pleased with some of the policies enunciated by Pyongyang, such as its decision to go nuclear. According to Chinese scholars, North Korea was deemed to be in breach of the Treaty when it declared itself a nuclear power without consulting with China.[23] However, the fact that both leaders have agreed to renew does speak volumes about the importance of the relationship, with China viewing it as a possible hold over DPRK, which not many countries can claim. It has been suggested that with this alliance continuing, 'the power dynamics on the Korean peninsula look set to follow a familiar pattern. China will leverage its alliance with North Korea to prevent Pyongyang from provoking a major crisis, while dangling the threat of a Chinese intervention to moderate US ambitions', while 'North Korea will continue to rely on Chinese economic assistance, especially to recover from the pandemic, and assume Chinese protection while advancing its nuclear program'.[24]

The close strategic ties between South Korea and the United States will always be a factor in ROK–PRC relations. Every time the leaders of both countries meet and touch on strategic issues, the Chinese will invariably react, sometimes with a warning or providing advice to Seoul. When US President Biden met with his South Korean counterpart, Moon Jae-in, in Washington on 21 May 2021, and a joint statement issued which mentioned the ultrasensitive issues of the South China Sea and the Taiwan Straits, it touched a raw nerve in China, even though Seoul's Foreign Ministry reiterated the country's continued adherence to the One-China policy and that it has refrained from making specific comments about China's internal affairs.[25] Obviously, Beijing saw this as 'interference' in its affairs by external powers. According to Chinese Foreign Ministry spokesperson Zhao Lijian, the very mention of Taiwan-related questions is 'playing with fire', while Chinese scholars, such as Lu Chao from the Liaoning Academy of Social Sciences, notes that 'From China's perspective, remarks from South Korea seem like a guilty look. It would be better if South Korea generously admitted that mentioning the Taiwan Straits is wrong… South Korea should have said nothing about the island of Taiwan, but should make practical efforts to prevent a setback in China-South Korea ties, and stop sliding into the trap of the US.'[26] Knowing full well the sensitive nature of the Taiwan Straits in China's eyes, and possible ramifications if Seoul makes reference to it, it is possible that either it was unable to prevent the United States from including it or it felt obligated to Washington and therefore played along—hence the joint statement from the two presidents. However, despite the mention of the South China Sea and the Taiwan Straits, according to one observer, 'the Moon government seems to have carefully coordinated with the US so that the outcome of the summit would not be interpreted as direct criticism against China'.[27]

Whilst part of the American alliance system in East Asia, South Korea was careful not to be seen to be dragged into the United States' Indo-Pacific strategy. Seoul knows full well that China is waiting to see ROK's reaction to Washington's defence strategy in this region. In that respect, while the strategy was mentioned in the joint statement following the Moon–Biden meeting, it fell short of Seoul's endorsement, making it more tolerable to the Chinese.[28] No doubt, the US factor will always be a complicating issue when it comes to China's relations with the Republic of Korea.

It is interesting to consider the South Korean view of the Americans, which might best be described as a kind of love–hate relationship. While the US military presence has caused some degree of discomfort as well as even growing resentment among Koreans, they also view the Americans with nostalgia, especially the older generation who still have a living memory of the United States standing by their side when faced with North Korean forces. There is indeed an element of ambivalence towards the United States. After all, the US military presence is both a curse and a blessing. It acts as a deterrent against North Korean aggressive intentions, while at the same time, it attracts aggression from Pyongyang.

Traditionally, Koreans have a negative perception and attitude towards Japan, mainly due to historical animosity. Throughout history, Japan had aggressive ambitions towards the Hermit Kingdom. For example, between 1592 and 1598, Japanese overlord Toyotomi Hideyoshi, known as Taiko, rather than Shogun—due to his humble background, which denied him that more coveted and exalted title—sent his forces across the Korean Straits, to invade the peninsula. However, the campaign, known as the Imjin War, proved to be a disaster for the Japanese when the defenders were able to repel the invading force. A few centuries later, in 1910, Japan annexed Korea and the peninsula came under Japanese rule until the end of Pacific War in 1945. Over the centuries, the hatred towards Japan grew and has become part of the Korean psyche.

However, recently, it would appear that China is fast competing with Japan to take over the number one slot, as the country most hated by the South Koreans. They were incensed when the Chinese media claimed that the uniquely Korean dish, *Kimchi*, originated in China. To Peter Charles of the Australian Lowy Institute, 'the kimchi incident was an example of China's "wolf warriors" scoring an own goal.... By picking a wholly unnecessary fight on a topic with no diplomatic stakes, Beijing has only further damaged its reputation with the South Korean population and made life more complicated for counterparts in Seoul who are otherwise eager to cooperate with China.'[29]

This popular tilt against China was further accentuated by the portrayal of Chinese culture and culinary traditions in a much-anticipated Korean drama series, the *Joseon Exorcist*. When the drama series first aired in March 2021, 'South Koreans weren't impressed. Instead, many were incensed those Korean characters were shown drinking Chinese liquor and eating Chinese food, such as dumplings, mooncake pastries and preserved "century eggs".'[30] Such adverse reactions by the viewers prompted the TV channel to apologise and subsequently take the series off the air. According to a report, 'The incident reflects growing animosity toward what many South Koreans feel is inappropriate Chinese influence in South Korean entertainment, as well as a manipulation of history in order to claim several beloved aspects of Korean culture.'[31]

This emerging wariness towards China was demonstrated by the US-based Carnegie poll conducted in Seoul in November 2019, which showed that only a quarter of those surveyed trusted China as a unification partner, while almost three-quarters did not trust Beijing very much or at all. In addition, when asked which countries were likely to be a unified Korea's biggest threat, more than half picked China.[32] In another poll, conducted in October 2020 by Pew global poll, as many as 83 per cent of South Koreans had no confidence that Chinese President Xi Jinping would do the 'right thing in world affairs'.[33] Notwithstanding the flaws of any polling process, such numbers reflect the general attitude amongst South Koreans towards China.

To some extent, South Koreans' increasing hatred towards the Chinese could stem from not only Beijing's support for Pyongyang but also its own regional ambitions. Such nascent negativity towards the Chinese could also develop from US influence, which constantly places China in bad light. China's aggressive behaviour towards Taiwan is probably a grim reminder for the South Koreans, given the similarity to the North's stance towards them. Perhaps, South Koreans feel some sympathy towards the Taiwanese, who find themselves on the receiving end of a bully's actions.

According to the US government-backed Voice of America, 'Underpinning the tensions are wider concerns about China's growing economic and military strength, and its more combative stance towards its neighbours, which analysts say is an attempt to reassert Beijing's position as a dominant regional power.'[34]

However, despite the various irritants, like many other regional countries, South Korea's relationship with China is mainly predicated on economic ties, as Beijing is Seoul's largest trading partner. During 2020, South Korean exports to China stood at US$132 billion, with electrical and electronic equipment being the largest sector. Based on such economic reality, South Korea has to balance its ties with China, although Seoul will often adopt the 'big picture' approach and not be swayed by economic and trade considerations. This is perhaps best illustrated by its attitude towards China's BRI, which might best be described as ambivalent. This position was demonstrated in June 2019, when presenting his credentials to Beijing as the new ROK's ambassador to the PRC, Jang Ha-sung delighted his hosts when he declared his country's support for this grand project. He was quoted as saying that his country hoped to participate actively in the vast infrastructure initiative. However, interestingly, back in Seoul, the Foreign Ministry was prompt in denying that to be the case.[35]

Maintaining ties with both North and South places China in a unique position to play a role as a peace broker between the two arch enemies.

Beijing arguably, tacitly, likes to be seen to be contributing to peace and stability in the Korean Peninsula. For example, amidst the North's usual sabre-rattling in reaction to an ongoing US–South Korean military exercise, the Chinese ambassador to Seoul, Xing Haiming, urged the two Koreas to get along better with each other. He said, 'Inter-Korean relations should be improved. After all, North Korea and South Korea are of the same Korean people and we just hope they make concerted efforts to get along well with each other.... It would be a good thing for them to do a lot of things that may help bring about peace and reconciliation on the Korean peninsula.'[36] To a large extent, Beijing could reap much regional goodwill if it takes concrete steps to play such a role. However, China also takes cognizance of North Korea's streak of independence and the South's American connection. Nonetheless, the PRC continues to balance its ties between the two Koreas while, at the same time, seeing them as part of a larger regional and global issue.

In his quest for a more positive regional and global image, President Xi will continue to pursue his 'charm offensive'. In a 40-minute phone conversation between the Chinese and South Korean leaders, in August 2021, Xi expressed his country's support for dialogue between the two Koreas as well as denuclearisation talks between the United States and North Korea. He also underlined Seoul's role in a political solution to the Korean Peninsula issue. Both leaders reaffirmed their strong commitment to implementing a wide range of projects to promote bilateral cooperation.[37] Periodic contacts at the top-most levels of leadership, between China and the two Koreas, will offer some measure of check and balance will prevail, with Beijing playing a crucial role as the moderator in this acrimonious relationship.

Cross-Straits Relations and the China Threat

The Taiwanese believe that China poses a direct threat to their existence. This is the Republic's reality. It has been argued earlier that, because China regards Taiwan as an integral part of its territory, it will never in any way cede the island. China does not have any qualms about saying categorically that it will resort to force to unite the two territories. What Beijing is most opposed to is any move within Taiwan towards independence. For China, even talk of independence spells trouble and is seen as pushing it into a corner. This is the line which Beijing will never allow Taiwan to cross. Of this the Taiwanese are fully aware and some elements within Taiwanese society use it as a rallying cry, much to the anger of Beijing.

In addition, the US factor is a critical consideration when it comes to any potential conflict over this issue. Given China's own rivalry with the United States, the involvement of the latter is a matter of strategic importance. It could be argued that this factor adds to the overall uncertainty of cross-straits ties, although its deterrent value cannot be easily diminished or dismissed. However, given the ultrasensitive nature of the Taiwan issue for the Chinese, the United States pursues a cautious policy towards the former. For instance, due to its recognition of the One-China policy, Washington is unable to maintain normal state-to-state ties with Taiwan. Like the American policy of 'neither confirm nor deny' whether its warships are carrying nuclear weapons while in Japanese territory—due to the three non-nuclear principles that Japan strictly adheres to—in as far as Taiwan is concerned, the United States pursues a position creatively known as 'strategic ambiguity' over whether it would defend Taiwan in the event of attack. However, in August 2021, President Biden breached this by suggesting that the United States would defend Taiwan in such an event, together with Japan and South Korea. This knee-jerk reaction by the new administration was more to defend and restore US prestige and commitment following criticisms of the way it had abandoned Afghanistan. Embarrassingly, Washington had to backtrack, with a senior Biden administration official saying that US 'policy with regard to Taiwan has not changed'.[38] Clearly, Washington did not want to cause a backlash from the Chinese, which could hurt the Taiwanese more than the Americans. Besides, the Biden administration probably felt that it did want to strain ties with China so early into the presidency.

Following the fall of Afghanistan into the hands of the Taliban, and the Americans' chaotic withdrawal, the Chinese exploited the events by telling the Taiwanese that the United States could not be relied upon and that it would not defend the island. According to the Chinese Communist Party's (CCP's) *Global Times*, based on what happened in Afghanistan, Taiwan 'should perceive that once a war breaks out in the Straits, the island's defence will collapse in hours and the US military won't come to help'.[39]

At a time that coincided with the fall of Afghanistan, the Chinese were conducting air and naval exercises around the Taiwan Straits. According to a US-based news report, 'The jingoistic rhetoric coincided with air and naval drills launched Tuesday by the Chinese military, which sent fighter jets and warships near Taiwan in response to what it called the "repeated collusion in provocation" by Washington and Taipei.'⁴⁰ It seems clear that Beijing will seize the opportunity whenever it arises to drive home the point to the Taiwanese of the unreliability of the Americans and that it would be far more profitable if it accepts the inevitability of coming back to the fold. After all, the Chinese leadership will never give up on this cherished goal of reuniting Taiwan with the mainland.

While Taiwan relies on the US defence umbrella, the latter's policies and actions as well as US–ROC joint statements could also result in the former paying a price. This was the case when the People's Liberation Army (PLA) launched joint live-fire assault drills in multiple locations near the island of Taiwan. According to official Chinese sources, this was a direct response to what it referred to as 'recent collusion and provocations made by the US and the Taiwan secessionists'.⁴¹ As stated in the previous chapter about a possible Chinese large-scale amphibious landing operation on Taiwan, experts believe this exercise was part of its practice for such a scenario, which would see the PLA seize air superiority and control of the sea. Such real threats will always be a critical factor in Taiwan's strategic calculations. China will remain steadfast in its 'dream' of joining the renegade Taiwan to the mainland, by force or by peaceful means.

Southeast Asia: Between History and Today's Economic Reality

Southeast Asia is often seen as China's backyard. In this respect, regional countries have had different experiences with Beijing—historically and in more contemporary times. They share some common features, chief of which is the presence of ethnic Chinese in their national make up. Many Chinese fled the mainland to escape the tumultuous and chaotic Qing China of the nineteenth and early twentieth centuries. Their commercial acumen and hard work has meant that many have contributed to the economic prosperity of the region, with the assistance and encouragement of the various colonial powers. It was the need to develop certain industries or plantations that caused the mass migration, not only from China but also from India. This was clearly the case in British Malaya, where the discovery of tin and the development of rubber plantations led to the direct influx of migrant workers from China and India.

However, while these incomers have brought some degree of economic prosperity and growth to their respective countries, they have also posed a major challenge to the wider society in which they live. Due mainly to the income gap between the ethnic Chinese and indigenous population, the former tended to be a convenient target for the frustrations of the latter. This has resulted in the periodic flare-up of local conflicts, such as in Malaysia in 1969, in Indonesia in 1998 following a major economic crisis, and in Vietnam in 1978, disruption that led to the boat people, who were mostly ethnic Chinese, fleeing persecution by the state and wider society.

Central to this issue is a supposed continuing connection to the mainland, leading to suspicions about the loyalty of ethnic Chinese to their new home and to possible justification for China to intervene in the domestic affairs of host countries. Given the increasing capability of China's long arm, the fear is that Beijing will interfere if ethnic Chinese are in jeopardy. This makes governments nervous. It is clear that, like other countries, China has the right to assist its nationals abroad if they are in distress. However, the key question is whether this obligation extends to ethnic Chinese, whose ancestral homes are on the mainland but who have given up their Chinese citizenship. This has resulted in caution and a general suspicion of local populations towards the presence of ethnic Chinese.

In addition to this and mainly as a result of the region's colonial history (with the exception of Thailand, which was never colonised), all the host countries have had to deal with national liberation movements, mainly spearheaded by communists, which appeared to have closer ties with Beijing than Moscow. This historical legacy has been a strong determinant in the perception of China, although this is now much less significant.

As Southeast Asia shares common land and maritime borders with China, trade and commercial links have been established over many centuries. More recently, with the opening up of China and its subsequent economic take-off, this region naturally became a fertile area for further commercial links to be established. Specific to the Belt and Road Initiative, Southeast Asia has become a major route and therefore a natural partner. Against such a backdrop, economic realities and exigencies become the driving force in bilateral ties being developed between China and the regional states.

Vietnam and China: On the Horns of a Dilemma

Vietnam and China share a long and often acrimonious history. Its origins can be traced as far back as 111 BCE when a Han dynasty army conquered the southern Kingdom of Nan Yue, which itself controlled vast lands.[42]

The Qin emperor also sent troops to this area, but his was an unsuccessful and unpopular campaign.[43] For centuries, Vietnam—then known as Annan, meaning 'Settled South', a name imposed by the Tang dynasty—was essentially part of China's dynastic territory but was under varying degrees of control from the centre. For instance, during the Tang dynasty, which brought about the greatest expansion of China's borders, Vietnam was regarded as a protectorate. However, it was a difficult area to control with numerous rebellions and battles taking place between rival leaders, such as Nanzhou, who undermined central control of the region's southern flanks.[44]

Even in contemporary times, bilateral ties have remained tense because of the invasion of northern Vietnam by Chinese troops in February 1979. Given this, one might argue that Hanoi views Beijing as a potential threat to its security. This perception is further reinforced by the presence of a small ethnic Chinese minority and the maritime territorial dispute over the South China Sea and the Paracel Islands.

While the ethnic factor is less significant at present, the disputed resource-rich areas remain prominent on the radar screen. Both countries have clashed over this and the rhetoric from Hanoi and Beijing remains loud. In July 2019, six heavily armed coastguard vessels—two Chinese and four Vietnamese—were involved in a week-long confrontation near Vanguard Bank, in the Spratly group of islands, despite both sides agreeing to settle disputes by negotiation following the Chinese Defence Minister General Wei Fenghe's visit to Hanoi just two months before.[45] In May 2014 the two sides had confronted each other, resulting in several boats being damaged and a number of Vietnamese being injured. According to one news report, Chinese ships rammed and fired water cannons at Vietnamese vessels trying to stop Beijing from building an oil rig in the area.[46]

During the 1980s, Vietnam began to establish closer strategic ties with the USSR, even housing the Soviet military, as part of its realignment between the two communist giants. It was a counter-weight strategy on the part of Hanoi. Today, the Russian connection is not as strong but remains significant. This could become an insurance policy for the Vietnamese against any untoward Chinese aggression. However, given the marked improvement in Sino–Russia ties, how Moscow would assist Hanoi in the event of a much more serious armed conflict between Vietnam and China is uncertain.

Given this overriding security concern, it is understandable that Hanoi will remain suspicious of Beijing despite the increased economic ties between the two countries. According to official Vietnamese figures, China invested about US$1.6 billion in Vietnam in the first quarter of 2019, making it the country's fourth largest source of foreign investment. Since 2004, China has been Vietnam's biggest trade partner and is its second largest export market after the United States. Vietnam is China's largest trading partner in ASEAN.[47] It seems clear that both sides have remained pragmatic—keeping security and economic factors separate. Despite the attraction of Chinese economic power, the Vietnamese have not been pressured to give in to Beijing. On the contrary, Hanoi has remained steadfast in exerting its claims over the disputed territories. This could be attributed to Vietnam's fiercely independent stance and nationalistic fervour. It did defeat the French and the United States and has been able, intermittently, to withstand the might of its giant neighbour.

Nonetheless, given the uneasy historical ties between the two countries, both remain cautious towards each other, but at the same time, they refuse to escalate issues that could lead to rising tensions. It is interesting to note that, in April 2021, the General Secretary of the Communist Party of Vietnam, Nguyen Phu Trong, during China's Minister of Defence Wei Fenghe's visit to Hanoi, declared that Vietnam will not follow others in opposing China, hinting to the American proposal for an Indo-Pacific Strategy which, to the Vietnamese, 'will undermine regional integration, unity and peace, as it uses the divergences between regional countries to hype up and escalate tensions, and Hanoi doesn't want to be made use of'.[48] Specific to the South China Sea dispute, Trong said the two countries should handle the issue properly based on mutual trust and respect and prevent any related negative effect on bilateral ties.[49]

While both Hanoi and Beijing have remained level-headed in managing their bilateral ties, outstanding issues do remain, such as their conflicting claims over the South China Sea. Given China's growing influence around the rest of Indochina, often regarded as Vietnam's backyard, new forms of tensions are likely to surface. This seems to be the case over Laos, where Hanoi and Vientiane have long-established cordial ties. However, China's increasing economic presence in Laos, and replacing Vietnam as the largest investor and lender, has created an element of rivalry. While Hanoi has remained cautious over China's BRI, Laos has been most enthusiastic, given the largesse that it has received from China, with projects such as the massive hydroelectric projects along the Mekong River as well as the

Kunming–Singapore railway which runs through Laos, all funded by the Chinese. According to some Vietnamese scholars, such projects 'are designed to isolate Vietnam from the rest of the region'.[50] Nonetheless, despite the emerging rivalry over Laos, both Hanoi and Beijing are realistic enough to recognise that they must manage the ties between them well. Both are aware that the United States will always be lurking in the background, waiting to exploit any cracks in the power rivalry between these two communist countries.

The Philippines: Ambivalence Towards China

Today the Philippines walks a tightrope—balancing between engaging the Chinese in its economic development and trying to exercise sovereignty in the South China Sea. Its maverick president, Rodrigo Duterte, has taken his country into unchartered waters and in just a few years his position has vacillated over China, from embracing it in 2016 in what was described as a 'love affair' to the point of wanting to abandon Manila's long-time ally the United States, to hitting out at Beijing over the South China Sea in 2018 and then moving back towards the Chinese later that year. The latter happened after President Xi's visit to Manila during which the two countries signed a joint oil and gas exploration deal and 29 other deals, including a memorandum of understanding to cooperate on China's BRI and to boost bilateral trade.[51] Duterte met Xi again, in Beijing in September 2019, where, according to China's official news agency, Xinhua, the latter said the two nations could take a 'bigger step' in joint offshore oil and gas exploration. Xi said, 'As long as the two sides handle the South China Sea issue properly, the atmosphere of bilateral ties will be sound, the foundation of the relationship will be stable, and regional peace and stability will have an important guarantee.'[52] It is clear that China is dangling a carrot to placate Manila's often loud voice over the disputed maritime territory, especially since the international arbitration tribunal in The Hague voted in its favour. Duterte himself made it abundantly clear when he said that Xi offered a quid pro quo—a generous offer over oil and gas exploration in lieu of the arbitration ruling. Rather amusingly, the Philippine president publicly admitted that he was running out of options in his efforts to press Beijing to adhere to The Hague court's ruling. Duterte even jokingly asked journalists at the media conference if they had any suggestions for persuading Chinese leaders.[53] Earlier, in July 2019, Duterte had announced that he had allowed Chinese fishing vessels to operate in Philippine waters in order to prevent war, stating that while the West Philippine Sea belonged to Manila, the region was under Chinese control.[54]

Despite Manila's positive overtures towards China, the latter continues to confront the Philippines over the disputed South China Sea, much to the chagrin of President Duterte. In an incident in May 2021, hundreds of Chinese fishing boats were gathered at several South China Sea islets, most notably at Whitsun Reef, within Manila's EEZ. Anticipating that the Chinese will use these boats as part of its militia force to occupy the reef, the Philippines decided to deploy its navy as well as coastguard to the area. In retaliation, China demanded that the Philippines withdraw its forces, to which Duterte replied in the negative, in his usual colourful manner. Prudently, the Chinese did not retaliate, resulting in Manila rescinding their harsh words. According to one report, soon after the outburst from the Philippines' leadership, Duterte 'reverted to form. He barred Philippine government officials from publicly commenting on the South China Sea dispute…. Nevertheless, the episode put a spotlight on the frustration among the most China-friendly Philippine leader.'[55]

Connected with its ties to China is the Philippines' relationship with the United States, its long-time ally. Ever since Duterte became president, he has been most critical of the United States, even chastising its leaders, both Obama and Trump. On his first trip to Beijing in 2016, he announced that he would not be going to America any more, due to the criticism he had received from Washington as a result of his war against drugs, which was linked to extrajudicial killings, and that it was time to say goodbye to the United States, which was received with delight and cheers amongst his hosts.[56] Since February 2020, Manila had been threatening to terminate its Visiting Forces Agreement (VFA) with the US military. The VFA essentially spells out the legality of American military forces stationed and operating in the Philippines. However, in July 2021, in conjunction with US Defence Secretary Lloyd Austin's visit to Manila, Duterte announced that the Philippines will continue the VFA, thereby ending months of tense relations between Manila and Washington. In retrospect, it was possible that Duterte had no intention of terminating the agreement with the United States, but rather was using such threats, in order to see whether China would make good its promise of enormous investments into the country. In addition, Manila was probably watching whether China would be less aggressive in the South China Sea. According to a scholar based in Washington, 'Had China delivered more on its promises of infrastructure and investment, it could have given Duterte a more solid ground and a solid push to stay adamant on the VFA.'[57]

Given the rise of China, many were expecting Manila to use its close ties with the United States, as leverage, although this proved not to be the case. The Philippines has actually been vacillating between Beijing and Washington, with a seeming lack of direction. Whether this is deliberate on the part of President Duterte, only time will tell.

It is clear that the Chinese will do what it takes to exert control when it comes to real estate. In relation to the Philippines, Beijing has used economic leverage to its advantage. It will continue to use all the advantages it has over other states to secure its interests. It decided not to use force but rather offer a more 'beneficial' route to the Philippines. However, while President Xi has achieved his objective, his Philippine counterpart has received severe criticism from some quarters domestically and has been accused of selling the country out. However, given the unpredictable nature and the often-impetuous manner of President Duterte, Beijing is probably as perplexed as others on how to deal with him. It would appear that as long as Duterte remains as president of the Philippines, bilateral ties between Manila and Beijing will continue to experience bouts of ups and downs.

Indonesia: Being Pragmatic

Indonesia is often regarded as the *primus inter pares* of Southeast Asia. This is due to geographical factors—its territorial vastness and dense population—and to the regional and even global role that Jakarta has played and continues to play. Its leading role in the non-aligned movement was confirmed by its hosting of the inaugural meeting in Bandung in 1955. This eponymous conference, which saw the assembly of a who's who of the developing world including host Sukarno, India's Nehru, Egypt's Nasser, Ghana's Nkrumah, Yugoslavia's Tito and Chinese Premier Zhou Enlai, is etched in our history books. Indonesia's current position is also significant in that it sees itself as pursuing an independent foreign policy. Jakarta has made this one of its major pillars and tries to pursue it vigorously, although not necessarily successfully.

Like some of its regional neighbours, Indonesia can also boast past glories, such as the Majapahit and Srivijaya empires which had considerable influence. More recent history, such as its war of liberation against the colonial Dutch which led to freedom in August 1945, gave the country an early start in becoming an independent nation. What followed, however, were tumultuous times, culminating in the abortive coup by the communists, who were seen to be supported by Beijing. Such accusations led Jakarta to suspend its diplomatic ties with the PRC in 1967, only for them to be restored 20 years later in 1990.[58] Given the presence of ethnic Chinese, suspicions towards China have remained with periodic anti-Chinese riots taking place, such as in 1998.

Primarily due to economic imperatives Jakarta pursues Chinese investors for its own economic benefit. The notion of the China threat, which was previously a consistent feature in Indonesian thinking, has been superseded by commercial reality. This does not mean that the ethnic factor has altogether disappeared. It is more a case of being placed on the back burner while the country pursues a much more pragmatic approach in its relationship with Beijing.

Like some other Southeast Asian countries, Indonesia has a direct territorial dispute with the Chinese—the Natuna Islands, located at the southern tip of the South China Sea and which many regarded as being outside those group of islands. Being a claimant, Jakarta could well be dragged into a conflict over the islands. Like other claimants, Indonesia has been at the receiving end of Chinese violations of its territories, with the former issuing formal protests to the Chinese ambassador in Jakarta. In one instance, in September 2020, the Chinese Coast Guard (CCG) cutter 5204 entered Indonesia's EEZ, with the latter issuing a protest note to Xiao Qian, the Chinese ambassador. While China recognises Indonesian sovereignty over its northernmost Natuna archipelago, it has always refused to provide the exact coordinates of the nine-dash line, a broad tongue-shaped swathe of the South China Sea extending into the North Natuna Sea.[59] In an earlier incident, in January 2020, Chinese vessels entered 100 kilometres inside Indonesian waters in a large-scale intrusion which resulted in the Indonesian Air Force deploying its F-16 jets from Pekanbaru, southern Sumatra, as well as the Navy sending eight vessels to the area.[60]

Despite such territorial disputes, more often than not economic reality plays a larger consideration in policy decision-making. Jakarta continues to benefit from trade ties, making China its largest trading partner and also participating in the latter's Belt and Road Initiative, such as its proposal for the Lambakan Dam in East Kalimantan with Chinese financing. It was reported that during a phone conversation with his counterpart, Indonesian President Jokowi referred to China as a 'good friend and brother'.⁶¹ Economic factors aside, China's pandemic diplomacy towards Indonesia—mainly by providing the Sinovac vaccine, as well as equipment to assist the Indonesian health authorities in their efforts to manage the pandemic—has indeed helped to improve ties, amidst conflicting territorial issues.

Singapore: Deriving Benefits from All Sides

Given Singapore's ethnic Chinese majority it has, perhaps in a humorous way, long been regarded as a Chinese outpost. However, it has hitched its wagon to the American star as a guarantee of continued peace and prosperity. This has resulted in the island city state hosting the permanent and rotational presence of US military assets at the Paya Lebar air and Sembawang naval bases.

Singapore has tended towards pragmatism when it comes to exercising its strategic interests, whether driven by economic or political imperatives. Singapore was one of the first countries to invest in China. After extensive discussions, the China–Singapore Suzhou Industrial Park was launched in February 1994. This was based on the model that Singapore would help the Chinese build an industrial park and eventually train them to manage the project. However, due to rival commercial groups within China and a lack of transparency and proper management and business procedures, the project became controversial and resulted in Singapore becoming more cautious in its business with China. This was one of the earliest projects undertaken by a foreign country in China and the absence of proper legal and business infrastructures proved to be insurmountable obstacles. Such dealings have improved vastly since then.

In strategic terms, Singapore knows where its interests lie. However, it is pragmatic enough to recognise the futility of regarding China with suspicion, at least openly, and instead has decided to engage Beijing in a multidimensional fashion, including in joint military exercises. In May 2019 the countries' defence ministers met in Singapore and agreed to a 'substantial programme' to deepen bilateral military ties, including holding a second bilateral naval drill in 2020.⁶² According to the Singapore Ministry of Defence, the increase in cooperation will include 'the establishment of frequent high-level dialogues, new arrangements for Services-to-Services cooperation, academic and think tank exchanges, and an increase in the scale of existing bilateral exercises'.⁶³ Such a marked enhancement of their 2008 defence cooperation agreement is significant because Singapore provides military facilities to the United States and, under the 1975 Project Starlight,[64] has a defence arrangement with Taiwan with Taipei providing facilities for the Singapore Defence Force. This does not mean that Beijing has not exerted pressure on Singapore to relinquish its military ties with Taiwan. On the contrary, it has consistently demanded Singapore respect its One-China policy. For example, in November 2016 Beijing insisted that Singapore end military ties with Taiwan after nine armoured troop carriers were intercepted in Hong Kong for not having an import licence. They had been used in a military exercise in Taiwan.[65] Interestingly, according to the head of Singaporean think tank the Singapore Institute of International Affairs, this matter should not be seen as a zero-sum game: 'It's not something that, to be my friend, you must be the enemy of other countries.'[66] Singapore has managed to maintain a close relationship with China and yet has also exercised a degree of independence. Whether this is primarily due to Singapore's own strength or Beijing preferring not to damage ties with this important state is debatable. Nonetheless, it is a tribute to Singapore's diplomatic dexterity that it has managed to benefit from its ties with both mainland China and Taiwan.

To some extent, Singapore is caught between the United States and China. While it knows that the island has to maintain cordial ties with Beijing, its strategic partnership with the United States has placed Singapore in the middle between these two rival powers. As prudence has it, Singapore is increasingly seen as more neutral in what appears to be a deterioration in US–China ties, with no significant improvement with Trump's successor at the White House, despite President Biden's stress on forming an overall 'constructive relationship' with China. Singapore Premier Lee Hsien Loong has warned the United States and China to de-escalate tensions, saying both powers presumed incorrectly they would win in any conflict. He said, 'The reality is, neither side can put the other one down', and 'that is a possible misunderstanding on both sides'. He went on to state that the United States is not in terminal decline, as some in Beijing believe, but equally 'China is not going to disappear. This is not the Soviet Union.'[67]

This more neutral position taken by Singapore was recognised by the Chinese as expressed in a news piece from the CCP-based *Global Times*, stating that Singapore is moving a little closer to a neutral position between China and the United States.[68] Following from this, it could be argued that despite Singapore's penchant for US security protection, the reality of growing Chinese power seems to influence the Lion City to tilt towards a much more central position, vis-à-vis, a tense Washington–Beijing relationship.

Malaysia: Economic Imperatives over Security Concerns

The emergency period ended in Malaya in 1960 when the communist uprising, which started in 1948, was successfully contained by a combination of British, Commonwealth and Malayan military forces. The defeated communists were not entirely eliminated and their struggle against the state continued until 1989 when a peace agreement was signed with the governments of Malaysia and Thailand.[69] Prevalent throughout this insurgency was the role of China, which supported the communists who were predominantly ethnic Chinese. This had been the main factor shaping the threat perception of Malaysian leaders for decades and was further influenced by the presence of a large minority of ethnic Chinese whose loyalty had long remained suspect. The fear was that this local population was a potential fifth column threatening the country.

When China began to open up in the 1980s, suspicions remained and did so until the mid-2000s when China's own economic miracle began to be felt globally. Malaysian concerns then began to shift from security to economic and commercial considerations, and despite criticism of China's pricing and hints of corruption, the leadership cannot now afford to push the Chinese away.

Even Malaysia's interests in the South China Sea have been somewhat compromised to avoid conflict with its giant neighbour, and there appears to be a tacit *modus vivendi* between the two countries over this area. Both countries have even agreed to set up a joint consultation mechanism for this disputed area. According to Chinese State Councillor Wang Yi, the establishment of this mechanism is 'for maritime issues, a new platform for dialogue and cooperation for both sides'.[70] According to an official Malaysian report, the annual report of the National Audit Department, Chinese coastguard and navy ships had intruded into Malaysian waters in the South China Sea some 89 times between 2016 and 2019 and often remained in the area even after being turned away by the Malaysian navy. The report also stated that, in response, Malaysia had sent six diplomatic protests to China over such encroachments.[71] It was also reported that, in 2020, a Chinese research ship spent a month surveying in Malaysia's exclusive economic zone, amid a standoff with a Malaysian oil exploration vessel near the disputed waters.[72]

Malaysia has been less vocal than others in its criticism of China's frequent infringements of its EEZ or territorial waters, especially by China's large fishing vessels. In one instance, Malaysia's Defence Minister Mohamad Sabu even said that such violations had 'not done anything that caused us trouble, so far'.[73] Surely such statements reflect a case of 'missing the point', since any such violations of an area that a country claims must be defended, even if only diplomatically. The very fact that Chinese vessels, military or otherwise, encroach into Malaysia's zones and seas is tantamount to challenging the country's sovereignty. Clearly Kuala Lumpur prefers to put aside its security interests for the sake of a business-friendly China. Such a position benefits Malaysia and its dealings with China seem to be pragmatic; to act otherwise could jeopardise the former's economic imperatives which have been accorded paramount importance. Kuala Lumpur's stance is justified by wider economic and commercial interests. Malaysia continues to receive huge Chinese investments. For example, in June 2021, the Malaysian Prime Minister Tan Sri Muhyiddin Yassin announced that a top solar tech Chinese corporation, Risen Energy Company Limited, will be investing some RM42.2 billion in Malaysia, over a five-year period, which is expected to generate 3000 jobs.[74]

However, this does not mean that Malaysia will not, when it suits its own interests, mainly the result of domestic imperatives, would voice its position. For instance, in December 2019, its foreign minister described China's claims over the entire South China Sea as 'ridiculous'.[75] Whether such a retort was influenced by the growing anger among the Muslim majority in the country over the Chinese alleged repression of the Uyghurs or the growing racial polarisation within Malaysia is debatable. However, an incident occurred on 31 May 2021, which was probably the most serious violation of Malaysia's air space to date to have been made public but, at the same time, does illustrate Malaysia's unwillingness to 'go all the way', in order to protect its territorial integrity. Due to the significance of this incident, it is worth looking into this episode further. Nonetheless, such a sudden rather uncharacteristic official remark does illustrate that Kuala Lumpur's behaviour could at times be dictated by various factors beyond economics.

Chinese Violation of Malaysian Air Space
Rather surprisingly, on 1 June 2021, the public relations division of the Royal Malaysian Air Force (RMAF) released a press statement indicating that 16 aircraft belonging to the People's Liberation Army—Navy (PLAN)

Air Force had entered the air space of the Malaysian Maritime Zone (ZMM), Kota Kinabalu, heading towards the country's national air space, the previous day, on 31 May. Their flights were detected by the RMAF Air Defence radar from the Air Defence centre (CRC 2) in Sarawak, East Malaysia. The Chinese aircraft were flying in tactical formation in trail 60 nautical miles from each other. At one stage, they were flying towards the air space of Beting Patinggi Ali or Luconia Shoals, located in the disputed South China Sea, which is claimed by Malaysia. The press statement further revealed that when the Chinese aircraft were located some 60 nautical miles from Sarawak's coastline, thereby threatening the country's sovereignty, and after repeated warnings from the Air Defence Centre were ignored by the Chinese, the RMAF deployed its Hawk 208s from 6 Squadron out of Labuan Air base, for the purpose of visual identification. It was revealed, with pictures, that the aircraft were Ilyushin Il-76 and Xian Y-20 types, mainly for strategic transport as well as other roles, such as maritime surveillance. The Chinese aircraft subsequently left the area. The statement, which was accompanied by a map showing the flight path of the PLAN aircraft, also stated that, through the Ministry of Defence, the Foreign Affairs Ministry was informed of this incident.

It is worth noting that such a detailed account was unprecedented. There had been previous reporting, but it never took the form of a statement released by the Air Force. A number of observations could be made here. Firstly, it was interesting that the RMAF issued the press release and not the Ministry of Defence, which would reflect a much-united position, including involving the political masters at the top. Did RMAF consult the headquarters of the Malaysian Armed Forces and the defence minister before releasing the statement? If so, did they consult other agencies such as the National Security Council and Ministry of Foreign Affairs or even the Prime Minister's Office? Could this be a manifestation of the frustrations of the armed services with the government's lackadaisical attitude to previous cases of Chinese violations of the country's territorial integrity as well as to illustrate the critical role of the armed forces towards national defence? It is also interesting to speculate what would the RMAF do if the Chinese aircraft continued to ignore warnings and entered the country's national air space. Would Malaysia up the ante, by deploying fighter jets, such as the Sukhoi Su-30MKM or the F/A-18 Hornets, to warn and possibly to intercept? It would be interesting to know the rules of engagement as well as any contingency plans of the Malaysian armed forces in the event of such a case.

While we could speculate on the reasons behind the RMAF's move, the subsequent turn of events does show that the Malaysian government is unwilling to take the Chinese to task. Immediately that evening following the press release, the Malaysian Minister of Foreign Affairs Datuk Seri Hishammuddin Hussein issued a statement to say that his ministry would issue a diplomatic note to protest against the intrusion of Chinese air force aircraft into Malaysian airspace to the government of China, as well as to summon the Chinese ambassador to Malaysia to provide an explanation regarding this breach. The minister also said that 'Malaysia's stand is clear—having friendly diplomatic relations with any countries does not mean that we will compromise our national security. Malaysia remains steadfast in defending our dignity and sovereignty.'[76]

The Chinese responded through Wang Wenbin, the spokesperson of the Ministry of Foreign Affairs, that the PLAN held a routine training operation in southern Nansha in the South China Sea and did not target any country and that the air force strictly abided by international law and did not enter the territorial airspace of other countries. It was also surprising that Wang mentioned that China has communicated with Malaysia over the matter.[77] Echoing this official stand, a Chinese military expert, Song Zhongping, said that PLA's strategic transport aircraft need to make long-distance flights to carry out their duties. To him, the South China Sea is a region where strategic transport aircraft need to cover both military airlift and humanitarian aid tasks, so it is normal for them to hold routine exercises there.[78] It was also mentioned by the Chinese official-backed *Global Times*, a news daily, under the auspices of the CCP's flagship, *People's Daily* newspaper, that these strategic cargo planes have been playing a key role in fighting the COVID-19 pandemic, and the PLA's Y-20 airlifts were dispatched to deliver vaccines and other medical supplies to several countries, including those in the South China Sea region.[79] The Chinese Embassy in Kuala Lumpur, apart from reiterating the official position, also added that 'China and Malaysia are friendly neighbors, and China is willing to continue bilateral friendly consultations with Malaysia to jointly maintain regional peace and stability'.[80] Notwithstanding such official statements, it is expected that Chinese vessels as well as aircraft will continue to violate the country's territorial integrity, as a way either to reinforce its own claims or to 'test' Kuala Lumpur's response.

From these Chinese official statements, they were in effect saying that the Malaysian Air Force made a false allegation, despite the RMAF providing visual proof of the violation. Although, technically, even based on the

RMAF press release, the Chinese aircraft did not actually violate the Malaysian national airspace, but were only flying close to the area. On the issue of flying over the disputed territory, as far as the Chinese were concerned, how could they have violated their 'own airspace' for the whole South China Sea belongs to them.

It remains unknown whether the Chinese ambassador was actually summoned to the Ministry of Foreign Affairs. If the meeting did take place, who from the Ministry of Foreign Affairs received the Chinese ambassador? In diplomatic action, the sending of a junior official to meet the ambassador would send a stern signal of the relegation of China in the eyes of Malaysia. This is most unlikely. In any event, nothing was mentioned by the Malaysian authorities after the release of the Chinese statement above, which seemed to suggest that either Kuala Lumpur had accepted the Chinese position or it decided that the matter should rest and not take the matter any further. Either way, the Malaysian government did not come out of this episode well.

No matter, the fact that the episode did not garner a satisfactory outcome does illustrate how far Malaysia was willing to go when dealing with China. Whether Malaysia feels intimidated by China is open to debate, but Kuala Lumpur probably decided that, on balance, and taking its economic and commercial interests into consideration, it would not jeopardise its good ties with China over such incident. It also suggests that Malaysia had admitted that being a disputed area, China, as much as Malaysia, can claim rights over the area. So, technically, Malaysia has probably conceded that the area is disputed and that it may not be willing to sacrifice its ties with China over a piece of real estate, contrary to public statements. Nonetheless, it would have given the Chinese the impression that Malaysia may not be willing to resort to the use of force, or even to the threat of the use of force, to assert its sovereignty over the disputed South China Sea, or at least against the Chinese. This seems to be the case, as we have seen continued infringements of the country's waters, by Chinese vessels. Clearly Malaysia places economic relations above its security interests. As stated earlier, it remains debatable whether it was a mere coincidence that the announcement by the Malaysian prime minister of an RM42.2 billion investment by the Chinese in Malaysia came less than a month after this incident.

Going Beyond East Asia

We have seen how a number of Asian countries perceive China, but we need also to look at powers that are considered rivals to China, namely the United States, Russia and India. The United States now faces its greatest challenge—the possibility that China could overtake it—and it is perhaps no surprise that the publication of Graham Allison's *Destined for War*[81] has stirred up such a debate among academics and policy makers. This well-known Harvard professor posits the argument that the United States and China are moving towards what he calls the 'Thucydides trap'—or the inevitable road to conflict. The phrase comes from ancient Greece in which Athens was a maritime power and Sparta had strength in land forces. These rival powers clashed in the Peloponnesian War which took place between 431 and 404 BCE. Will the intense rivalry between the United States and China also end in a major confrontation?

The second half of the twentieth century was dominated by US–Soviet rivalry, and there is little doubt that today and for the foreseeable future the world will be mesmerised by the competition between America and China. This has manifested itself in several forms, most openly through trade rivalry. The trade war which President Trump started in 2019 is symptomatic of the intensity of the struggle between these two giants. Given the strong narrative being pushed by the West, the rivalry is often portrayed in Manichean terms—a fight between the good Americans and the bad Chinese. It is no surprise that part of this, though not universally accepted in the West, is the view that whatever China does is bad. Conversely, what the West does is usually good, and even if it is negative, its intentions are good.

It is safe to assume that these two powers see each other as threats to their continued prosperity and peace. This perception goes beyond ideology and involves a whole array of factors, from military and commercial concerns to trying to win allies globally. The situation is more urgent from Washington's standpoint because China is still rising; there are some who believe that the United States is a declining power.

Does China really pose a threat to the interests of the United States? If the primary interest of the United States is to maintain its superiority over others, and in this case China, then the answer has to be no because while the Chinese are gaining power, they are still far behind the Americans. This is not only in the military sphere but also economically and in terms of political influence. There is no doubt that China is expanding its military and its economy is second only to the United States and that it is already a global powerhouse. Its political influence will continue to grow as its economic development takes root worldwide. However, these developments are taking place not in isolation, as the United States is still a superpower and there are no signs that it will withdraw or reduce its activities, military or economic. The possibility that the United States will withdraw into an isolationist shell, as it did after the Great War, is zero, as its interests are far too global. And after all, Trump's mantra, 'Make America great again', had struck a chord with many citizens and illustrated that the United States is not about to withdraw from its top position. It could be argued that the election of President Trump and the anti-establishment trends sweeping the Western world suggests that voters feel the United States has given up too much at its own expense.

Furthermore, various pressure groups in America are using the China threat as justification for further expansion or at least the maintenance of its apex position. Beijing is now the new bogeyman for Washington.

After the roller-coaster presidency of Trump, many expected ties between the United States and China to improve. However, with Biden in the White House, matters appear to have taken a turn for the worst. This is predicated on the firm belief that the Chinese will be competing with the Americans and that the former aspire to dominate the world. According to a leader article in the *Economist*, there is now a new China doctrine coming out from the Biden administration. It argues that they have based 'their doctrine on the belief that China is "less interested in coexistence and more interested in dominance". The Task of American policy is to blunt Chinese ambitions. America will work with China in areas of common interests, like climate change, but counter its ambitions elsewhere.'[82] Whether this is rhetoric on the part of the Biden administration so as not to appear weak—especially when compared to the gung-ho image of his predecessor, Trump—only time will tell. This new doctrine is a clear indication of the United States' recognition that its top global position is being challenged, and if it does not take measures to apply the brakes on China, it will indeed wake up one day and find itself left behind. This is indeed a 'wake-up call' for the Americans.

Will the United States and China go to war in the future? No one can answer that question with any certainty, just as the leaders, who put their signatures to the Treaty of Versailles in 1919, could not foresee that, even before the ink was dry, the seeds of the next global conflict had been sown. The punitive treaty provisions of 1919 paralysed Germany and paved the way for the rise of fascism, which rode on the hatred of World War I victors. However, like all governments, the defence of the homeland is a necessity, and to have a credible military is a necessary evil. An arms race, therefore, however asymmetrical, will ensue between the United States and China. This will involve the other spheres of power. However, it is also clear that while both countries are fully aware of the direct competition as well as strategic rivalry that exists between them, both are prudent enough to recognise that war must be averted at all costs. Interestingly, despite its new doctrine targeted against China, the Biden administration is examining the possibility of establishing a hotline that would directly link the two leaders, along the lines of the US–Soviet hotline during the Cold War. According to a news report, 'the Biden administration wants to develop a rapid communication tool that could be folded into a broader effort to reduce the risk of conflict between the US and China.'[83] Even though it is still early days, as this idea has not been officially conveyed to the Chinese, such a notion, which actually can be traced back to the Obama presidency, does illustrate the critical importance of the opening of a communication channel between these two rival powers. It is indeed a recognition on the part of Washington of the 'coming of age' of the Chinese and placing them at the same level as the United States. In addition, it shows that the Americans are sufficiently worried that the Chinese are fast moving up the ladder and have now become a global player, alongside the once only superpower.

Then there is Russia. Although power rivals historically, there is today some kind of tacit understanding between Russia and China—they have put aside their differences for a common enemy in the United States. This does not eliminate all the negative perceptions that one might have of the other. Territorial disputes and conflicting interests will ensure that, beneath the present veneer of cordial ties, underlying suspicions remain. However, these once comrades in arms are unlikely to turn back the clock and revert to a more hostile bilateral relationship. Currently both countries' leaders are pragmatic enough to ensure this more cordial stance prevails, at least for the foreseeable future. The regular joint military exercises between these once-arch enemies, which started in 2005, illustrate the changing balance of power on the present world stage and the convergence of security interests of these countries. The latest China–Russia military exercise took place in August 2021, involving some 10,000 troops from both sides, in a combined tactics training exercise in the former's inland Ningxia Hui autonomous region. It also involved the establishment of a command centre as well as training to improve joint reconnaissance, early warnings, electronic and information attacks and joint strikes.[84] According to a Russian-based military specialist, the exercise is 'sending a powerful signal to the US about their ability and willingness to operate together, which serves as a deterrent'.[85] To a retired Chinese colonel, Yue Gang, 'China and Russia have to stick together when facing the United States. We are not allies but as good as allies with our collective capabilities.'[86] Following on from the joint exercises, which appear to be growing larger and larger, the United States could be forced to consider a future scenario of facing two powerful military forces, with the possibility even of a two-front conflict.

The final power that needs to be examined is India. Does this second most populous country in the world view its giant neighbour as a threat? The answer is yes. The two countries fought a border war in the early 1960s and are rivals economically, and China supports India's arch-enemy, Pakistan. The power rivalry between them is strong enough to have prompted India to initiate its own version of the BRI. The concept remains nebulous, but the fact that the Indian leadership has articulated its desire for its own grand strategy speaks volumes about this sense of competition and the need for India not to fall behind. India harbours its own great power ambitions and believes it should be a permanent member of the UN Security Council. Such a mentality will inevitably lead to a clash with the Chinese and the power rivalry between these two countries will only intensify. Unresolved territorial disputes between China and India could well lead to a major conflict. The border skirmishes in 2020 near the disputed region of Ladakh, which saw troops from both sides engaged in aggressive melee, in one instance, involving clubs, stones and fists, resulting in casualties, including 20 Indian troops dead, are constant reminders of the potential for confrontation between these two giant neighbours. While talks between both sides have been ongoing, the ties between China and India will remain tense, as the border areas are heavily militarised.

THE CHINA THREAT: AN OVERALL ASSESSMENT

It is not the intention of this study to examine comprehensively the perceptions of most countries and powers towards China. The situation today is markedly different from the Cold War period when the line between the two opposing camps was clearly drawn. Alliances and security arrangements were formed primarily to contain, combat and counter the might of the other, so much so that both sides were locked in confrontation. There were two large military alliances, NATO and the Warsaw Pact, which faced each other with conventional and nuclear forces along the thin red line that separated the West from the East. The threat facing each side was clear and unambiguous.

The situation involving China is fundamentally different. Although ideologically China and the Western powers are diametrically opposed, pragmatism prevails. One could argue that no such dividing line exists between China and the rest of the world. This makes a big difference in alleviating and mitigating any threat perception that exists. It could be further argued that this situation is much more benign, although there will always be some who would like to see the opposite happening. This might explain why there is a strong and often unfair narrative against China. This does not suggest that China should not be above criticism.

The above narrative of the threat perception of some countries towards China is primarily to show that despite strong historical animosity, most countries are now adopting a more pragmatic approach; history has given way to economic and commercial considerations. This pragmatism has also been driven by a notion of fatalistic acceptance—countries have little choice when their economic growth is dependent on continued healthy ties with their giant neighbour. This is compounded by the situation in the West, where economies are under strain and threatened by economic stagnation. We have seen that Japan and others are investing in the region. However, unlike Japan or for that matter Western powers, China is often viewed with jaundiced eyes, even among states that appear to enjoy cordial ties with Beijing. There is a prevailing view that states cannot be certain how China will behave when it reaches its apex. Given this uncertainty, most countries have concluded that it is better to be pragmatic and not view China as a threat because this could turn out to be a self-fulfilling prophecy. If there are any lessons to be learnt from the Cold War, states should not allow themselves to be caught up as part of the great power rivalry. If they do, they risk being trampled on. On the whole, due to practical considerations, most if not all states view China optimistically, even if that view is tempered with a large dose of caution.

Notes

1. It is no surprise to hear, on an almost comical level, the emotions expressed by both sides as to what belongs to them. Perhaps unfairly many Chinese see what Japan claims to be part of their cultural life to originate from China, including the sakura flower—which has been associated with the land of the rising sun.
2. Ever since the Japanese invasion of Manchuria in 1931 which was essentially to gain control over its vast resources, Japan had been expanding its military presence on the mainland. The Marco Polo Bridge incident occurred when there was a standoff between Chinese and Japanese forces, resulting in the exchange of fire from other sides, of which the cause was unknown. Nonetheless, it was alleged that during the standoff on 8 July 1937, the Chinese side fired on the Japanese, hence triggering the much-needed justification for Japan to attack China, on a much bigger scale. See Xiaobing Li, *China at War: An Encyclopedia* (Santa Barbara, California: ABC—CL10. 2012).
3. Take moto, Tadao and Ohara Yasuo, *The Alleged 'Nanking Massacre': Japan's Rebuttal of China's Forged Claims* (Tokyo: Meisei-sha, Inc, 2000).
4. Peter Duus, Ramon H. Myers, and Mark R. Peattie (eds.), *The Japanese Informal Empire in China, 1895–1937* (Princeton, New Jersey: Princeton University Press, 1989), p. xiv.
5. See Jonathan Clements, *Admiral Togo: The Nelson of the East* (London: Haus Publishing, 2010).
6. In the case of Japan, the establishment has had a powerful influence on the way Japan has behaved. The bureaucracy is the bulwark of Japan and is highly homogenous. However, whether there will be a backlash against this powerful group—as we have seen in a few Western countries, where anti-establishment votes have resulted in almost chaotic developments, is debatable.
7. Due to the time difference, Japanese troops landed in parts of Malaya (Kota Bharu) and the Siam Kingdom (Patani and Singora) a few hours before the first Zero fighters began their assault on Pearl Harbour across the international dateline.
8. This has been the subject of much public discussion, both academic and non-academic. Interestingly, a few films have been made recently focusing on the role of the emperor including Alexander Sokurov's *The Sun* (2005), Masato Harada's *Emperor in August* (2015) and Hollywood's *Emperor*, directed by Peter Webber (2012).
9. Quoted in *The Japan Times*, 14 August 2021, www.japantimes.co.jp
10. Ibid.

11. The Japanese established the puppet state of Manchukuo as a political entity in northeast China, with the last Chinese emperor, Puyi, at its helm. Although not recognised by the nationalist government, its existence provided evidence of Japan's imperial design over China. For an interesting work on Manchukuo, see Prasenjit Duara, *Sovereignty and Authenticity: Manchukuo and the East Asian Modern* (Maryland: Rowman & Littlefield Publishers, 2004).
12. For instance, in its 2000 edition, it made explicit how the Soviets would mount an invasion on the northern-most island of Hokkaido.
13. *Defense of Japan 2018* (Tokyo: Ministry of Defense, 2018), p. 28.
14. Ibid., p. 108.
15. Ibid., pp. 108–109.
16. Laura Zhou, 'Japan weighs in on South China Sea dispute, adding to pressure on Beijing', South China Morning Post, 21 January 2021, www.scmp.com.
17. 'US-Japan Joint Leaders' Statement: US-Japan Global Partnership for a New Era', 16 April 2021, The White House, www.whitehouse.gov
18. Ibid.
19. Cleo Paskal, 'Indo-Pacific strategies, perceptions and partnerships', Chatham House, 23 March 2021, www.chathamhouse.org
20. See J. Berkshire Miller, 'Japan is taking on China in Africa', *Foreign Policy*, 22 August 2019. foreignpolicy.com.
21. Panos Mourdoukoutas, 'Japan, not China, is the Biggest Investor in Southeast Asia's Infrastructure', *Forbes*, 26 June 2019. Forbes.com.
22. First signed in July 1961 when both Mao Zedong and North Korea's Great Leader Kim Il Sung were leading their respective countries.
23. Khang Vu, 'Why China and North Korea decided to renew a 60-year-old treaty', theinterpreter, 30 July 2021, www.lowyinstitute.org
24. Ibid.
25. Reported in Global Times, 26 May 2021, www.globaltimes.cn.
26. Ibid.
27. Wongi Choe, 'The Quest for Strategic Balance and South Korea's Indo-Pacific Conundrum', The Diplomat, 13 August 2021, thediplomat.com.
28. Ibid.
29. William Gallo, 'In South Korea, Antagonism Toward China Is Growing', Voice of America, 20 April 2021, www.voanews.com.
30. Ibid.
31. Ibid.
32. Chung Min Lee, 'South Korea Is Caught Between China and the United States', *Carnegie Endowment for International Peace*, 21 October 2020, carnegieendowment.org.
33. Ibid.

34. William Gallo, op. cit.
35. John Power, 'What does South Korea think of China's belt and road? It's complicated', *South China Morning Post*, 1 June 2019, www.scmp.com.
36. Quoted in Park Chan-kyong, 'China urges Koreas to get along, as North warns of "crisis" over US-South Korea military drills', *South China Morning Post*, 11 August 2021, www.scmp.com.
37. Reported in *The Korea Times*, 2021-01-26, m.koreatimes.co.kr.
38. Reported in *The Guardian*, 20 August 2021, www.theguardian.com.
39. 'Afghan abandonment a lesson for Taiwan's DPP: Global Times editorial', Global Times, 16 August 2021, www.globaltimes.com
40. Nectar Gan and Steve George, 'Chinese state media sets sights on Taiwan as US' Afghan retreat stokes nationalism', CNN, 18 August 2021, amp.cnn.com.
41. Global Times, 2021/8/17, www.globaltimes.cn.
42. Kathlene Baldanza, *Ming China and Vietnam: Negotiating Borders in Early Modern Asia* (Cambridge: Cambridge University Press, 2016), p. 13.
43. Valerie Hansen, *The Open Empire: A History of China to 1600* (New York: W.W. Norton and Company, 2000), p. 104.
44. Wang Zhenping, *Tang China in Multi-Polar Asia: A History of Diplomacy and War* (Honolulu: University of Hawai'i Press, 2013), pp. 120–126.
45. *South China Morning Post*, 12 July 2019, scmp.com.
46. 'Tensions rise in South China Sea as Vietnamese boats come under attack', *the Guardian*, 7 May 2014, amp.theguardian.com.
47. 'Viet Nam, China trade ties continue to develop', *Viet Nam News*, 25 April 2019, vietnamnews.vn.
48. Global Times, April 27, 2021, www.globaltimes.cn
49. Ibid.
50. Nguyen Khac Giang, 'Vietnam's tug of war with China over Laos', East Asia Forum, 12 May 2021, www.eastasiaforum.com.
51. *South China Morning Post*, 20 November 2018, amp.scmp.com.
52. Reported in *CNN*, 12 September 2019, amp.cnn.com.
53. *South China Morning Post*, 6 September 2019, scmp.com.
54. *South China Morning Post*, 23 July 2019, scmp.com.
55. 'Hot and Cold: The Philippines' Relations with China', Foreign Policy Research Institute, 7 July 2021, www.fpri.org.
56. 'Duterte in China: Xi lauds "milestone" Duterte visit', BBC News, 20 October 2016, bbc.com.
57. Quoted in Ralph Jennings, 'Why the Philippines Picked America over China', Voice of America, 5 August 2021, www.voanews.com.
58. For background to this often-difficult relationship, see Rizal Sukma, *Indonesia and China: The Politics of a Troubled Relationship* (London: Routledge, 1999); and Dewi Fortuna Anwar, 'Indonesia's Relations with

China and Japan: Images, Perception and Realities', *Contemporary Southeast Asia*, Vol.12, No.3 (December 1990), pp. 225–246.
59. John Mcbeth, 'China, Indonesia sea dispute hot and getting hotter', Asia Times, 15 September 2020, asiatimes.com.
60. Ibid.
61. Derek Grossman, 'Indonesia Is Quietly Warming Up to China', *Foreign Policy*, 7 June 2021, foreignpolicy.com. It must, however, be pointed out that the usage of the term 'brother' is commonly used by Asian leaders when referring to their Chinese counterpart. In one instance, the Malaysian foreign minister added the word 'big/elder brother', which was heavily criticised by several groups for appearing subservient to the Chinese. The minister explained that the term was used out of respect for his counterpart, who was much older than him. See, for example, 'Malaysia is independent, says Hishammuddin who called Chinese counterpart "elder brother"', Channel News Asia, 3 April 2021, www.channelnewsasia.com.
62. *South China Morning Post*, 30 May 2019, amp.scmp.com.
63. 'Singapore and China to Step Up Defence Cooperation through Enhanced Defence Interactions', MINDEF Singapore, 29 May 2019, mindef.gov.sg.
64. Starlight is a Singapore base camp located in southern Taiwan and used primarily to house Singaporean infantrymen for their training.
65. *South China Morning Post*, 6 October 2017, amp.scmp.com.
66. Quoted in *South China Morning Post*, 6 October 2017, amp.scmp.com.
67. Quoted in Philip Heijmans, 'Singapore's Lee Urges China, U.S. to Stem Deteriorating Ties', *Bloomberg*, 3 August 2021, www.bloomberg.com.
68. *Global Times*, 5 August 2021, www.globaltimes.cn.
69. The various elements of the military arm of the Communist Party of Malaya, as well as factions that were part of the larger conflict with Malaysia, were operating along the Malaysia–Thailand borders.
70. 'China, Malaysia to set up South China Sea dialogue mechanism', Reuters, 12 September 2019, www.reuters.com.
71. Reported in Reuters, 14 July 2020, www.reuters.com.
72. Ibid.
73. Reported in Reuters, 12 September 2019, www.reuters.com.
74. Reported in *Malay Mail*, 24 June 2021, www.malaymail.com.
75. 20 December 2019, https://www.nst.com.mynation.
76. Reported in *New Straits Times*, 1 June 2021, and *Malay Mail*, 1 June 2021.
77. *Global Times*, 2 June 2021, www.globaltimes.cn.
78. Ibid.
79. Ibid.
80. Ibid.
81. Graham Allison, *Destined for War: Can America and China escape Thucydides's Trap* (London: Scribe, 2018).

82. 'Biden's new China doctrine', 17 July 2021, *The Economist*, www.economist.com.
83. Kylie Atwood, 'Biden administration looks to set up "red phone" to China for emergency communications', CNN, 14 July 2021, amp.cnn.com.
84. *South China Morning Post*, 8 August 2021, www.scmp.com.
85. Quoted in ibid.
86. Quoted in *South China Morning Post*, 13 August 2021, www.scmp.com.

CHAPTER 6

Conclusion: Balancing Between Domestic and International Imperatives

The official flag of the Qing dynasty was a colourful dragon chasing a magical pearl. To the Chinese, the mythical dragon exercised strength but was also benign and intelligent. The pearl symbolises wisdom, prosperity and power. With such qualities, the dragon is diplomatically dexterous. It is because of these attributes that this book has identified China as engaging in dragon diplomacy. It has managed to harness its economic might to extend its influence globally. Its military power is increasing, but China is being prudent in its use. Although China often talks about resorting to force, it has exercised restraint because it is conscious of its image abroad. Besides, it is wise enough to know that resorting to force may not necessarily be the right route to take. As we have seen in many instances throughout history, using force is one thing, but to withdraw gracefully may be a different ball game altogether. Both superpowers during the Cold War had to 'cut and run' from their ill-conceived occupation and involvement in foreign territories—for instance, the United States from Vietnam and the Soviet Union in Afghanistan.

The Chinese leadership is painfully aware of how Western leaders and Western media jump at the sight of the People's Liberation Army assets being deployed aggressively. China's reluctance to intervene in the prolonged, chaotic protests in Hong Kong during the summer of 2019 was based on the leadership's belief that to do so would be to fall into a trap. The leadership in Beijing must be ever mindful of how former Premier Li Peng was dubbed the 'Butcher of Beijing' by the Western media for his use of the military to crush the Tiananmen demonstrators. No Chinese

© The Author(s), under exclusive license to Springer Nature Switzerland AG 2021
A. R. Baginda, *The Global Rise of China and Asia*, https://doi.org/10.1007/978-3-030-91806-4_6

leader would want to be remembered, at least from a Western perspective, as the 'Butcher of Hong Kong'. However, given the level of violence in Hong Kong, especially by the protesters, who have used Molotov cocktails and destroyed and vandalised properties, the use of force by the police may well be justified. When the Los Angeles riots occurred in 1992, both the National Guard and the US Army were deployed. In the case of Hong Kong, the authorities appear to be on the defensive as they have been severely criticised by the international media.

How can one draw any conclusions about China when the country is still developing? Assumption, speculation and conjecture abound about how China will progress in the foreseeable future, but this much we know: China is undeniably a great power—whether it has yet reached superpower status is disputed, but this book asserts that it is a superpower.

Like all great powers, we can at least project the path that it will take. As we have seen, President Xi did not mince his words about the country's aspirations in becoming a great power. The frequent history lessons set out in his speeches, albeit a highly selective choice, glorify its long civilisation. Although he never fails to mention the West's attempts to dominate the country, leading to its humiliation, the main thrust of these lessons is to instil sentiments of nationalism amongst China's 1.4 billion people. There is a sense that the Chinese leadership is out to encourage patriotism in its population, in the midst of the internationalisation of the country and its peoples—with the focus on China's glorious past and the richness of its culture and civilisation, propped up by its incredible modern-day achievements. After all, the huge investment in space exploration is nothing more than playing to a nation's insatiable appetite for glory and all the prestige that comes with it. Just imagine what such resources could have achieved if channelled into research on cancer and other diseases. As we have seen, China has sent its unmanned Mars rover *Zhurong* to the red planet and hopes to begin human exploration there in the 2030s. No doubt, such a Mars mission is part of China's quest for greatness in the eyes of its own population and the world at large. No longer is China in the global backwaters, but rather, as in its glorious past, is exactly where Chinese leaders want the country to be—at the centre of the world—*Zhongguo*.

Whether such enthusiasm is shared by the rest of the world is doubtful as it is unclear whether a future China will be a hegemon. If we are to look at the behaviour of the dominant superpower for more than half a century, the United States, as an indication of how a future superpower will behave, most will be pessimistic. The Taliban's swift advance to seize Kabul in August 2021, thereby gaining control of Afghanistan, in light of a precipitate withdrawal of American forces, was reminiscent of how the United States left Vietnam, after committing as many as half a million American troops on the ground. The graphic images of US helicopters hovering on top of the US Embassy in Kabul trying to pick up Americans fleeing the capital drew comparisons with what happened in Saigon in April 1975, when Vietcong forces were at the gates of the capital of South Vietnam. There is little doubt that while the Americans have brought progress to the world, it has equally, if not more so, caused death, destruction and chaos to many parts of the world. If China was to be a hegemon, it will be quite difficult to outdo the Americans. In other words, even if China ended up being a hegemonic power, with what the world has gone through in the twentieth and the early years of the twenty-first centuries, things can't get any worse.

The rise of China has challenged the global order, which, hitherto, has been dominated by the United States, especially after the end of the Cold War. Although Russia remains a rival power to the United States, the growing global strength of China has catapulted it to centre stage. China is now seen as a power that could strip the United States of its number one position.

Clearly the United States is not about to simply relinquish this position. American leaders, such as Trump and Biden, have given notice that the United States is not done yet. As we have seen, it would appear that Washington will continue to use the big stick approach towards China, in an attempt to exert its continued dominance in the international order. President Biden has gone on record to say that 'on my watch', China will not achieve its goal 'to become the leading country in the world, the wealthiest country in the world, and the most powerful country in the world'.[1] Biden has also expressed concerns over the ideological competition between democracy and authoritarianism, in which the latter is gaining ground. He seems to recognise this when he said, 'We're kind of at a place where the rest of the world is beginning to look at China', even arguing that the world was at an inflexion point in determining 'whether or not democracy can function in the twenty-first century'.[2] Such concerns expressed in Washington could well be welcomed in Beijing. After all, as we have seen, President Xi wants to make China a great nation, with all the trappings of power—including in the ideological arena, where the China model is gaining popularity at the expense of the democratic path, which has been experiencing a rough patch of late. The world has seen too many instances where the United States and Western countries have been pressing democracy on states that are ill-equipped in many ways to adopt an alien system and culture, ending in dismal failure. The chaotic pull-out from Afghanistan, leaving a half-baked system behind which easily collapsed, adds to the countless examples of the Western-based democracy experiment that have gone sour and, in some instances, horribly wrong.

It might be that allies of the United States, and those that harbour concerns about China, could also be urging this once sole superpower to provide some form of check and balance, or even a counter-weight, to China's power and influence. However, China is conscious that with its growing power and influence globally, through its economic, military and soft power, as an ascending power, it will have to manage its position carefully. We have seen the growing confidence on the part of China, with its 'China Dream' and the employment of soft power, in order to make the country much more acceptable by the rest of the world. As President Xi has said on several occasions, China wants to be liked and accepted and that its positive contributions to the world's prosperity and security are acknowledged. In this respect, it is quite impressive how the Chinese were able to turn around its position vis-à-vis the COVID-19 pandemic. At the initial stage of the pandemic, China was heavily criticised for its inertia in alerting the World Health Organisation (WHO), and as the original source of the virus, although this is highly contentious. However, a few years into the pandemic, not only was it able to overcome the 'guilt' image, but it has been providing massive assistance to countries needing protective gear as well as the made-in-China vaccines, Sinovac and Sinopharm. In this respect, Beijing was able to move its position from being the cause to becoming a saviour through what has been dubbed China's pandemic diplomacy. Such a turn of events could well be attributed to a much more sophisticated employment of its soft power, through its public diplomacy.

Today most countries are engaged in some way with China. Through its vast Belt and Road Initiative, its economic and commercial tentacles have spread across the world. While the need to exercise prudence is axiomatic, countries are preferring to dance rather than wrestle with the dragon. In a world where economic realities dictate policies, this is the best way to move forward. This does not mean that countries should blindly follow their economic instincts, but rather they should do so with their eyes open.

We have seen how China has exercised its influence, using its economic leverage to neutralise security issues, such as those in the South China Sea. This is the latent nature of Chinese power, and it will remain so for years to come. Whether this is the surreptitious and insidious objective of China's grand strategy is uncertain.

Apart from this external dimension, it is the domestic imperative that poses the greatest challenge to the Chinese leadership and to the country's future. Like the Chinese emperors, communist leaders are obsessed with internal matters. If there is one consistent theme that runs throughout Chinese history, it is the occurrence of rebellions, uprisings, dissident cabals and intrigues at the imperial court and beyond. For instance, the Taiping rebellion between 1850 and 1864 involved a challenge to the Qing dynasty by the Taiping Heavenly Kingdom, which resulted in a civil war that caused the death of around 20 million people. Even after the collapse of imperial China, many decades of tempestuous political and economic upheaval followed. During the 'warlord' period of the 1920s and 1930s, countless rival generals fought each other and changed sides while the population suffered from poverty and famine. According to one account, being poor and sick in 1928 was a death sentence, with medical care reserved for the rich and a few working people; there were 30,000 official hospital beds available for 400 million people.[3] Famine caused starvation and three million deaths. Nationalist rule only brought further deprivation.

The triumph of the communists in 1949 did not bring the much-desired peace but instead, mainly as a result of mismanagement, further chaos ensued, with mass famine and economic dislocation. It was only in the late 1970s that things began to improve, although economic success has brought its own set of challenges for the Chinese leadership.

Despite its impressive economic growth from the late 1970s, until reaching the top two position in the global economic food chain, the position of the Communist Party of China has remained strong, if not stronger. Through its leadership, the country has been able to bring about prosperity with stability, an achievement only very few countries can boast. The CCP has been able to balance the contradictions of an open economy with a closed political system. It has zero tolerance to any challenge or rival to its power, even at the level of individuals. This was probably what happened to Jack Ma, the founder of the multibillion tech company, Ali Baba. Apart from his enormous wealth, he was fast becoming a mega-superstar, within China and beyond. The fact that hundreds of millions of

Chinese use his applications in their daily lives meant that, for the first time perhaps, the population could be under the control of someone outside the powerful Communist Party. Jack Ma was becoming too powerful for the likes of the Chinese leadership. It did not help matters that he led an almost cult-superstar celebrity lifestyle, with a personality that was displaying elements of hubris. According to Song Qinghui, an economist, Jack Ma amassed far too much power; this is understood by everyone in China.[4] As a result, he had to be muted and put in his place. President Xi had already come down firmly on corrupt officials, and it would appear that he was also not comfortable with large corporations, and egocentric entrepreneurs, with great wealth. According to the *Wall Street Journal*, Xi 'has displayed a diminishing tolerance for big private businesses that have amassed capital and influence—and are perceived to have challenged both his rule and the stability craved by factions in the country's newly assertive Communist Party'.[5] It could be argued that President Xi decided that high-profile entrepreneurs, such as Jack Ma, could have a negative impact on the general population—on the upper and middle classes who aspire to move up the wealth ladder, while the masses are appalled by the kind of conspicuous consumption and wanton display of unimaginable wealth and power.

China is still grappling with the need to provide the most basic living standards to all its citizens. Its ever-growing population, now over 1.4 billion people, magnifies the gravity of the challenge. While Beijing or cosmopolitan Shanghai might seem affluent, travel a few miles outside these ultra-modern cities and witness the plight of the Chinese masses. Their condition remains the country's single biggest challenge.

There have been calls from various quarters, mainly the West, that China should seek a more democratic path, but the leadership is more concerned with the bread-and-butter issues of managing the country. India, the other highly populous nation, will not provide much comfort to the Chinese leadership. There, despite being the largest democratic country in the world, abject poverty and underdevelopment are ubiquitous. A compelling argument is that for the population at large it is the basic necessities of life that are a far more serious goal than being part of any political process. Democracy has certainly not solved the perennial issue of poverty, nor has it put an end to conflict.

The gap between the rich and the poor is so wide in China today that there seems little hope that it can be narrowed. The problem for China will always be numbers; to house, feed and clothe 1.4 billion people will remain a challenge of arguably insurmountable proportions. The government has instituted many reforms to tackle this challenge, including an excellent communication network and infrastructure which connects the disparate parts of China. It seems axiomatic that any Chinese government will need to do more to alleviate the plight of the masses. While peace has been achieved, wealth still seems to elude the average Chinese citizen.

Economics aside, there is the question of how one deals with dissenting views which will inevitably follow economic progress and higher levels of education. How does China deal with dissent or deal with a possible challenge against the polity? Given its authoritarian nature, China will resort to what it believes is the best method—control. One of the Chinese state's most serious challenges comes from its Muslim population. There are 20 million Muslims in the country, mainly in the Xinjiang region. Revelations about their persecution by the state, including the establishment of sites euphemistically referred to as education camps, have put the Chinese leadership in the spotlight. While individual Muslim countries and societies at large have protested vehemently at Myanmar's persecution of its own Muslim Rohingya population, including countries in ASEAN of which Myanmar is a member, their silence on the persecution of the Uyghurs is deafening. Malaysian Prime Minister Tun Dr Mahathir had once said that Muslim countries are silent about the persecution of Uyghurs because China is a powerful nation and so it is best not to antagonise the Chinese when they can provide economic benefits.[6]

The position taken by regional countries is symptomatic of the effects of China's power. One does not have to flex one's muscles when others recognise the power one can wield. The ancient strategic thinker, Sun Tzu, once noted, 'For to win one hundred victories in one hundred battles is not the acme of skill. To subdue the enemy without fighting is the acme of skill.'[7] This seems true of China.

The Chinese have remained dogmatic in their approach to dissent. Beijing must be all too aware of how opening up the country to dissenting views contributed to the collapse of the Soviet Union—15 of its republics became independent overnight. This possibility haunts the Chinese leadership. The problem is that Chinese leaders are not willing to give an inch on, for example, demands for more democratic decision-making, for they know that further demands will follow. This is fuelled by the pressure from the West for China to embark on a more democratic path and adds to the fear of the Chinese leadership that such demands are being encouraged and even financed by elements in the West. It may well be in the interest of all if the West were to lower the volume of its call for democracy in China. The louder those call the greater the pressure will be on the Chinese leadership, which could lead to a further tightening of its grip on society. Besides, the position of the CCP is unassailable and remains supreme in the country.

China has a good story to tell but is often not very good at telling it, although Beijing is placing much more emphasis on its public diplomacy. It would benefit from engaging the media when there is negative news, such as the treatment of the Uyghurs, rather than taking the easier route of resorting to censorship.[8]

The more one censors, the deeper the proponents of an issue dig in; it is better to deal with a problem and disprove negative claims. The suppression of dissenting views or groups is not sustainable in the long run. It is better to address grievances—to engage rather than suppress.

It is the domestic agenda that will be the ultimate determinant of how China progresses in the future. No matter how much pressure the international community applies, the Chinese leadership will follow its instincts in trying to balance internal and external strategies and goals.

However, as China becomes increasingly integrated into the international economic and political mainstream, it is the belief of this book that it will become benign power that contributes to international security and order, which would be, to use the words of English philosopher Jeremy Bentham, 'for the greater good'[9] of everyone, not just the Chinese.

Notes

1. Thomas Wright, 'Joe Biden worries that China might win', Brookings, 9 June 2021, brookings.edu.
2. Ibid.
3. Philip S. Jowett, *The Bitter Peace: Conflict in China 1928–37* (Gloucestershire: Amberley Publishing, 2017), p. 3.
4. Quoted in *Financial Times*, 15 April 2021, www.ft.com.
5. 'China's President Xi Jinping Personally Scuttled Jack Ma's Ant IPO', *The Wall Street Journal*, 12 November 2020, www.wsj.com.
6. *New Straits Times*, 28 September 2019, nst.com.my.
7. There are many works on the writings of Sun Tzu; see Stephen F. Kaufmann, *The Art of War: The Definitive Interpretation Sun Tzu's Classic Book of Strategy* (Tokyo: Tuttle Publishing, 1996).
8. There are exceptions of course. The Chinese ambassador to the United Kingdom, Liu Xiaoming, has been quite articulate and appeared frequently

in the British media. Though keeping to the 'party line', his eloquence is welcomed, whether one agrees or not with his comments. Not shying away from the media should be the norm rather than the exception for those representing the Chinese government.
9. See Charles Milner Atkinson, *Jeremy Bentham: His Life and Work* (London: Forgotten Books, 2018).

Select Bibliography

Allison, Graham, *Destined for War: Can America and China escape Thucydides's Trap* (London: Scribe, 2018)
Blasko, Dennis J., *The Chinese Army Today: Tradition and Transformation for the 21st Century* (Oxford: Routledge, 2012)
Bowei, Lu and Wang Guoping, *The Revolution of 1911: Turning Point in Modern Chinese History* (Beijing: Foreign Language Press, 1991)
Brautigam, Deborah, *The Dragon's Gift: The Real Story of China in Africa* (Oxford: Oxford University Press, 2009)
Brown, Kerry, *The World According to Xi* (London: I.B. Tauris, 2018)
Brown, Kerry, *CEO, China: The Rise of Xi Jinping* (London: Tauris, 2016)
Ch'en, Jerome, *Yuan Shih-K'ai* (Stanford: Stanford University Press, 1972)
Cheng, Pei-Kai and Michael Lestz (eds.), *The Search for Modern China: A Documentary Collection* (New York: W.W. Norton & Co., 1999)
Chesneaux, Jean, Marianne Bastid and Marie-Claire Bergere, *China from the Opium Wars to the 1911 Revolution* (New York: Random House, 1976)
Chinghua, Tang, *The Ruler's Guide: China's Greatest Emperor and his timeless secrets of success* (New York: Scribner, 2017)
Chow, Tse-tsung, *The May Fourth Movement: Intellectual Revolution in Modern China* (Cambridge, Massachusetts: Harvard University Press, 1960)
Cliff, Roger, *China's Military Power: Assessing current and future capabilities* (Cambridge: Cambridge University Press, 2015)
Dardess, John W., *Ming China 1368–1644: A Concise history of a resilient empire* (Lanham, Maryland: Rowman & Littlefield Publishers, Inc., 2012)
Dreyer, Edward L., *Zheng He: China and the Oceans in the Early Ming Dynasty, 1405–1433* (London: Pearson Longman, 2006)

Duiker, William J., *China and Vietnam: The Roots of Conflict* (Berkeley: University of California, 1986)
Durschmied, Erik, *The Military History of China: From 1218 to the Present Day* (London: Andre Deutsch, 2018)
Economy, Elizabeth C., *The Third Revolution: Xi Jinping and the New Chinese State* (Oxford: Oxford University Press, 2018)
Elleman, Bruce, *China's Naval Operations in the South China Sea: Evaluating Legal, Strategic and Military Factors* (Folkestone, Kent: Renaissance Books, 2018)
Esherick, Joseph W., *The Origins of the Boxer Uprising* (Berkeley: University of California Press, 1987)
Esherick, Joseph W., and C.X. George Wei (eds.), *China: How the Empire Fell* (London: Routledge, 2014)
Fairbank, John King and Merle Goldman, *China: A New History* (Cambridge, Mass., The Belknap Press, 2006)
Fravel, M. Taylor, *Active Defense: China's Military Strategy since 1949* (Princeton, New Jersey: Princeton University Press, 2019)
Fenby, Jonathan, *The Dragon Throne: China's Emperors, From the Qin to the Manchu* (London: Quercus Publishing, 2015)
Fishman, Ted C., *China Inc.: How the rise of the next Superpower challenges America and the World* (New York: Scribner, 2005)
Foot, Rosemary, *Rights Beyond Borders: The Global Community and the Struggle over Human Rights in China* (Oxford: Oxford University Press, 2000)
Frankopan, Peter, *The New Silk Roads: The Present and Future of the World* (London: Bloomsbury Publishing, 2018)
French, Howard W., *Everything Under the Heavens: How the Past Helps Shape China's Push for Global Pow*er (New York: Vintage Books, 2017)
Gittings, John, *The Changing Face of China: From Mao to Market* (Oxford: Oxford University Press, 2005)
Goncharov, Sergei N., John W. Lewis and Xue Litai, *Uncertain Partners: Stalin, Mao and the Korean War* (Stanford, CA: Stanford University Press, 1993)
Gries, Peter Hays, *China's New Nationalism: Pride, Politics and Diplomacy* (Berkeley: University of California Press, 2004)
Hayton, Bill, *The Invention of China* (New Haven: Yale University Press, 2020)
Hibbert, Eloise Talcott, *K'ang Hsi: Emperor of China* (London: Kegan Paul, Trench, Trubner and Co Ltd., 1940)
Ho, Alfred K., *China's Reforms and Reformers* (Westport, Connecticut: Praeger Press, 2004)
Holslag, Jonathan, *China's Coming War with Asia* (London: Polity Press, 2015)
Hu, Bo, *Chinese Maritime Power in the 21st Century: Strategic Planning, Policy and Predictions* (Oxford: Routledge, 2019)
Ji, You, *China's Military Transformation* (Cambridge: Polity Press, 2016)

Kaczmarski, Marcin, *Russia–China Relations in the Post-Crisis International Order* (London: Routledge, 2015)

Kroeber, Arthur R., *China's Economy: What Everyone Needs to Know* (Oxford: Oxford University Press, 2016)

Lai, Benjamin, *The Dragon's Teeth: The Chinese People's Liberation Army* (Hong Kong: Casemate Publishers, 2016)

Lai, Hongyi and Yiyi Lu (eds.), *China's Soft Power and International Relations* (London: Routledge, 2012)

Lampton, David M., *Following the Leader: Ruling China, From Deng Xiaoping to Xi Jinping* (Berkeley: University of California, 2014)

Lewis, Mark Edward, *China's Cosmopolitan Empire: The Tang Dynasty* (Cambridge, Massachusetts: The Belknap Press of Harvard University Press, 2009)

Li, Xiaobing, *China's Battle for Korea: The 1951 Spring Offensive* (Bloomington, Indianapolis: Indiana University Press, 2014)

Lovell, Julia, *The Great Wall: China Against the World, 1000 BC–AD 2000* (London: Atlantic Books, 2006)

Lukin, Alexander, *China and Russia: The New Rapprochement* (Cambridge: Polity Press, 2018)

McReynolds, J. (ed.), *China's Evolving Military Strategy* (Washington, D.C.: The Jamestown Foundation, 2017)

Menges, Constantine, *China: The Gathering Threat* (Nashville, Tennessee: Nelson Current Books, 2005)

Meisner, Maurice, *Mao's China: A History of the People's Republic* (New York: The Free Press, 1977)

Miller, Tom, *China's Asian Dream* (London: Zed Books, 2017)

Mote, F.W., *Imperial China, 900–1800* (Cambridge, Massachusetts, Harvard University Press, 1999)

Navarro, Peter, *The Coming China Wars: Where they will be fought and how they can be won* (London: Financial Times, 2008)

Nolan, Peter, *Transforming China: Globalization, Transition and Development* (London: Anthem Press, 2004)

Paludan, Ann, *Chronicle of the Chinese Emperors: The Reign-By-Reign Record of the Rulers of Imperial China* (London: Thames and Hudson, 1998)

Parello-Plesner, Jonas and Mathieu Duchatel, *China's Strong Arm: Protecting Citizens and Assets Abroad* (Oxford: Routledge, 2015)

Parritt, Brian, *Chinese Hordes and Human Waves: A personal perspective of the Korean War, 1950–1953* (Barnsley, S. Yorkshire: Pen and Sword Military, 2011)

Raine, Sarah, *China's African Challenges* (Oxford: Routledge, 2009)

Ringmar, Erik, *Liberal Barbarism: The European Destruction of the Palace of the Emperor of China* (New York: Palgrave Macmillan, 2013)

Rowe, William T., *China's Last Empire: The Great Qing* (Cambridge, Massachusetts: The Belknap Press of Harvard University Press, 2009)

Ryan, Mark A., et al. (eds.) *Chinese Fighting: The PLA Experience Since 1949* (London: M.E. Sharpe, 2003)

Saunders, Phillip C., et al, (eds.) *The Chinese Navy: Expanding Capabilities, Evolving Roles* (Washington, D.C.: National Defense University Press, 2011)

Scobell, Andrew, *China's Use of Force: Beyond the Great Wall and the Long March* (Cambridge: Cambridge University Press, 2003)

Segal, Gerald, *Defending China* (Oxford University Press, 1985)

Shambaugh, David, *China Goes Global: The Partial Power* (Oxford: Oxford University Press, 2013)

Shambaugh, David (ed.), *Power Shift: China and Asia's New Dynamic* (Berkeley: University of California Press, 2005)

Shambaugh, David, *Modernizing China's Military: Progress, Problems, and Prospects* (Berkeley, University of California Press, 2002)

Sheng, Hu, *From the Opium War to the May Fourth Movement* (Beijing: Foreign Language Press, 1991)

So, Alvin Y., and Yin-Wah Chu, *The Global Rise of China* (Cambridge: Polity Press, 2016)

Spence, Jonathan D., *The Search for Modern China* (New York: W.W. Norton and Company, 1999)

Storey, Ian, *Southeast Asia and the Rise of China: The Search for Security* (Oxford: Routledge, 2013)

Taylor, Ian, *China and Africa: Engagement and Compromise* (Oxford: Routledge, 2006)

Taylor, Jay, *The Dragon and the Wild Goose: China and India* (Westport, Connecticut, 1987)

Timperlake, Edward and William C. Triplett, II, *Red Dragon Rising: Communist China's Military Threat to America* (Washington, D.C.: Regnery Publishing, 1999)

Topgyal, Tsering, *China and Tibet: The Perils of Insecurity* (London: C. Hurst & Co., 2016)

Tsai, Shih-Shan Henry, *Perpetual Happiness: The Ming Emperor Yongle* (Seattle: University of Washington Press, 2001)

Vogel, Ezra F., *Deng Xiaoping and the Transformation of China* (Massachusetts: Harvard University Press, 2013)

Walters, Derek, *Chinese Mythology* (London: The Aquarian Press, 1992)

Wang, Yiwei, *The Belt and Road Initiative: What will China Offer the World in its Rise* (Beijing: New World Press, 2016)

Wang, Zhenping, *Tang China in Multi-Polar Asia: A History of Diplomacy and War* (Honolulu: University of Hawai'i Press, 2013)

Whiting, Marvin, Imperial Chinese Military History: 8000 BC–1912 AD (iUniverse, 2002)

Xi, Jinping, *The Governance of China* (Beijing: Foreign Language Press, 2014)

Xiang, Lanxin, *The Origins of the Boxer War: A Multinational Study* (London: RoutledgeCurzon, 2003)
Yang, Benjamin, *Deng: A Political Biography* (Armonk, New York: M.E. Sharpe, Inc., 1998)
Yoshihara, Toshi and James R. Holmes, *Red Star of the Pacific: China's Rise and the Challenge to US Maritime Strategy* (Annapolis, MD, Naval Institute Press, 2010)
Zhao, Qiguang, *Dragons, East and West* (Beijing: Dolphin Books, 2013)

Index[1]

A
Acton, Lord John, 27
Aden, Gulf of, 64, 93
Afghanistan, 31n52, 64, 113, 149, 175, 177, 179
Africa, 23, 26, 36, 44, 47n11, 61, 63, 64, 76, 96, 100, 121–124, 143
 See also Individual countries
AliBaba, 179
Allen, Craig, 111
Allison, Graham, 21, 165
Amur, 119
Anglo–Chinese War (Opium War), 9, 43, 44
Asian Development Bank, 56, 66
Asian Infrastructure Investment Bank, 65
Association of Southeast Asian Nations (ASEAN), 21, 24, 86, 153, 181
Australia, 24
Azerbaijan, 65

B
Bandung Conference, 121, 124
Bangladesh-China-India-Burma Economic Corridor, 64
Baogang He, 5
Baruah, Darshana, 73
Beja, Jean-Philippe, 55
Belgium, 36, 125
Bell, Daniel A., 5, 15
Belt and Road Initiative (BRI), 10, 26, 37, 58, 60–77, 131, 138, 147, 151, 153, 154, 157, 168, 178
Bentham, Jeremy, 182
Biden, Joe, 111, 142, 144, 149, 159, 166, 167, 177
Blair, Tony, 16
Borodin, Mikhail, 120
Boshin War, 49n39
Boxer rebellion, 44
Brexit, 62
Brooking Institution, 57

---

[1] Note: Page numbers followed by 'n' refer to notes.

© The Author(s), under exclusive license to Springer Nature Switzerland AG 2021
A. R. Baginda, *The Global Rise of China and Asia*,
https://doi.org/10.1007/978-3-030-91806-4

Brown, Kerry, 19
Brunei, 86

C
Cambodia, 93, 122, 123, 125, 126, 129
Camdessus, Michael, 67
Canada, 10
Canton, 42
Caspian Sea, 65
Center for Global Development, 66
Charles, Peter, 146
Cheng Li, 12
Chiang Kai-shek, 45, 115, 120
Chile, 22, 130
China Construction Bank, 69
China-Mongolia-Russia Economic Corridor, 64
China–Pakistan Economic Corridor (CPEC), 37, 64, 68
China-Singapore Suzhou Industrial Park, 158
Chinese Communist Party (CCP), 4, 7, 11–13, 15, 17, 18, 20, 34, 48n38, 53, 55, 92, 94–96, 120, 122, 149, 163, 179, 182
Chinese People's Volunteers (CPV), 115
Chow, Gregory, 52
Churchill, Winston, 8
Clancy, Tom, 22, 30n52, 108n91
Clinton, Hillary, 16, 61
Corbett, Julian, 79
Cousin-Montauban, General Charles, 42
Cuba, 28n3
Cyprus, 67

D
Daim Zainuddin, 69
Dalai Lama, 113, 114, 132n9
Democratic People's Republic of Korea (DPRK), 144

Democratic Republic of Congo, 93, 124
Deng Xiaoping, 19, 46, 50n50, 51–58, 98, 102n5, 125
Development Bank of China, 65
Dibb, Paul, 59
Dien Bien Phu, battle of, 129
Djibouti, 66, 80
Duterte, Rodrigo, 154–156

E
East Coast Rail Link (ECRL), 68, 69
East India Company, 42
East Kalimantan, 157
Economy, Elizabeth, 18, 19
Egypt, 39, 124, 156
Engels, Frederick, 3, 103n12, 119
Ethiopia, 124
European Central Bank, 67
European Commission, 67
European Council, 17
European Union, 17
EXIM Bank of China, 65

F
Facebook, 26
Falkland Islands, 114
Fenby, Jonathan, 36
Finlandisation, vi, 22
Forbidden City, Beijing, 39, 45
Foreign Direct Investments (FDI), vii, 54, 58, 91, 143
Four Modernisations Programme, 52
France, 59
Fudan University, 94

G
Gang of Four, 46, 50n48, 51, 52
Germany, vii, 27, 64, 92, 132n6, 166
Ghana, 124, 156

Gibbon, Edward, 35
Gorbachev, Mikhail, 57
Gordon, General Charles George, 42
Grant, General James Hope, 42
Great Leap Forward, 45
Greece, 39, 165
Grenada, 22, 107n81
The Guardian, 17, 172n38
Guinea (Republic of), 124

H
The Hague, 86, 154
Hambantota (Sri Lanka), 74
Han dynasty, 61, 151
Harding, Harry, 57
Hayton, Bill, 33
Hirohito, Emperor, 140
Hishamuddin Hussein, 163
Ho Chi Minh, 129
Hong kong, 26, 44, 49n40, 52, 53, 74, 82, 97, 159, 175, 176
Hua Chunying, 66
Hua Guofeng, 46, 51
Huawei, 2, 26, 27
Hu Jintao, 95
Hungary, 64

I
India, 14, 21, 24, 43, 64, 68, 71, 73, 107n72, 112–114, 116–118, 121, 150, 156, 165, 168, 180
Indian Ocean, 64, 73, 107n72
Indonesia, 61, 67, 123, 129, 151, 156–158
International Institute for Strategic Studies, 91
International Monetary Fund (IMF), 48n36, 66, 67
Iran, 34, 46–47n4, 64, 130
Iraq, vii, 16, 22, 64

J
Japan, 21, 24, 34, 36, 44, 59, 66, 87, 88, 92, 105n50, 128, 129, 139–143, 146, 149, 169, 170n1, 170n2, 170n6, 171n11
Jardine, William, 43
J Capital Research, 66
Jiangnan Shipyard, 78
Jiang Qing (wife of Mao), 46
Johnson, Boris, 6
Jokowi (Joko Widono), 157

K
Kangxi, Emperor, 40
Kazakhstan, 60, 61, 64
Kennedy, John F., 3, 6, 109n105
Kennedy, Paul, 35
Khan Imran, 68
Khmer Rouge, 123
Khrushchev, Nikita, 50n47, 120
Kim Il Sung, 84, 115, 116
Kim Jong Un, 143
King, Martin Luther, 18
Kishi, Nobuo, 140
Kong Zi Institute, 97
Korean Peninsula, 36, 84, 121, 128, 142–144, 148
Korean War, 115, 129, 143
Kunming-Singapore railway, 154
Kuomintang, 82, 120, 126
Kyrgyzstan, 66

L
Lambakan Dam, 157
Laos, 66, 90, 122, 129, 153, 154
Layang-Layang Island (South China Sea), 88
Lee, Bruce, 49n40
Lee Hsien Loong, 159
Lee Teng-hui, 127

Lianhuashan Park, 54
Liaoning Academy, 145
Liberia, 93, 124
Libya, 124
Lin Biao, 92, 115, 116
Li Peng, 61, 175
Liu Huaqing, Commander Admiral, 78
Liu Shaoqi, 51
Liu Xiaobo, 99
Liu Xiaoming
  treaty of, 182n8
Lovell, Julia, 37
Lu Chao, 145
Lumumba, Patrice, 124

M
MacArthur, General Douglas, 115, 116, 129
Macartney, Lord, 37, 41
Macau, 82
Mahan, Alfred Thayer, 79, 80
Mahathir Mohamad, Dr., 68, 69, 181
Ma, Jack, 179, 180
Malaya, vi, 106n57, 123, 129, 150, 160, 170n7
Malaysia, v, vi, 24, 67, 86, 88, 100, 107n68, 151, 160–164, 173n61, 173n69
Malaysia Maritime Zone, 162
Maldives, 66
Manchukuo, 171n11
Manchuria/Manchus, 38, 41, 48n35, 119, 121, 170n2
Mandate of Heaven, 38, 45
Mao Zedong, 5, 7, 45, 52, 74, 92, 115, 119, 120, 171n22
Marco Polo Bridge Incident, 139, 170n2
Maritime Silk Road, 61
Marshall Plan, 60, 71

Marxism/Karl Marx, 3, 26, 55, 103n12, 119, 125
Matheson, James, 43
May Fourth Movement, 44
McCarthyism, 128
McMahon Line, 117
Mekong incident, 89–91
Mekong River, 90, 153
Merkel, Angela, 27
Ming dynasty, 1, 80
Mongolia, 64, 66
Montenegro, 66
Moon Jae-in, 144
Muhyiddin Yasin, 161
Myanmar (Burma), 80, 90, 181

N
Nanjing
  massacre of, 139
  Treaty of, 43
Nathan, Andrew J., 6
National People's Congress, 13, 62
Natuna Islands, 157
New Eurasian Land Bridge, 64
New Zealand, 24
Nguyen Phu Trong, 153
Nkrumah, Kwame, 124, 156
North Atlantic Treaty Organisation (NATO), vii, 169
North Korea, 115, 143, 144, 148, 171n22
Nye, Joseph, 94, 95
Nyerere, Julius, 124

O
Obama, Barak, 155, 167
Opium War (Anglo-Chinese War), 9, 43, 44
Organisation for Economic Co-operation and Development (OECD), 63

P

Pacific War, 8, 34, 59, 140, 146
Pakistan, 64, 66–68, 168
Paracel Islands, 152
Patriot Act, 27
Peng Dehuai, 115
People's Liberation Army (PLA), 21, 81, 117, 150, 175
People's Liberation Army–Air Force (PLAAF), 80, 126
People's Liberation Army–Navy (PLAN), 78, 80, 107n68, 161–163
Percival, General Arthur, 8
Persian Gulf, 1, 64
Philippines, 86, 129, 154–156
Project starlight, 159
Putin, Vladimir, vii, 17, 112
Puyi, emperor, 45, 49n44, 171n11
Pyongyang, 116, 143, 144, 146, 147

Q

Qamdo, battle of, 113
Qianlong, emperor, 37, 40
Qin dynasty, 34
Qing dynasty, 40, 41, 175, 179
Qin Huangdi, emperor, 34
Quanzhou, 64

R

Reagan, Ronald, viii
Republic of China (ROC), 38, 82, 126
Reuters, 91
Rosenberg, Ethel, 128, 135n51
Rosenberg, Julius, 128, 135n51
Ross, Wilbur, 63
Rowen, Harry, 6
Royal Malaysian Air Force (RMAF), 161–164
Runciman, Professor David, 16
Russia, vii, xii, 8, 34, 64, 68, 112, 119, 120, 129, 141, 152, 165, 167, 168, 177
See also Soviet Union (USSR)
Russo-Chinese war (1900), 119
Russo-Japanese Wars (1904–1905), 8

S

Saigon, 177
Saudi Arabia, 28n1
Scotland, 17
Senkaku/Diaoyu islands, 141
Shaanxi, 61
Shang dynasty, 37
Shanghai, v, 44, 54, 78, 107n68, 180
Shenzhen, 53, 54, 69
Shunzhi, emperor, 113
Silk Road Economic Belt, 61, 104n22
Silk Road Fund, 65
Singapore, 8, 24, 52, 92, 154, 158, 159, 173n64
Sinopec, 64, 105n49
Socialism in China, 19, 53, 57
South China Sea, vi, 24, 31n59, 58, 64, 80, 82, 85–87, 92, 93, 106n57, 107n73, 128, 131, 137, 141–143, 145, 152–155, 157, 160–164, 171n16, 179
See also Indonesia; Malaysia; Philippines; Singapore; Vietnam
South Korea, 52, 84, 92, 116, 140, 143–148
Soviet Union (USSR)
and the US, 93, 101, 124, 125, 152, 175
and Vietnam, 126, 152, 175
See also Russia

Spain, 64
Spratly Islands, 78, 152
Sri Lanka, 66, 74, 76
Stalin, Joseph, 50n47, 120, 134n35
Sudan, 42, 93, 124
Suga Yoshihide, 142
Sukarno, President, 123, 156
Sun Tzu, 181, 182n7
Sun Yat-sen, 45, 120

T
Taiping rebellion, 179
Taiwan, 52, 53, 78–80, 82–85, 93, 106n60, 106n64, 126–127, 131, 141, 142, 145, 147–150, 159, 173n64
Taizong, emperor, 39
Tajikistan, 66
Tang dynasty, 36, 113, 152
Tanzania, 124
Thailand, 15, 90, 123, 129, 151, 160, 173n69
Thatcher, Margaret, 114
'Thucydides's trap,' 165
Tiananmen Square, 54–56, 61, 99
Tianwen-1, 3
Tibet, 112–114, 117, 132n6, 132n9
Till, Geoffrey, 79
Togo, Admiral, 139
Tolkien, J.R.R., vi
Toyotomi Hideyoshi, 146
Trump, Donald, 3, 5, 16, 21, 85, 93, 111, 130, 131, 143, 155, 159, 165, 166, 177
Turkey, 64
Turkmenistan, 65
Tusk, Donald, 17

U
United Kingdom (UK), vi, 16, 24, 27, 62, 96, 97, 104n23, 104n26, 182n8
United Nations (UN)
  Convention on Law of the Sea, 86
  UN Security Council, 59, 93, 114, 128, 168
United States (US), vii, 1–4, 7, 10, 16, 21, 22, 26, 27, 28n1, 28n3, 28n4, 54, 56, 57, 59–63, 70, 77, 78, 80, 82, 84, 85, 87–93, 96, 101, 105n49, 105n50, 107n81, 111, 112, 115, 116, 118, 124, 125, 127–131, 138–140, 142–150, 153–156, 158, 159, 165–168, 175–178
USSR, *see* Soviet Union
Uyghur, 99, 161, 181, 182
Uzbekistan, 65

V
Varoufakis, 67
Versailles, Treaty, 166
Vietnam, vi, 22, 28n4, 36, 56, 86, 112, 122, 123, 125, 128, 129, 151–154, 175, 177
Vogel, Ezra F., 56

W
Wang, Xuejun, 23, 24
Wang Yi, 71, 86, 160
Wang Yiwei, 63
Wei Fenghe, General, 152, 153

Wen Jiabao, 13
World Bank, 20, 53, 56, 66
World Health Organisation (WHO), 178
World Trade Organisation, 58
World War One, 16, 167
World War Two, 2, 22, 59, 129, 132n6
Wu Bangguo, 13

X
Xiao Qian, 157
Xi Jinping, President, 3–5, 9, 18–21, 26, 33–35, 37, 44, 54, 60–62, 64, 70–72, 76, 77, 86, 88, 91, 94–96, 98, 112, 147, 148, 154, 156, 176–178, 180
Xing Haiming, 148
Xinjiang, 40, 99, 181

Y
Yalu River, 8, 115–116
Yasukuni Shrine, 140
Yeltsin, Boris, 57
Yongle, Emperor, 1, 38–40
Yuan Shikai, 38, 45, 49n45
Yue Hu, 11
Yugoslavia, vii, 156
Yu Keping, 13

Z
Zhang Qian, 61
Zhao Lijian, 145
Zheng He, Admiral, 1, 40, 80
Zheng Wang, 55
Zhong Guo, 33, 34
Zhou dynasty, 37, 38
Zhou Enlai, 37, 49n44, 51, 52, 116, 121–124, 134n36, 156
Zhurong, 3, 176